Politics of
the Meiji Press

# Politics of the Meiji Press

## The Life of Fukuchi Gen'ichirō

James L. Huffman

THE UNIVERSITY PRESS OF HAWAII
*Honolulu*

FRONTISPIECE: FUKUCHI AS A WAR CORRESPONDENT
COVERING THE SATSUMA REBELLION IN 1877. WOODBLOCK
BY KOBAYASHI KIYOCHIKA. *(Photo courtesy of Mainichi Shim-
bunsha Shi Henshūshitsu)*

*Library of Congress Cataloging in Publication Data*

Huffman, James L      1941–
   Politics of the Meiji press.

   Bibliography:  p.
   Includes index.
   1.  Fukuchi, Gen'ichirō, 1841–1906.   2.   Journalists
—Japan—Biography.   I.   Title.
PN5406.F77H8      070.4'092'4 [B]      79–3879
ISBN 0–8248–0679–4

*To Judith—*
*and our children,*
*James and Kristen*

# Contents

# Acknowledgments

It was with more than slight fear that I plunged into Japanese-language research early in 1970. Characters were strange, Japanese library techniques new, sources sometimes baffling and hard to find. Had I not enjoyed the gracious assistance of more persons than I shall ever be able to thank, I should have failed utterly. But they gave me their help, and the present work, though certainly not their responsibility in its many failings, has been finished because of that help.

I want first of all (need it always be last?) to thank my wife, Judith, who has shared so completely my immersion in both Japan and Fukuchi, providing fresh insights, useful criticism, and unbounded encouragement over the years in which I have been engaged in this work. The end product is, in a real sense, hers as much as it is mine. Our children, James and Kristen, deserve thanks too—for their forbearance of a work that has consumed much too much of Dad's time and for their ability to appear interested when I am certain they really could not have been.

Then, thanks go to a number of individuals who gave a great deal of assistance during my three years in Japan. Professor Ikeda Mayako of the Inter-University Center for Japanese Language Studies in Tokyo guided me in initial readings there on the history of Japanese journalism. Professor Koito Chuichi of Sophia University and Dr. Nagai Michio, then of *Asahi Shimbun,* suggested a number of approaches and opened doors to helpful sources. Two other professors, Nishida Taketoshi of the Meiji Shimbun Zasshi Bunko and Sugiura Tadashi of *Mainichi Shimbun,* greatly enhanced the final product with concerned

and knowledgeable observations from their own study of Fukuchi. Fujita Nobukazu of *Mainichi* also gave useful advice, as did
Professors Uchikawa Yoshimi and Ga Motohiko of Tokyo University. And at a later stage Kano Tsutomu of *The Japan Interpreter* provided both inspiration and provocative insights into
the world of Meiji thought. To Miss Oguchi Michiru I must express a special sense of gratitude for many hours of assistance
with translating problems.

I am particularly pleased to be able at last to express publicly
my debt to several former professors who have done much to
make the world of scholarship come alive for me. Thanks—to
Richard Gray at Northwestern University (now at Indiana University), for first sharing with me the excitement possible in the
study of journalism; to Robert E. Ward, whose early tutelage
made modern Japan such an inviting place; to William B.
Hauser, now of the University of Rochester, for bringing such
human warmth into Japanese history; to the late Joseph Yama-
giwa, for his patient direction in my earliest readings in Japanese history; and—especially—to my mentor, friend, and
adviser, Roger F. Hackett at Michigan, without whose encouragement, suggestions, criticism, and patience the study never
would have been completed.

For financial assistance thanks are due to the U.S. Office of
Education (for Fulbright-Hays and National Defense Foreign
Language grants), to the U.S. State Department (for a postdoc-
toral Fulbright grant that enabled me to complete this manuscript), to the Horace H. Rackham School of Graduate Studies
at the University of Michigan, to the Josephine dé Karman
Foundation of El Monte, California, and to the Research Council of the University of Nebraska. Grants from each provided the
backing to complete various stages of the research and writing.
Librarians also have placed me under a debt. I cannot begin to
name them all, but I would be inexcusably remiss not to thank
the staff at Tokyo University's Shimbun Kenkyūjo; Ishii Shirō
and Kitane Minoru at the Meiji Shimbun Zasshi Bunko; Naomi
Fukuda and Saito Masaei at the University of Michigan Asia Library; and Betsy Hadden at the Wittenberg University Library.

And then there are the scores of friends, advisers, and fellow scholars who have given both frequent and occasional suggestions, critiques, leads, and advice—teachers from my early days at Marion College, associates in the history department at the University of Nebraska, colleagues in the history department and East Asian Studies program at Wittenberg, and numerous other friends in the United States and Japan. To begin to name each would be to start a list that could not be completed—a fact that I regret. But to each of you, thank you!

Thanks, finally, go to my editors, Janyce Blair and Stuart Kiang, and their assistants at The University Press of Hawaii. I cannot imagine more patience, graciousness, and painstaking care than they have given me—and my manuscript. I am indeed a debtor!

J.L.H.

*Wittenberg University*

# Introduction

If one cares sufficiently to search among several rows of tumble-down curio and clothing shops just west of Tokyo's largest temple, the Asakusa Kannon, he may chance upon a fifteen-foot-high memorial marker jutting above the roofs of back-to-back shirt booths. And if he dares to climb over one shop's tin roof, he will find on the marker a tribute to one of Japan's most influential early journalists, Fukuchi Gen'ichirō, an inscription put there in 1919 by Fukuchi's noted friend, Yamagata Aritomo. Fukuchi, says the epitaph, was a ''never-to-be-forgotten man,'' one whose ''honor and integrity we deeply miss'':

A great teacher was he on the stage of learning.
His vision penetrated the ages;
His knowledge spanned both East and West.

The great essayist of *Nichi Nichi*
—He wrote with clarity and precision.
His was the outspoken voice of the prophet.

Undergirded by talent and ability,
He dominated the stage of life.
Still today he shines from the realms of death.

It is a striking marker, partly because of its size and message, partly because of the irony suggested by its imposing loneliness. Was not its inscription commissioned by one of Meiji Japan's most powerful oligarchs? Was not Fukuchi one of that era's more influential public figures—prominent as an author, journalist, playwright, diplomat, politician, even economist? The marker's location was revered once as an honored part of the temple grounds. Yet, by the last quarter of the twentieth century, the memorial's place had been usurped by crowding commercialization, the honor of a great man lost amid the new tastes and preoccupations of a different generation.

History, one suspects, is too often like that, a serpentine and unpredictable science through which one person lives on for centuries while a worthy colleague fades, forgotten by all but the specialist. Whereas the contrast in their fates sometimes may result from a genuine difference in stature and contribution, just as often it springs from a paucity in written records left by the forgotten figure, from political changes in the atmosphere of the times, from the existence (or nonexistence) of disciples to publicize a mentor's role, from the emergence (or lack of it) of a later scholar to call attention to a given person's contributions, or (more often than one wants to admit) from factors too complex to analyze. The contrast may even result from pure chance. All of these latter reasons certainly played a role in the case of Fukuchi, modernizer of the Japanese press and leading popular proponent of orderly, "gradual" progress in the first half of Meiji Japan (1868–1888).

In recent years, much has been written about various groups that influenced the remarkable economic, political, and cultural transformation of the early Meiji period—about the oligarchs who charted the course of that development, about the leaders of "popular rights" movements who opposed the oligarchs, about the businessmen who did so much to lay the groundwork for industrialization, about those writers and intellectuals who advocated "liberal" causes. One significant group, however, has been almost completely overlooked by historians of the period: that small but influential corps of journalists who advocated, not antigovernment "liberalism," but a moderate course of "progress and order" labeled "gradualism" *(zenshin-shugi)*. While their competitors in the press have gained the full attention of scholars as visionaries and harbingers of reform, these "gradualists" followed a less dramatic yet perhaps more influential road, generally supporting the government's slower pace of national transformation, attempting to dampen public clamor, and often clarifying the rationale behind government moves.

These men were, in a certain sense, outsiders holding themselves aloof from the traditional bureaucratic power structure and seeking to influence events primarily with their pens. They remained a minority, even within the world of the press. But more than any other segment of the journalistic world—indeed, as much perhaps as any broad, opinion-leading group except the oligarchs—they exerted a key influence on the development of early Meiji Japan, articulating, reflecting, and defending the general course followed by the nation. As one of Fukuchi's competing editors said, their editorials "guided society."[1]

Among this small group, no man approached the personal power of Fukuchi Gen'ichirō,[2] editor of the newspaper *Tokyo Nichi Nichi* from 1874 to 1888. An experienced traveler in the West, a promising (though overly frank) young bureaucrat in the Finance Ministry, an intimate of leading oligarchs, Fukuchi decided early in life that "if one could not be prime minister, one had best become a newspaper writer."[3] Accordingly, he accepted an offer in 1874 from *Nichi Nichi,* and during the next decade he made the newspaper into one of the nation's most powerful voices. Calling vigorously for a kind of national progress that would be rooted in strong central leadership rather than in Western-style popular sovereignty, he exerted an extraordinary influence on the broad political, economic, and diplomatic movements of his times, even while mirroring in his personal life the more tempestuous side of Japan's social and intellectual transformation. An examination of his life thus becomes essential to any full understanding of the course of the early Meiji era.

The study of Fukuchi's public career does pose certain obstacles, any of which might trap the unwary or frighten off the timorous. His interests, for example, were so broad as to preclude a complete understanding of the man. During more than forty years of public life, he made major contributions to the fields of diplomacy, history, economics, politics, drama,

public finance, journalism, constitutional thought, and fiction
—too many areas to handle even in perfunctory manner in a single monograph. Indeed, for this reason the present study will
bypass significant portions of his life, concentrating on only the
two key focuses of his middle years—journalism and political
thought.

A second, even more difficult obstacle lies in the complexity
of Fukuchi's personality and thought. As subsequent pages will
show, his mind was like an artesian well, spewing out ideas and
proposals as diverse and seemingly incongruous as the varied
elements of the national soil that produced them. He might
boast of his government connections one day, then advocate
journalistic independence the next. Or he might support imperial sovereignty and genuine popular rights in the same newspaper series. There was an underlying consistency in his
thought. To find it, however, and to grapple with its relation to
the apparent paradoxes, is at first glance a fearful challenge.

A third problem lies in the difficulty of trying to correct the
glib and frequently inaccurate generalizations that have characterized most historical references to Fukuchi. Students of the
Meiji era, including some of Fukuchi's biographers, have created a stereotype, then given in to the temptation to emphasize
only those facts that fit the accepted image. Thus, for most,
Fukuchi becomes a brilliant but eccentric journalist who gave
unquestioning support to government positions—a man willing
to sell his soul (or at least his mind) for a bit of influence, a man
of minor political impact in the 1870s and 1880s. As with all
stereotypes, this description is not without basis in fact. Yet a
more careful study of Fukuchi shows it to be essentially incor-
rect. Fukuchi was not, as we shall see, an unflinching supporter
of government policies; nor did he ever put a price on his basic
philosophies. He was indeed brilliant and eccentric, but, in
contrast to the image, his influence in Tokyo in the 1870s was
vast. The image has strayed rather far from reality, a fact that
makes a study of his life both treacherous and essential.

The study of Fukuchi's life promises thus to serve at least two
functions. It should provide greater understanding of the politi-

cal thought of Japan's out-of-power gradualists, and it should clarify the biographical details of the leading representative of this important group. But the study hopefully will not stop with those somewhat narrow goals. Fukuchi's life also provides at least two other motivations for research, both of them broader in significance.

The first of these is the aim of developing, through the mirror of his life, a clearer picture of early Meiji society in general. Fukuchi, among all the individuals of his era, seems particularly well equipped to give us such a picture. It has become a truism that no person lives in isolation from society, just as no society exists apart from those individuals who populate it. Consequently, those most worth the historian's attention are those who shed the brightest light on the times in which they lived. The "great man," said Hegel, is the one whose activities represent "the heart and essence of his age," the individual who "actualizes his age."[4] Fukuchi was, in many respects, such a man.

Through a study of his life we can hope to discover, for example, a fuller picture of the evolution of the early Japanese press. Japan's modern press might be said to have experienced three major periods of development during the nineteenth century: the period of birth in the late 1860s, the period of emergent political influence in the 1870s, and the period of growing independence and commercialization from the late 1880s onward. As the nation's most powerful editor in the first two of these periods, Fukuchi clearly represented "the heart and essence" of Japan's early journalistic development. His attitudes, philosophies, and practices—perhaps more than those of any other individual—shaped the early press.

His work also sheds a brilliant light on the gradualist policies adopted by the government prior to the promulgation of the Meiji constitution in 1889. Robert N. Bellah has noted that journalism probably provided the prime reservoir of intellectuals in the early Meiji period.[5] Most of these intellectuals wrote in opposition to the evolving oligarchic policies. Fukuchi, by contrast, espoused a position that was generally consonant with government policies—a position characterized by emphasis on national strength, constitutionalism, assembly government, limited popular rights, protection of essential national traditions, and imperial sovereignty. At the *Nichi Nichi,* he articulated this position regularly, indeed almost daily, for fourteen years—presenting the reading public with a cogent rationale for the "progress and order" approach to national policymaking that characterized most official actions. His editorials thus become important windows onto the world of thought and rationality that produced the peculiarly Meiji course of action.

Fukuchi's experiences also have a great deal to say about the overall tenor of the times, about the general fabric we call early Meiji society. These were tempestuous, dynamic times. The first twenty years of Meiji rule brought to Japan a rapidity of change that defied tranquil or reasoned integration, and few individuals more fully mirrored those times than did Fukuchi. His roller-coaster-like ascent and descent of the peaks and valleys of public life illustrated the stress-ridden, precarious nature of life in an era of change. His inability to rid himself of numerous "feudal" attitudes highlighted the persistence of traditional culture even in a society that sometimes seemed hell-bent on transformation. His life also gave vivid insight into the importance of Western learning in Meiji Japan, the difficulty of balancing the traditional and the contemporary, and the important role intellectuals play in such an era. And the increasingly emperor-centered conservatism of his mature journalistic years presaged the "search for moral surety" and the "quest for a national mission" that would engulf most Japanese later in the century.[6] Fukuchi, as we have noted, was a man of many spheres. That fact alone enabled him to mirror his own times with special clarity and force.

Fukuchi's life deserves study, finally, as a basis for comparing the development of the Japanese press with that of journalistic institutions elsewhere in the world. This point need not (indeed, it *dare* not!) be elaborated, because such a comparison lies outside the competence and limits of the present study. Its potential must, however, be raised.

Even the most facile consideration raises tantalizing parallels between Fukuchi and his contemporaries or near contemporaries in the Western press. Like Joseph Pulitzer, for example, he saw the press as an instrument of national reform and as a medium of information for *all* the people. Like Horace Greeley, he used the press as an instrument for helping to develop the "greatness" of his country. Yet, unlike Pulitzer, he eschewed sensational news, mass circulations, and antigovernment crusades. And unlike Greeley, he never considered using his power as a journalist as a steppingstone to governmental office. What do such similarities and differences say about the comparative nature of the Japanese and U.S. presses at that time? Or, to probe a bit more deeply, would it be more logical to consider the Defoes and Franklins of eighteenth-century Britain and the United States as Fukuchi's true counterparts, since they, like he, were the actual shapers of their nations' earliest press traditions? If so, might not the similarities between the approaches of each of these be more significant in a comparative study than the differences between Fukuchi, Pulitzer, and Greeley? Such questions are, at this point, somewhat fanciful. Their answers must await a later study. But they do suggest several fundamental questions about the comparative development of national institutions in variant societies at divergent stages. And even to begin the consideration of such questions, an understanding of individuals such as Fukuchi is essential.

CHAPTER I

# The Clash of Two Worlds:
# 1841–1868

> *When I observed the traditional bakufu*
> *students . . . no one was pursuing anything*
> *worthwhile; so I decided that I would not*
> *waste my life by advancing with them.*[1]

Fukuchi Gen'ichirō, like the Japan in which he came of age, was a child of two worlds. Born and trained in the home of a Confucian scholar, he early threw himself into the study of Dutch and the translation of English. Convinced as an adult of the validity of Western political forms, he nevertheless insisted that traditional cultural values were superior. At age eighteen, Fukuchi became one of the youngest members of Japan's new diplomatic corps; and from his first day on the job he alternately cursed the rudeness of Western merchants and praised their business acumen. By age thirty-four, he had become acknowledged as Japan's foremost newspaper editor—a position based partly on his ability to martial Western theories in support of traditional Japanese concepts of government. Even at age fifty-seven, when he had emerged as one of Japan's leading dramatists, he advocated Western-style plots but traditional Japanese stage settings. Indeed, no single theme more consistently dominated Fukuchi's life than the painful yet exhilarating struggle to integrate the best of both East and West into a single formula capable of propelling Japan to a position of worldwide respect.

The mature Fukuchi developed a label for this policy of conscious balancing. He called it "gradualism" *(zenshinshugi)*, a policy that would assure deliberate, Western-oriented change based on the salient features of Japanese tradition. The key to success in the modern age, he asserted again and again throughout life, lay in the twin pillars of gradualism: progress and order.

It hardly need be stated that such a broad philosophy was capable of widely differing interpretations when it came to the specifics of policy formation. And Fukuchi did indeed go through a certain evolution in his own view of what policies were best for Japan. Nor is it necessary to discuss the fact that it took Fukuchi several decades to perfect his gradualist formula, several decades of excruciating experimentation and grappling with the paradoxes that dominated his educational upbringing. But, though the formula itself emerged slowly, the strands that produced it were present almost from the beginning of Fukuchi's life—so much so that a look even at his formative years must concentrate, above all, on that very clash of two worlds that eventually would make him Japan's foremost private spokesman for gradualism.

Actually, it was the accident of time and birthplace that first suggested that Fukuchi would be involved in a world broader than that of his ancestors. He was born on Tuesday, May 13, 1841,[2] in Nagasaki, Japan's most "international" city at the time. As the one place where merchant ships from abroad (China and the Netherlands) could dock, this port town provided cosmopolitan contacts unavailable anywhere else in Japan. Here alone, on the tiny harbor island of Deshima, a handful of perhaps a hundred resident Dutch merchants had mingled regularly for two centuries with a similar number of Japanese interpreters. And although the interpreters rarely displayed an intellectual bent, they had been responsible through the years for stimulating Western consciousness in a number of scholars and officials.[3] They, above all others, had made sure that a "faint current of the intellectual storm raised by Galileo and Newton would continue to blow" into Japan.[4]

Nagasaki's unique position actually had been established early in the seventeenth century through several edicts of the Tokugawa government, or bakufu, banning all types of Japanese intercourse with other lands, except for the limited Chinese and Dutch trade at Nagasaki. Determined to control foreign trade and suppress heterodox ideologies, the Tokugawa had even proscribed foreign books. The result was that all parts of the nation, with the sole exception of Nagasaki, had been almost totally cut off from knowledge of the rest of the world. None but the elite, it would appear, even possessed an active knowledge that an outside world existed. And the Dutch at Deshima were treated more like prisoners than merchants. Ships were allowed into the harbor only once a year. Resident merchants were prohibited from venturing into Nagasaki proper.[5] The colony itself boasted but two streets, and most officials spent evenings conversing languidly in the hall of their Dutch chief—"a very disagreeable way of life, fit only for such as have no other way of spending their time than droning over a pipe of tobacco."[6]

Nevertheless, the mere presence of a continuing Dutch colony in Nagasaki harbor assured a constant and growing seepage of Western science and ideas into Japan. As the crack through which that learning oozed, Nagasaki became the center of Japan's international consciousness.[7] Bastardized foreign words dotted local dialects. Dutch interpreters gossiped about Western customs they observed on Deshima. Eighteenth-century Western scholars such as Maeno Ryōtaku and Hayashi Shihei came to Nagasaki to study. By the time of Fukuchi's youth, when the quest for Western learning was taking hold in various parts of Japan, a number of the country's most promising, ambitious youths—men such as Ōkuma Shigenobu and Fukuzawa Yukichi—had begun to choose Nagasaki as the center for early studies and political maneuvers. There they could observe the West, acquire weapons, or study Dutch. So great, by contrast, was the cosmopolitan mood introduced by two centuries of Dutch presence that in 1859 England's first minister to Japan exclaimed: "Nagasaki to Yeddo: Two centuries lie between these points."[8]

The Dutch were not alone, however, among the foreign powers exerting an influence in Nagasaki at the time of Fukuchi's childhood. Beginning late in the eighteenth century, such other Western nations as England, Russia, France, and the United States also had begun making rather frequent, though unsuccessful, efforts to open Japan to foreign commerce. The port to which their ships usually sailed was Nagasaki. Each visit was repulsed, and in 1825 the bakufu attempted to strengthen its isolation policy with an expulsion decree stating that "any foreigners who should land anywhere must be arrested or killed, and any ships approaching the shore must be destroyed."[9] But the Western challenge refused to abate, and by 1844, just three years after Fukuchi's birth, the Dutch king felt it necessary to send a letter to the Japanese shogun, by way of Nagasaki, informing him of the recent Opium War in China and warning of similar disaster in Japan if the country failed soon to open its ports to Western trade.[10]

It should hardly seem surprising, then, that Fukuchi remembered his youth as a period when "many Western ships were coming to Nagasaki,"[11] nor that one of the earliest stories of his childhood recounted how, when playing with neighborhood children, he pointed one day toward the blue water in the distance and wondered aloud what one would find if one could fly across the sea. Someday he would build a big boat and go to the other shore, he boasted: "So remember it well; I will bring back beautiful, rare flowering trees and divide them among you."[12]

No matter how limited international intercourse may have been in the 1840s and 1850s, Nagasaki was the center of what there was, and as such it gave many a dreaming child and aspiring young man a sense that the future lay outward, in a world much larger than the tiny islands in which he was born. Fukuchi was no exception.

He was not, however, shaped merely by fascination with Western things. If the place of birth dictated an interest in the new world, the family into which he was born dictated a corresponding exposure to the more traditional, Chinese-inspired philosophies that had long dominated Tokugawa society. For Fukuchi's samurai father, though a doctor by profession, was a Confucian scholar by inclination and avocation.[13] Trained in the Osaka school of Rai San'yō (1780–1832), the influential poet-historian whose writings sparked so much emperor-centered loyalism in the waning years of the Tokugawa,[14] he continued to death to practice calligraphy and study the classics, insisting that his only son be given a traditional upbringing based on standard works. So though the times were too tempestuous, too much dominated by Western incursions, to allow classical training ever to become normative in Gen'ichirō's life, his father, Kōan, like most other samurai of his day, made sure it would not be ignored either.

### An Insatiable Student

Gen'ichirō's birth, following that of seven daughters, brought more joy and excitement to the Fukuchi household than perhaps any event since his grandfather, Yoshimasa, had moved to Nagasaki decades earlier. Though the youngest of eight children, Gen'ichirō was the family's first natural-born son in three generations and, as such, his father's unbounded joy. "To see accomplished in a son that which is lacking in one's self is the earnest desire of all fathers," wrote Goethe[15]—and few fathers could have felt that sentiment more deeply than Kōan in a hierarchical society that had frustrated many of his own efforts to achieve fame. Accordingly, Kōan gave the newborn his own infant name, Yasokichi.[16]

The young Yasokichi's formal education began at age four, when his father commenced oral instruction in such classics as *Hsiao ching* ("Classic of filial piety") and *San tzu ching* ("Three character classic"), requiring that he memorize major sections of each work by rote in the manner of the day. Most biographers, following traditional stylistic clichés, have the lad reading Chinese and practicing calligraphy by age five. In 1848, when Fukuchi turned seven, they relate that Kōan sent him to the prominent Osagawa household to begin studying history. Fukuchi spent nearly a decade at the Osagawa school, developing a fascination with Japanese history that would prompt him in later years to describe himself as "not so much a journalist, nor a politican nor dramatist, as an historian."[17]

The fact that Fukuchi excelled in his studies at the Osagawa school is important largely because this early grounding in traditional Confucian ideals, though submerged during most of his young manhood by Western learning, would vividly color his mature philosophical concepts. Although a knowledge of the West was to be the chief support of his drive to national prominence, Eastern concepts would moderate and bend that knowledge once the drive itself had brought him success. Many of Fukuchi's adult contemporaries would puzzle and argue over the reasons for his refusal to join them in demanding rapid westernization. An important reason lay in the solid traditional education he had received in Nagasaki.

His life would be dominated by two worlds: the East and the West. One of the early indications of that fact was the traditional poetry for which he grew mildly famous at the Osagawa school. Written in *classical* Chinese, again and again it evidenced *modern* themes unimaginable at the time of his father's adolescence. One of the best examples was composed when he was just fifteen:

| | |
|---|---|
| Masts of barbarian ships | *Isen no hanshō* |
| Line up in the channel. | *Kaimon ni tsuranaru* |
| A soldierly mood, evoking | *Shinzen taru heiki* |
| trees in a forest, | *Nami o asshite kurashi.* |
| Falls darkly across the | |
| waves. | |
| | |
| Jackals and wolves | *Sairō gi naku* |
| Know neither justice nor | *Kanete rei nashi* |
| propriety. | *Shinsui ikukai ka* |
| How oft' they plunder | *Nao on o karu.* [18] |
| our fuel and water— | |
| All in the name of | |
| kindness. | |

Fear and resentment would not, however, remain dominant for long when Fukuchi saw the "barbarian ships." After the forced opening of Japan by Comdr. Matthew C. Perry in 1853, his father gradually began to sense that success could not much longer lie solely in the study of Chinese classics. The barbarians might be "jackals and wolves," but they were also *shrewd* plunderers who had introduced unsettling elements into the traditional political equilibrium. The man who knew their ways and tongues might find in that knowledge the key to the future. As a result, Kōan decided late in the summer of 1855 to place Gen'ichirō in the home of his friend Namura Hachiemon, one of Nagasaki's best Dutch interpreters. His son would learn a new language. The Western world would replace the East, for a time at least, as his consuming passion.

Namura, a senior translator and interpreter for the Nagasaki shogunal commissioner *(bugyō)*, was known locally as both a boisterous man and a "very strict" mentor—a superb teacher.[19] That fact did not intimidate his new pupil, however; for if Namura ranked among the best teachers, Fukuchi soon became one of the teacher's favorite students. So impressed was Namura with the young poet's language aptitude that when his own son was summoned to bakufu service in Edo, he proposed that Fukuchi be adopted into the Namura household, with the prospect of eventually marrying the master's daughter. That Kōan would agree to such an adoption hardly seemed likely, given the fact that Gen'ichirō was the first Fukuchi male heir in three generations. Yet consent he did, due to the ambition he harbored for his son,[20] and early in January 1856 Fukuchi took a new name—Namura—writing a fitting poem that referred to his new "father and teacher" from whom he got "warm, pure knowledge."[21]

By 1857, Fukuchi's knowledge of Dutch had progressed sufficiently to enable him to teach at the Namura school and begin translating for the shogunal office. In the latter capacity he went regularly to Deshima, the island where the Dutch resided, and where he encountered his first newspaper, an event of no little signficance for a teenager who would one day be known as father of the modern Japanese press. As Fukuchi later recalled, Namura was responsible at that time for translating the annual *fūsetsugaki,* or summary, of the state of the Western world prepared for the shogun by the Dutch at Deshima, and on occasion he would ask the teenage Fukuchi to take notes as he translated. When he was first asked to do so, probably early in 1857, Fukuchi puzzled over the document's wide range of subject matter and asked how a single person, particularly an isolated captain living at Deshima, could know so much about the world. Namura replied that "in Western countries they publish daily what is called a newspaper, a sheet that informs men of the events of other lands and, of course, of their own country. The captain reads these newspapers and roughly summarizes their most important items for presentation to the shogunal administrator."[22]

It was a startling explanation. Never had Fukuchi heard of such a thing. Few in all Japan had so much as encountered the notion of newspapers. When sensational events such as earthquakes or fires occurred, enterprising people would occasionally print the facts on a sheet called *yomiuri*, then hawk the sheet through the streets for a small fee. But Japan's first sustained news publication was still half a decade away, and the nation's first daily newspaper did not appear for nearly fifteen years. Adding to this the fact that no Japanese, except a few shipwrecked sailors, had been abroad in well over two hundred years, one can readily understand the effect Namura's explanation had on the impressionable Fukuchi.

After thus introducing him to the idea of Western journalism, Namura picked up a discarded Amsterdam paper and gave it to Fukuchi. "Again and again I attempted to read it, consulting a dictionary," the youth recalled, "but the prose was difficult and the events hard to understand. So, lacking sufficient skill, I abandoned it."[23] With that, his first involvement with the press ended. But the initial contact was important, the earliest link in a chain of experiences that eventually would convince Fukuchi that newspapers were essential to the development of effective government.

The next year, in mid-1858, another of Fukuchi's proclivities —a proneness to abrasive self-confidence—also surfaced. But instead of firing his imagination, this quality simply forced him out of the Namura household and threatened to cut off his career as a Dutch scholar. Like so many of the scheming, climbing young samurai of late Tokugawa Japan, Fukuchi boasted openly about his intellectual abilities, and as a result he frequently stirred the ire of his language-school colleagues—particularly those who were his seniors in age and experience but his juniors in talent and position. Thus, when Namura was summoned by the bakufu to Edo in mid-1858, leaving Fukuchi alone in charge of the Nagasaki household, simmering resentments boiled over into a fierce power struggle. Members of the household and school, including even his promised wife, accused him of arrogance and irreverence. They refused to submit to his leadership, and normal activities slowed nearly to a halt. When Namura returned to the confused scene some months later, he was faced with a choice of either dismissing Fukuchi or losing all his students. He chose the former course, although reluctantly, and severed familial relationships with Gen'ichirō, asking him to resign from the interpreter's role. The seventeen-year-old lad accordingly returned to Kōan's houschold, taking back the family name of Fukuchi.[24]

Fortunately, however, demands for the use of Dutch were too great and translators with his ability too few to bar Fukuchi long from public service. So work quickly resumed. He began teaching one group of interpreters at the Nagasaki *bugyō* and supervising another group involved in Nagasaki's foreign shipping. But, despite the resumption of work, the ambitious teenager began to find Nagasaki life less and less satisfying. Perhaps it was the proximity of so many colleagues with whom he had quarreled at the Namura school that disturbed him. Perhaps it was Nagasaki's declining role, as the focus of international affairs began shifting to Edo, the bakufu headquarters a thousand miles to the northeast. He became especially aware of this shifting role when he was assigned about this time to teach Dutch to the ambitious young samurai at the government's new ironworks in Nagasaki. Their talk was of power, of driving the Western barbarians from Japan; and the locus of their conversations was the bakufu in Edo.

Stories of Edo pointed to a place where bright youths, especially those who knew Dutch, might advance further and faster than they could in Nagasaki. They spoke of adventure, of the excitement of a new life among hundreds of other idealistic young patriots, the freedom of living in an area where many of the old restraints had been removed. As an old man Fukuchi might recall his Nagasaki youth as "a full moon in a clear blue sky,"[25] but now, late in his teenage years, that city began to suggest a fading moon in a heaven rife with storms. The morning, he at length concluded, lay to the east. So in January 1859 he boarded the *Kanrin-maru* in Nagasaki harbor[26] and set sail for a new life in Edo. He arrived there within the month and, on disembarking, left the innocent years forever behind.[27]

### An Edo Dilettante

Historian George B. Sansom has pictured the Japan of Fukuchi's youth as a country "full of restless spirits, dissatisfied with their condition and thirsting for activity." It was, he said, a land where nobles "wanted independence and foreign trade," samurai "wanted opportunities to use their talents," merchants "wanted just a little freedom"—a land where "every force but conservatism was pressing from within."[28]

If such could be said of the nation as a whole, the mood of unrest was doubly intense in the Edo to which Fukuchi now came. No longer was the bakufu a unified or stable force. No longer were the stronger *han*, or fiefs, willing to submit passively to every shogunal desire. The increasing difficulty with which the Tokugawa administration found itself confronting economic and international problems highlighted a marked deterioration in leadership. The result, particularly in the power center of Edo, was a new assertion of vitality and competition among those outside the shogunal administration. Even the imperial court, which for centuries had submitted docilely to bakufu rule, was beginning to assert itself, encouraged by rival lords who sought not only the expulsion of the West but the accumulation of greater personal influence in the rule of Japan.

In the year before Fukuchi's arrival, for example, combined court, antiforeign, and anti-Tokugawa pressures had forced the bakufu to stall and compromise on the signing of its first commercial treaty with the United States and to dismiss the senior minister, Hotta Masayoshi, for his role in supporting the treaty.

Even a number of high-handed, forceful moves on the part of Hotta's successor to power, Ii Naosuke, had served primarily to emphasize the increasingly tenuous nature of shogunal rule. For despite Ii's near dictatorial assumption of administrative control, his main effect was to stir antibakufu resentments and resistance to new peaks. In the month of Fukuchi's arrival in Edo, the Kyoto court had granted its "forbearance" in the opening of treaty ports only after receiving bakufu assurances that Japan would be reclosed to foreign intercourse as soon as possible. Even then, the once pliable court had to be strenuously coerced.

Nor was Edo's dynamism and appeal at the time of Fukuchi's arrival limited to high-level political intrigue. The youth's new home also offered the attractions of a massive population (well over a million);[29] lively entertainment areas with drama, geisha, and ample companionship; fine eating; ostentatious estates of leading *daimyō,* or feudal lords, from each of Japan's *han;* the congestion that comes from packing too many people into a limited area.[30] By 1859, it had become home to an assortment of new groups that a youth like Fukuchi was to find stimulating. Many of the country's most ambitious young samurai, for example, were coming to the capital in search of quick routes to personal success. *Shishi,* young anti-Tokugawa zealots willing to sacrifice life itself in their struggle against the old regime, gathered in Edo's fencing schools. Institutions for instruction in gunnery and swordsmanship flourished. Slogans like "expel the barbarians" *(jōi)* and "revere the emperor" *(sonnō)* were heard everywhere. Dutch-language schools provided havens for those who wished to learn about the West. Shibusawa Eiichi, Fukuchi's friend who would later become one of Japan's leading businessmen, proclaimed himself more "overwhelmed" by an initial visit to Edo about this time than by his first trip to New York a few years later.[31] It was this environment in which the seventeen-year-old Fukuchi, away from his hometown for the first time, found himself in February 1859.

During the first weeks in Edo, he slept nights at the home of Yadabori Keizō, the *Kanrin-maru* captain, and he spent the days in an aggressive effort to contact various persons to whom his father or Nagasaki friends had sent letters of introduction. Among them were such bakufu officials as Mizuno Tadanori, lord of Chikugo; Iwase Tadanori, lord of Higo, several Confucian scholars; and a number of former Nagasaki friends, including Moriyama Takichirō, now the bakufu's leading interpreter.[32] Mizuno, who had become one of Kōan's friends during a stint as shogunal commissioner in Nagasaki, invited Fukuchi to live with him; soon the two became fast friends, consulting together on everything from currency problems to Tokugawa resistance at the time of the Restoration.[33]

Most of all, Fukuchi spent his early months in the capital tasting the pleasures, the freedom, the anonymity. Until now he had lived under the rigid discipline of parents and teachers, all of them hard taskmasters and stern disciplinarians; and though he had shown few signs of rebellion, the new freedom and range of opportunities at first intoxicated Fukuchi. He became known among young companions as a brash, bright climber, a "leader of mischievous students,"[34] as well as an expert at divination and palmistry. He loved to sit and argue, to dazzle (and irritate) Dutch scholars with individualistic, flashy translations. Also, he rapidly developed a fondness for the Yoshiwara prostitute quarters. In later years Fukuchi would be known as a dandy, a man entertained by no fewer than three thousand women during his life.[35] From the day of his first introduction to brothel life—reportedly by a doddering old Confucian classics teacher—he quickly developed a reputation as a "first-rate student of the Yoshiwara."[36] Indeed, the pseudonym Ōchi, by which he was later known as a Meiji novelist, likely came from the name of Ōji, a geisha to whom he was particularly attracted.[37]

Fukuchi began his formal studies at the school of Asaka Gonsai, a gentle, aged Confucian scholar known primarily for never scolding his disciples.[38] He had decided, before reaching Edo, that it would be wise to continue the pursuit of Eastern scholarship, at least until he could test the direction of the city's intellectual winds. Thus, he entered the Asaka school shortly after arriving in the city and began, somewhat sporadically, to study the Confucian classic *I Ching* ("Book of changes"). He showed considerable aptitude, and early in the spring a scholar-friend named Hayashi urged him to put his knowledge of the classics to use as a means of entering the bakufu and starting on a "rapid road to success." "Buy connections into a group of vassals as a lowly *kurokuwa*," suggested Hayashi, "then request an examination right away. With your ability you are sure to pass and thus raise your status at a bound. . . . There is no better way."[39] Becoming a *kurokuwa*, or menial laborer, he assured Fukuchi, would be the easiest possible way to enter the Confucian-oriented Tokugawa house. Once inside, he would be in a position to commence a rapid climb on the ladder of success.

It was not an unreasonable suggestion. The problem, however, was that, to a somewhat iconoclastic idealist like Fukuchi, Confucian studies—at least the traditional, staid kind taught by Asaka—offered little real excitement or enticement. Once the source of Japan's greatest scholarly creativity and even yet the nominal support of philosophical "orthodoxy," Neo-Confucianism had grown moribund. As Maruyama Masao has so incisively pointed out, Neo-Confucianism's evolution had been constantly downward since the heyday of Ogyū Sorai's articulation of "ancient studies" early in the eighteenth century. Ogyū's assertion that the once normative ancient Way had relevance only as reinterpreted within the historical context of one's own day had robbed Neo-Confucianism of its absolute nature and had led to the rise of a myriad of schools and forces outside the rigid early Tokugawa Confucian framework.[40]

As a result, by the time Fukuchi reached Edo, the most creative intellectual developments were no longer in traditionalist schools, such as those to which Fukuchi was introduced by Asaka, but in the spin-offs and in non-Confucian intellectual traditions. Advocates of Dutch learning, or *rangaku*, for example, had developed a heterodox tradition calling for trade and intercourse with other lands. National learning scholars *(kokugakusha)* had grown more and more vociferous in demanding new respect for the emperor, contending that the imperial institution merited recognition as the Japanese equivalent of the ancient Chinese Way. Scholars from the Tokugawa family *han* of Mito were even now insisting on a restoration of the traditional order, emphasizing antiforeignism and more respect for the imperial institution.[41] And charismatic individuals like Yoshida Shōin were making powerful waves by demanding *both* loyalty to the throne *and* greater personal commitment or action.[42] The staid images of an all-pervasive, early Tokugawa intellectual orthodoxy may themselves have been illusory. But by Fukuchi's day even the illusion was gone. With the very pretense of orthodoxy now a sham, its adherents looked, at least in his eyes, more like anachronisms than champions of The Way.

What was more, Fukuchi quickly came to realize that Edo society precluded the simultaneous study of both Chinese classics and Western languages. Hayashi's eagerness for him to become a Tokugawa vassal, he saw, stemmed as much from a desire to remove Fukuchi from the influence of Western ways as from any wish to help him along the path of success. For the enmity between Eastern and Western orientations was keener in Bakumatsu Edo than any quarrel born of mere theoretical disagreement. It involved maneuverings for influence, challenges to time-hallowed traditions, warfare over the very way of life in which men now found or envisioned themselves. As Fukuchi put it:

> Chinese and Western scholars became bitter enemies. The Chinese scholars would ridicule Western scholars as "alien barbarians," while students of the West would call their Eastern counterparts "old fashioned round-abouts." . . . Since I was not yet twenty years old and had become a leader among the brattish, bohemian student types, I began to sneer at the idea of using Chinese learning to achieve success. When I observed the traditional bakufu students in their peaceful havens of tranquility, I saw that no one was pursuing anything worthwhile; so I decided that I would not waste my life by advancing with them. I rejected Hayashi's advice and began taunting those peace-loving traditionalists with heterodox ideas. It got so bad that I became estranged even from Asaka.[43]

To most, it would have seemed more sensible for Fukuchi to have followed the course suggested by Hayashi, since Chinese scholars enjoyed far brighter prospects in the bakufu circles of the 1850s. But, as a youth, he valued ideas and ideals more than "sensibility." And in the long run it was to Fukuchi's advantage that he rejected the Confucian world. For, as it turned out, the bakufu would last less than another decade, and after its fall only those Tokugawa retainers with a knowledge of the West would have much prospect of success, a point to be discussed later. His apparent "mistake" actually proved auspicious. And that too, it should be noted, was an eventuality that would repeat itself in Fukuchi's career.

Fukuchi also acted wisely in choosing a specific field within the realm of Western studies. For while nearly everyone else studied Dutch, Fukuchi, having observed the widespread use of English by foreigners in Nagasaki, decided to take up the language of the United States and Great Britain. In this respect, the friendship of his old master Namura with the interpreter Moriyama proved helpful. Moriyama was one of only two Edo residents "proficient in English," and for this reason he was kept too busy as an interpreter to have much time for teaching. Indeed, even as bright and persistent a young man as Fukuzawa Yukichi would be totally frustrated in a series of efforts to secure lessons from the willing but "always-too-busy" Moriyama.[44]

Thus, Fukuchi was elated when Moriyama invited him in May to enter his household and learn English while assisting with interpreting duties and serving as head of the master's Dutch school. At the same time, Moriyama also suggested that he study English on alternate days at the home of Edo's other English teacher, Nakahama Manjirō, a shipwrecked fisherman who had spent ten years in the United States and then returned to Japan to become an English instructor at the bakufu's Naval Training School in Edo. Realizing (gloating in!) his favorable situation, Fukuchi would comment later that many future leaders, includiing Fukuzawa, Tsuda Sen, and Numa Morikazu, came and went at his gate "seeking the benefit of Moriyama's instruction."[45] But Fukuchi alone received it.

With entry into the Moriyama household, Fukuchi took a decisive step toward becoming a bakufu vassal. As a foreign office interpreter, Moriyama was deeply involved in negotiations over the scheduled opening of a Yokohama harbor in July and the expected arrival of Rutherford B. Alcock as England's first full-fledged foreign minister in Japan. Quite naturally, Moriyama enlisted Fukuchi's aid in translating materials related to these negotiations. So in less than two months the young scholar, newly turned eighteen, found himself enmeshed in foreign office work. He was not yet a Tokugawa vassal; but once the value of his services became known, official entry into the shogunal administration would be but a formality.

It was, as has been suggested, a turbulent government that Fukuchi's master, Moriyama, was now serving. The commercial treaties had drastically changed life in the capital. Plans were under way to send a mission to Washington to ratify the U.S. treaty. *Jōi* hotheads were engaging in more and more violent opposition to the bakufu's stance toward the foreigners, arguing that advocacy of "Western science and Eastern ethics" was like saying that "although the source of the river contains poisonous water, there is no poison in the lower tributaries so it is alright to drink the water."[46] *Han* such as Satsuma were carrying out internal reforms that appeared to be strengthening their hand vis-à-vis the Tokugawa.[47] The intellectual world was in ferment. Yoshida Shōin described Japan during this very summer as "an old, decaying house" ready to be "blown down by a great wind."[48]

It was the seething nature of these very times that was reflected in the eighteen-year-old Fukuchi as he concluded his student life in mid-1859. He was ambitious—because the turbulence gave energetic, talented iconoclasts a feeling that they might be able to "make a difference." He was Western-oriented—due to his birth in Nagasaki, his study with Namura, and his enmeshment in the chaotic life of Edo. Yet he remained rooted in traditional philosophy—because his education had begun in a home and at a time when traditional values still held sway. Fukuchi was, moreover, brashly self-confident, both because of success in his studies and because he had already enjoyed sufficient close contact with upper-echelon officials to become convinced that they were no more capable than he. He was enamored of gaudy, promiscuous living, because that was the style of Edo's "male culture." Fukuchi had become, in short, a promising product of numerous worlds: of the West and the East, of the feudal and the progressive, the traditional and the modern, the scholarly and the pragmatic. Each of those worlds would play its own important role in the renaissance-like versatility, the personal flamboyance, the gradualist orientation that would typify him in the years to come.

### A Novice Bureaucrat

Fukuchi's actual entry into the bakufu came on June 26, 1859, when he was but eighteen years old. He entered as an interpreter for the foreign office *(gaikoku bugyō)* at Shinagawa on the day that Rutherford Alcock sailed into Edo Bay as Japan's first official foreign minister.[49] It was the beginning of an important period for the youth—an incubatory period of alternating successes and failures, a period in which the *yin-yang* contradictions of Eastern and Western thought would begin to become integrated into something approaching a recognizable system.

That the youthful Fukuchi should have been asked to enter the foreign office was natural, since in 1859 the number of Japanese even slightly acquainted with Dutch or English was far from adequate for all of the diplomatic work being forced on the bakufu. Furthermore, most of Fukuchi's friends were affiliated with the foreign office, and few routes to government position in those days were more direct than that of personal sponsorship. Yamagata Aritomo, for example, had been boosted into public recognition by a personal friend who recommended him to the influential Chōshū revolutionary, Yoshida Shōin.[50] Shibusawa Eiichi's early climb in the bakufu was facilitated instrumentally by the personal patronage of an adviser to the shogun. Fukuchi was to find a similar situation pivotal in his own life. In 1859, his first mentor, Mizuno, was a commissioner of the foreign office; his second patron, Moriyama, was chief of interpreters. Thus, when the foreign *bugyō* learned of Alcock's coming and the impending arrival of the

U.S. minister Townsend Harris, who had been vacationing in Shanghai, it was quite natural to summon Fukuchi into service.

The freshman bureaucrat worked for just one week at the Shinagawa office before being sent to the new port site at Yokohama. But before that week was out, he already had begun to develop a rather arrogant contempt for bakufu officialdom, a contempt that ultimately would prove his undoing as a bureaucrat. He was disillusioned first of all, he said, by the private lives of the officials, especially by their "secret" affairs at Shinagawa brothels despite regulations against prostitution while on official assignment. He was also "disgusted" by the "mediocrity" of most of his colleagues. Even as a teenager he saw himself as their intellectual superior. Most, he felt, were incapable of decisive action and devoid of administrative talent.[51]

On Saturday of his first week as a bureaucrat, after having helped to make domestic arrangements for Alcock's movement to Edo,[52] Fukuchi was ordered to report to Yokohama, site of Japan's newest commercial port and source of the ministry's first intense dispute with the new foreign envoys. The dispute, in which Fukuchi's mentor, Mizuno, was centrally involved, centered on the specific location of the new port on Edo Bay. The treaty of 1858 had called for a port at Kanagawa,[53] and foreigners quite naturally inferred that the first trade relations would be opened at the town that bore that name. The Japanese officials, on the other hand, decided to build the port some three miles away from Kanagawa station, at the small fishing village of Yokohama. When Alcock and Harris arrived at the end of June, they found Yokohama ready for trade, complete with "residences for the Consuls and merchants, shops, a custom house, a governor's office" and two landing docks.[54]

Both Alcock and Harris reacted angrily to the shift in sites, calling it a blatant violation of the treaty. In Alcock's view, Yokohama was nothing but an isolated outpost (more than a mile away from the major traffic route, the Tōkaidō) designed by officials to prevent "any communication with the foreigner, except such as they might choose to allow, and under such conditions as the Government might see fit secretly to impose."[55] To Harris, it was a "second Deshima."[56]

The Japanese, on the other hand, argued more or less candidly that the choice of Yokohama, originally the vegetable field of a bakufu foot soldier, was based simply on a desire to find the site most advantageous to foreigner and Japanese alike. As Mizuno outlined the bakufu case: (1) Kanagawa, located directly on the heavily traveled Tōkaidō, was too easily accessible to antiforeign *(jōi)* zealots; (2) the selection of Yokohama did not violate the spirit of the treaty, since it was located in the general area commonly known by local residents as Kanagawa; (3) Yokohama, possessing greater land area and a deeper harbor than Kanagawa, would make a better port.[57]

Logical as Mizuno's arguments may have sounded, they failed to satisfy Harris and Alcock, who continued throughout July to press for the Japanese to move the port back to Kanagawa. In August, however, Ii Naosuke decided finally that the port would remain in Yokohama, dismissing Mizuno from office to placate the foreigners. Before many weeks had passed, the practical Western merchants had moved their own residences to Yokohama, and the issue had died a natural death, though the bakufu continued to the end to call its Yokohama office the "Kanagawa *bugyō,*" to avoid accusations as "treaty violators."[58]

The brash youth who made his way to this controversial site on July 3 was, in so many ways, more naive than his Japanese superiors must have imagined. The story of Fukuchi's first official trip to Yokohama stands in delightful contrast to the self-confidence for which he was well known. As he described it, he returned home on Saturday night, July 2, after receiving the commission to Yokohama, packed his clothes and a few books, and retired. The next morning, unaware that bakufu officials were allotted two coolies and a horse for such trips, he rose at dawn, had his baggage sent ahead, and began walking toward Shinagawa. The Shinagawa attendants refused to believe him when he claimed to be "Mr. Fukuchi, the official." He was too naive, too young and unpretentious. "I hadn't conjectured, even in dreams, that as an official I should be allotted horses and men," he later recalled. "I wondered why the coolies didn't demand money."[59]

The young Fukuchi's assignment to the Yokohama Customs Bureau (Unjōsho) was a significant one; for it was there, at one of the most hectic offices in the entire Tokugawa bureaucracy, that he began more seriously than ever before to adopt the attitudes, form the friendships, and develop the life-style that would characterize his role in Meiji Japan. By now, he already had formed most of the basic skills on which his contributions would depend; from this summer on, he would seriously begin gathering the practical knowledge and forming the philosophies that would shape those contributions.

One of Fukuchi's first practical lessons—and frustrations— was the absolute necessity of becoming proficient in English. According to a clause in the treaties, Dutch and Japanese were to be the official languages of diplomacy and trade until 1864, but since most Western merchants could not use Dutch and refused to hire translators, it proved an untenable article. The Japanese could have insisted on the letter of the law, but, as Fukuchi noted, to have done so would have been "extremely difficult for both sides. It seemed better, instead, to learn English."[60] Interpreters like Fukuchi thus were forced to put as much effort as time would allow into improving their knowledge of the lingua franca of Western commerce. In the process, Fukuchi learned a rather important lesson on the necessity of fitting the ideal to the possible—a concept that would forever dominate his thinking.

A second lesson, equally important, was that Western "progress" was a two-sided phenomenon, not entirely admirable but not completely reprehensible either. Fukuchi's writings show an admiration for the merchants' levelheaded, no-nonsense approach to business. They got things done, refusing to be intimidated by meaningless traditions. Unlike traditional Japanese, they recognized the practical need for commerce and respected those who engaged in it. Even their contempt for Japanese insistence on form at the expense of efficiency won Fukuchi's admiration.

On the other hand, that same hard-nosed practicality frequently came through to Fukuchi as crudeness or insensitivity.

In Japan, merchants were supposed to remain standing on the earthen portion of a bureaucrat's office when dealing with government officials. Yet Western merchants not only walked onto the *tatami,* or matted flooring; they let their dogs accompany them. And the Westerners showed themselves completely lacking, at least by Japanese standards, in subtlety and public refinement. They even expressed anger openly, noted Fukuchi. As he described the tensions at Yokohama:

> We officials grew indignant, some of us angrily declaring the barbarians' haughtiness and rudeness toward officials to be simply monstrous. There was a very real danger that the violent murder of foreigners would not have to await the coming of irresponsible *jōi* rogues; it appeared that it might occur at the hands of the very officials working at the foreign office and the Kanagawa *bugyō.* But the foreign merchants also frothed in indignation. Prevented by the difficulties of language from fully understanding commercial operations and suffering from indiscretions on the part of customs officials, they often reacted in anger. They protested vigorously against the constant procrastinations in negotiations. And they were not always unjustified in those protests. We did many things to invite their scorn. The only thing that kept matters from getting out of hand was the samurai spirit of the Japanese, the tendency of even lesser officials to bear the situation quietly and with dignity.

Foreign ways and attitudes, he concluded, were a mixed blessing—not to be scorned but not to be aped either.[61]

The last half of 1859 also proved significant in providing Fukuchi's initial introduction to the complex world of economics. Both his writings and his practical involvement in the world of finance would make him one of Japan's most influential economic spokesmen during the first decade and a half of the Meiji era. For that reason, the problems that first piqued his interest at the Yokohama customshouse in 1859 deserve at least cursory consideration.

Most important among these problems was the currency question. According to the treaties, all foreign coins were to be exchanged by the government for Japanese coins, weight for weight, during the first year of commerce.[62] Accordingly, in preparation for the coming of foreign trade, the bakufu decided to mint a new coin that would, hopefully, offset a recent inflation-induced plunge in the value of Japanese currency vis-à-vis the standard Mexican dollar. What the Japanese officials decided upon was the dainishi, a coin somewhat heavier but worth only half as much in token value as the silver ichibu that had been current until then. As a result, when the foreign merchants took their Mexican dollars to the customshouse for exchange, they received (in keeping with the treaty's "weight-for-weight" stipulation) just two of the dainishi, instead of the three ichibu they had expected—yet found the new coins worth only half as much as the ichibu. This meant, in concrete terms, that a three-ichibu vase, which could have been purchased for the equivalent of one Mexican dollar with the old coin, now cost three dollars with the new dainishi.⁶³

The westerners reacted furiously. The Japanese move might be "legal," they admitted, but it was unethical and unacceptable. And by the time Fukuchi arrived in Yokohama, they had forced the foreign ministry to begin negotiations over what to do about the new coin. The Japanese remained intransigent for a time, but by mid-July it had become clear that the new dainishi would not be accepted on domestic markets. So, with great reluctance, Mizuno agreed to its discontinuance.⁶⁴

Even more of a problem, Fukuchi found, was foreign exploitation of Japan's "abnormal ratio of silver to gold."⁶⁵ Elsewhere in the world, silver was normally exchanged for gold at a rate of 16 to 1, whereas in Japan the rate was nearer 6 to 1, and since the treaty stated that foreign gold and silver "may be exported from Japan,"⁶⁶ the resultant gold drain hurt Japan seriously—so seriously that it concerned Harris nearly as much as it did the Japanese. On his advice, the Japanese gold was recast to alter the ratio. But parity with Western standards was long in coming, and the Japanese suffered severely.

Unfortunately, neither Fukuchi nor available records shed much light on his specific roles in connection with these problems. But that he became deeply involved with the issues themselves is clear from the great detail he devotes to them in his memoirs. At the very least he spent long hours discussing them with his mentor, the foreign *bugyō*, Mizuno, and his position in the customshouse most assuredly meant that he often heard (and most likely took part in) the acrimonious disputes occasioned by the currency issues. But the most significant aspect for us is the role these episodes played in introducing Fukuchi to an area that would one day become one of his fortes—economic analysis. His own *Kaiō jidan* ("Recollections") makes it clear that already, in his first summer as an official, he was gaining an unusual grasp of the nature and complexity of economic affairs.[67]

Fukuchi also learned practical lessons about the internal workings of the bureaucracy, and much that he learned disheartened him. He came to hate the petty bickering and clique rivalries that characterized and often paralyzed the bakufu bureaucracy. Promotion, he found, depended more on patronage than on talent. Decisions related more to the groups espousing a solution than to the merits of their proposal.

Fukuchi noted in *Kaiō jidan,* for example, that since the treaty had forbidden the export of copper coins but not of copper utensils, customs officials approved the export of scores of heavy copper tools, such as fire shovels. The censor's office *(ōme-tsuke),* on the other hand, saw this as a violation of the spirit of the treaty and frequently seized items that had already passed through customs. "It became absurd," Fukuchi said. The customs office continued approving the utensils, and the indignant censor's office kept right on seizing them.[68]

A second feature of clique politics affected Fukuchi more personally. When he entered the bakufu, members were already being selected for an embassy that would go to Washington the next year to exchange ratifications of the 1858 commercial treaty. According to the initial plans the leader of the mission was to be Mizuno, commissioner of both the Kanagawa and the foreign offices. Included in the party would be his protégé, Fukuchi. But as a result, first of the dispute regarding the placement of the new port at Yokohama, and second of the embarrassing August murder of two Russian sailors by antiforeign zealots,

Mizuno was dismissed from office. This dismissal, in turn, forced a change in leadership of the embassy to the United States; and when the new makeup was announced, it did not include Fukuchi.

The omission bitterly disappointed the young interpreter who had seen the trip as a chance to help make history as one of Japan's first official foreign travelers. As he wrote to a friend: "I will never be able to make a name for myself unless I travel abroad. . . . I cannot sleep on these winter nights."[69] But it was also a significant lesson in the realities of Bakumatsu politics, the importance of fostering the "right" alliances.

It seems clear then that the initial baptism into the world of Edo officialdom left Fukuchi a markedly changed man by the end of 1859. Chronologically he had advanced by less than twelve months, but psychologically he had spanned a chasm. Until the move to Edo his intellectual quest smacked largely of the simple search for "warm, pure knowledge," a search soured only by occasional personality disputes. But by the end of the year curdles of disillusionment and cynicism had begun to appear. The West no longer seemed so utterly good; Confucian studies (if not traditional ideals) had become a sham; the bakufu seemed overburdened with incompetents and indecisive officials. These feelings were not yet dominant or well articulated, partially because the day-to-day work load was heavy enough to demand most of his attention, partly because mentors like Mizuno and Moriyama continued to provide support and encouragement. But their very appearance meant that Fukuchi would not always be able to work easily within the bureaucracy. That fact, as we shall see, would have important bearing on his career and contributions.

The omission from the trip to the United States was an important source of this awakening disillusionment, but viewed in hindsight it also had its auspicious aspects; for antiforeign sentiment increased so sharply in Japan throughout 1860 and 1861 that, given his propensity for unguarded conversation, a foreign trip likely would have made him a sharp target of the *jōi*, or antiforeign zealots', wrath, perhaps immobilizing him before his public work had really begun. As it was, Fukuchi's life in 1860 and 1861, like that of most Japanese officials involved with foreign affairs, was shaped and shaken more by the tense, xenophobic atmosphere in which he was forced to work than by any of the immediate or specific problems of diplomacy that faced him day after day at the foreign office.

A major explosion came on March 24, 1860, with the assassination of Regent Ii Naosuke by antiforeign extremists. Fukuchi was in Edo when the bloody attack occurred, enjoying a brief holiday. On seeking out his young samurai friends to discuss the incident, he found them overjoyed. Most progressive young bureaucrats saw Ii's administration as reactionary in intent, a severe impediment to long-term improvement in international relations. The only "mourner" Fukuchi encountered, in fact, was Mizuno, who feared that the leadership vacuum caused by Ii's death would give extremists a chance to create even more havoc.[70]

Mizuno's fears proved correct. Throughout 1860 and 1861 foreign office work was hindered constantly by the agitation of *jōi* extremists. Interpreters came to be "ostracized like a special breed of people." The translators' office was known as "outcast village" *(eta machi)*. Foreigners were subjected to threats and assassination plots. Fukuchi even found old friendships suddenly evaporating in the heated atmosphere. Once, when he made a lighthearted call on his old Confucian scholar-friend Hayashi, Hayashi sent a servant to the gate with the message: "I don't deal with barbarians like you. . . . Don't ever again disgrace my place of learning by setting foot in this gate."[71]

Fukuchi's most direct personal encounter with this new *jōi* sentiment came on the night of July 5, 1861, when he was working as an interpreter at the British legation. "There had been a great deal of confusion that day," he recalled, "but after dusk things quieted down amid a gentle rainy season shower." About 10:00 P.M. Fukuchi and his associates had just hung mosquito netting in preparation for going to bed when they heard a sharp commotion outside, followed by shouts: "Ruffians! Break-in!"

Dashing barefoot into the courtyard, Fukuchi was startled by the sight of a panting guard striking down one of the *rōnin*, or masterless warriors, who had broken into the legation. "A blood-stained sword in his hand, [the guard] took the freshly-severed head from which blood was gushing and put it on the veranda," Fukuchi said. "It was a meritorious deed; for he was a guard, . . . but this was the first freshly-severed neck I had ever seen and, at the time, I was stunned."[72]

It became clear in the aftermath that the attack had been carried out by a group of *rōnin* from the xenophobic Mito *han*, and that the Japanese guards had fought them off vigorously and effectively. Nonetheless, the fact that twenty-three persons had been killed or wounded left both the foreign community and *gaikoku bugyō* employees more jittery than ever.[73] A knowledge of things Western might one day ease the route to success and political influence for men like Fukuchi, but in the summer of 1861 it provided excitement at best and alienation or death at worst. One wonders if Fukuchi ever questioned the wisdom of his decision two years earlier to opt for a career in Western studies.[74]

One other significant development during Fukuchi's first two years as an interpreter was a revival of his interest in newspapers. Now, for the first time, he had a chance to see a wide range of papers. He would borrow newspapers occasionally from foreign legations to study the development of affairs in the West. But their prose style defied easy reading, and more often than not he gave up after a paragraph or two.[75] Then in mid-1860, when members of the embassy to the United States sent back news accounts of their activities, Fukuchi's superiors ordered him to translate them. Seeking help from secretaries at the U.S. legation, he finally succeeded in reading his first articles from start to finish.[76] A deeper understanding of newspapers would have to await a trip to the West, where he could peruse them regularly. But his interest was growing.

That trip was not far off. After the U.S. embassy was dispatched in 1860, British and French diplomats began calling for a similar mission to their countries to avoid the appearance of favoritism. At first, the *rōjū,* or senior bakufu councillors, expressed misgivings about such a trip, fearing reactions of the antiforeign elements. But early in 1861, Townsend Harris suggested that the United States might be willing to postpone the opening of ports in Edo, Osaka, Hyogo, and Niigata (scheduled by treaty for 1863); and the *rōjū,* afraid of violence if the ports had to be opened on schedule, responded with an announcement that they would send a mission to Europe to seek consent there for postponement. Again Fukuchi's mentor, Mizuno, was bypassed as mission leader in favor of Takenouchi Yasunori, lord of Shimotsuke. Fukuchi was more fortunate this time, however, and when the membership of the embassy was announced his name was on the list as an interpreter.

From the beginning of preparations, Fukuchi's attitudes and comments gave evidence of his already considerable contacts with Western ways.[77] When others insisted on taking "mountains" of supplies, he was appalled—and said so. He laughed openly when officials decided to take along a thousand pairs of straw sandals for "foot travel" in Europe. He also ridiculed plans to take along javelins, stirrups, saddles, white rice, soy sauce, and pickled vegetables. And he told his superiors that their decision to take five hundred bottles of *miso* (bean paste) was impractical. They told him, in turn, to remember his rank and keep quiet. But when the "imperishable" *miso* began to "stink so badly" between Hong Kong and Singapore that they had to "throw jars and all into the sea," Fukuchi laughed again.[78]

As in the early months at Yokohama, the trip's importance lay not in Fukuchi's particular role (as a twenty-year-old interpreter, his opinions hardly shaped Japan's future!) but in its impact on Fukuchi himself. This was the youth's first direct contact with a foreign land, and as such it provided a welter of stimulating ideas, new experiences, and puzzling encounters that would shape his powerfully influential editorials a decade later. For that reason, it deserves more than passing notice.

The itinerary of the trip was exciting. In early March the mission landed at Suez, giving Fukuchi and his colleagues a chance to take their first train rides, across Egypt. On April 3 they docked at Marseilles, and two weeks later met Napoleon III. From France they went to England in May; to Holland in June; and then to Russia, Germany, and Portugal before returning to Japan in late December.[79]

The diplomatic efforts of the group yielded rather positive results in England. The British government, at the belated urging of Alcock, agreed in June to a five-year delay in opening the ports, and the other treaty powers followed suit. Fukuchi was not totally happy with the agreement, since it included patronizing warnings about Japanese maintenance of each clause in the 1858 treaty and proposed additional items for inclusion in a 5 percent tariff limit.[80] But he saw it as the best solution possible, the only way of "extinguishing the sparks before our eyes," and accordingly declared himself satisfied.[81]

Far more frustrating to Fukuchi were the delegation's efforts at diplomacy in Moscow. For years Japan and Russia had disagreed over the right of suzerainty and the boundaries of Sakhalin (Karafuto),[82] the island north of Hokkaido where a number of Japanese hunters and fishermen lived. In Moscow, the Russians rather unexpectedly offered to accept the forty-eighth parallel as Sakhalin's Russo-Japanese boundary. Since Russia had always before claimed the entire island (it extends from the forty-sixth to the fifty-fourth parallels), while the Japanese had claimed only the portion south of the fiftieth parallel, it seemed a reasonable compromise.

The Takenouchi mission had not, however, been formally commissioned to deal with the Sakhalin issue; so a major dispute arose over whether they should assume the authority and sign an agreement or wait for specific authorization from the home government. Takenouchi favored the former position, but several of his subordinates argued that to make such an agreement would be traitorous, equivalent to giving up national territory without proper authority. Fukuchi took an active part in the debate, arguing in a rather lengthy memorandum that the Russian offer was eminently fair and should be accepted, since such an opportunity might not soon come again.[83] To his dismay, the advocates of caution triumphed, and Japan and Russia agreed merely to send plenipotentiaries to Sakhalin for on-site inspections before the conclusion of any treaty.

To Fukuchi, this incident was another example of general ignorance and ineptness on the part of Japan's leading diplomats. He referred to the three leaders of the embassy, none of whom knew any Western languages, as "blind-deaf pilgrims."[84] Early in the Moscow negotiations he had cringed when the Russians "sneered" at the Japanese offer of an ancient Dutch map as serious evidence that world geographers recognized the fiftieth parallel as Sakhalin's proper Russo-Japanese boundary.[85] Then the embassy's "weakness" in refusing to sign an agreement seemed but an embarrassing capstone. As a powerful newspaper editor, Fukuchi would call often for diplomats to be more decisive, better informed about the ways and techniques of the West—a point that will become clear later on. It was in Moscow that such ideas began to take new root.

Even more important than these diplomatic lessons, to Fukuchi personally, was the face-to-face confrontation the months brought with the great technological and cultural gap between Japan and the Western world. In Hong Kong, he saw Western dancing for the first time—that form of entertainment where "several couples come forward, . . . separate and meet, assemble and disperse, advance and retire, then suddenly went [sic] swiftly round and round" to music that sounded "very die away."[86] In Egypt he took his first train ride, saw "lightning-news-long" telegraph wires, and went through a tunnel. In Paris, he expressed astonishment at the size of hotels ("thousands of rooms and dining halls capable of serving 3,000 people"); at the gas lights (evening streets "looked as if it were daytime"); at the cameras, the circus, the kangaroos at the zoo, the theater.[87] And in England, he and his companions were amazed at such things as an international exhibition; weapons factories; the British Museum; a Birmingham glassblowing factory; and, most confounding of all, British politics.[88] "Truly," commented Fukuchi in a letter to his father, "I could not possibly record in my diary all the strange talk and rare things I daily encounter."[89]

Everywhere Fukuchi encountered newspapers. On getting up

in Ceylon on Friday morning, February 28, embassy members were dumbfounded to see, already delivered to their hotel, a newspaper account of their entrance into port on the previous day. This newspaper "is very light and flimsy, and not to be relied on; but the quickness of its appearance was astonishing," observed one of Fukuchi's companions.[90] Fukuchi reported buying an English-language paper after arriving in Paris and being amazed at the rapid printing, as well as at the detailed knowledge reporters had gained concerning the embassy. By the time he reached London, where he visited his first newspaper office, he was reading newspapers frequently, interviewing reporters, and "envying" the freedom and skill of the British press.[91]

It was, in fact, a different Fukuchi, a radically altered young man of twenty-one, who returned to Edo at the end of 1862. He had read as much as possible while abroad about the history of England, the United States, and France. He had seen the power of the Western military, and he had encountered new and difficult political concepts—democracy, republicanism, independence, freedom, elections, people's rights, representative government. He had seen Japan's own diplomatic "weakness," born both of ignorance and of a lack of military and economic strength. He had seen, at first hand, the Western press—its speed in reporting, its detailed coverage, its freedom. Not everything appealed to him; but there was no denying the technological superiority of the West, no denying that Japan could learn much from her new international "friends." He would, he decided during the trip, become a more active proponent of that Western learning.

### A Frustrated Bureaucrat

The dreams that occupied Fukuchi on his return voyage were exhilarating. Unaware until near the end of the journey of the growth of antiforeignism at home, he gave himself to bright speculation about the future. There would, he imagined, be a "promotion in rank." There also would be a significant new leadership role in foreign office decisions, perhaps even a hero's welcome. And surely his tales would enrapture friends for months into the future.

> Being of low rank, I did not entertain the thought of being queried by the shogunal family, but I was sure I would be asked about Western conditions . . . in intimate conversations with some *rōjū*. For though it may be rude to say so, we translators and interpreters were really the only ones capable of drawing a true picture of the situation in the West since the leaders of the mission could neither speak nor read in Western languages.[92]

One can imagine what must have been his surprise, then, on returning to work the day after arrival in Edo in January 1863, when "only two or three friends, besides my wife and an old servant . . . came by to visit, while the others acted as if they did not know me." Even when it came time to leave the foreign office that day, "not a soul asked me about foreign matters."[93]

They acted as if he had never left the country. Yet it was not the same country. If the antiforeign sentiment had seemed like an erratic but spreading bonfire before, it now had become a blazing conflagration, fanned by a series of incidents and developments during 1862, all of which had given the *jōi* forces increasing confidence. In February of that year, for example, several *shishi* had made an attempt on the life of *rōjū* Andō Nobumasa. Early in May the modernizing Tosa leader, Yoshida Tōyō, was assassinated by loyalists. The bakufu itself had been forced by court factions in Kyoto to promise the eventual expulsion of all westerners—despite the mission's commitment in Europe to prevent obstacles to foreign trade. Even the marriage of the royal princess Kazunomiya to the Tokugawa shogun had merely agitated *jōi* sentiments, since some *shishi* saw it as an evidence of bakufu strong-arm tactics and others interpreted it as a sign of shogunal weakness. The sensational killing in September of Britisher Charles Richardson by members of the Satsuma *daimyō*'s procession had inflamed passions among Japanese and foreigners alike.

In short, what had essentially been a relatively unorganized, extremist force when the embassy left early in 1862 had by the end of the year become a powerful, increasingly well organized movement supported more and more openly by several powerful *han*, as well as by the court itself. Kyoto, rather than Edo, "had become the center of national politics,"[94] and *jōi* forces, as Mizuno told Fukuchi, were now pursuing a "scorched-earth" policy, intent upon driving out the foreigners at any cost.[95] Moderates in both the court and the bakufu were increasingly showing themselves impotent before the spreading flames. In fact, by March 1863, violence would reach a peak where extremists would act with impunity in killing three retainers of leading probakufu nobles, in each case sending the victim's severed ears or head to the "offending" courtiers.[96] The bakufu, not strong enough to openly oppose the foreign forces, now was finding its authority equally endangered by antiforeign forces at home. It was not a period for passionate—or even dispassionate—talk about foreign affairs.

Members of the returned embassy thus found themselves in the frustrating position of possessing exciting new knowledge about which they could engage no one in conversation. Most precarious of all, perhaps, was Fukuchi. He had become too enamored with Western progress to join the xenophobes. At the same time, he was temperamentally unfit to be as "moderate in speech and manner" as his colleague on the trip, Fukuzawa Yukichi.[97] A braggart, a frequenter of geisha quarters, an argumentative type who "loved" to "engage in such sharp debates that even my colleagues began seeing me as an enemy," Fukuchi became a threat both to the bakufu and to his own advancement.[98] On at least three occasions following the mission's return, extremists made attempts on Fukuchi's life, in one instance inviting him to a "group discussion" to hear his views, then later telling him they had planned to murder him after the session and had changed their plans only because his direct conversation (he had been warned by a secret friend in the group to be "most circumspect") had convinced them that he was "loyal."[99]

As a result, Fukuchi spent most of the remaining Tokugawa years in varying depths of depression and personal frustration, a victim of the explosive nature of rapidly changing times. Early in 1863, the foreign office ordered him not to speak about foreign matters, even in private,[100] and instructed Moriyama that Fukuchi "should, as much as possible, do his investigating at home . . . and should be told not to meet with other people." The instructions were carried out, and although he continued to receive periodic raises in rank and salary, most of his work for the next five years had to be done away from the official spotlight. Such restrictions were, of course, excruciating to an extrovert like Fukuchi. But what made them even worse was the fact that once removed from opportunities for direct contact with the official world he also tended to be forgotten. The result was half a decade of eclipse. Records show him called to work in times of diplomatic crisis such as the negotiations over the Richardson affair in the summer of 1863. They also point to a certain amount of involvement with old friends like Mizuno, even taking part covertly in an attempted probakufu march on Kyoto led by *rōjū* Ogasawara Nagamichi.[101] And they reveal a number of private projects launched by Fukuchi, the most significant of them being the creation in 1866 of a French- and English-language school. The school quickly attracted over fifty students, but it too proved abortive when bakufu officials, noting the presence in its ranks of a number of anti-Tokugawa students, ordered it to close.[102] On the whole, Fukuchi's life from 1863 to 1867 was thus one of nearly unmitigated frustration. Damned to the realms of oblivion, he described life as being "like a prison."[103]

The one escape from all this frustration came in 1865, when he spent half a year in Europe again, this time as an interpreter for the Shibata Gochu mission that had been commissioned to lay the groundwork for the construction of a naval shipyard at Yokosuka.[104] Even on this trip, his services were not overly taxed, partly because naval matters were outside his ken, and partly because the Frenchman François L. Verney accompanied the group and handled most of its business affairs. Leisure in Europe was different, however, from leisure in Edo, and instead of complaining Fukuchi professed those months to be "among the most enjoyable'' of his life. He gave his time to studying international law (until he found it ''too difficult'' for his limited French); to sampling such Western thinkers and writers as Herbert Spencer, Thomas Henry Huxley, Alfred Tennyson, and John Stuart Mill; to spending long hours in conversation with an eccentric Frenchman named Leon de Roni, who taught Japanese, spoke Japanese (''thirty percent was understandable''), drank Japanese tea, smoked Japanese tobacco, and grew indignant if anyone criticized Japan;[105] to attending the theater; and to studying the press. It was this last activity that was to have the most direct bearing on his later life. As Fukuchi put it:

> I was not particularly pressed with official duties; so, finding time on my hands, I questioned a number of leading men in London and Paris about the newspaper world. I learned just how powerful a newspaper could be in shaping public opinion about domestic and foreign political issues. *And, as a result, I began pondering the thought that, should I have the opportunity and should my literary talents prove adequate, I might sometime become a newspaper reporter myself, so as to taste the pleasure of discussing current events in public.* In other words, I envied the newspaper reporters of France and England, and as a result I began entertaining new and wild ideas about my own future.[106]

Once back in Japan, Fukuchi's life returned to its own ''new normalcy'' of boredom and oblivion, a state not to be fully shaken off until the fall of the Tokugawa two years later. It should not be assumed, however, that these years were a total waste. They may well have played a role almost as significant in shaping Fukuchi's later contributions as did the feverish period that preceded them. Now, for the first time, he found (was forced into!) time for contemplation, for assimilation and evaluation. The pace of his life until 1863 had been frenetic, almost beyond the point of belief for a lad not yet twenty-two. Busy studying foreign languages, interpreting and reacting to new experiences, he had had no time to evaluate or think through his philosophies. Now, consigned to leisure, he had a chance to ponder and record his impressions of Europe. He had time to visit with Mizuno. And after each visit, he also had time to reflect on what the senior official had said, to mull over Mizuno's exasperation with bakufu unwillingness to take drastic steps (such as "nationalizing" *han* military forces), as well as his hope that the nation's traditional order could yet be salvaged or revived. "At first I would think him too radical," Fukuchi noted; "but then I would think over what he had said and realize he was right." Mizuno, already a professed advocate of "progress for the sake of order," influenced Fukuchi most in these years simply because the youth had time now to listen to his expostulations and then think them through.[107]

These years also gave Fukuchi a chance to brood over the slow pace, the frustrations, and the incompetence one might expect to encounter if he devoted his career to a bureaucracy. He saw most officials as "wooden monkeys" who spent much of their time "bluffing," too "paralyzed" by traditions, mediocrity, and fear to act decisively.[108] Their reactions to his own loquacity did nothing to moderate his contempt. If he would one day express general cynicism about the bureaucracy, the origins of that cynicism may well have lain in the broodings of these years.

To overemphasize the role played by periods of idleness would, of course, be a mistake. But to overlook their impact, as is often done, is greater folly. It is difficult to say precisely where they led Fukuchi intellectually, since he left almost no writings in these years. One can only look at the influences that touched him—the thought of Europe, the traditional pragmatism of Mizuno, the frustrating strictures of the bureaucracy, the press of England and France—and then look ahead to the stances of his mature life. As one examines those mature attitudes—the dependence on Western logic to support even Japanese premises, the concern for "progress and order," the tempestuous love-hate relationship with the bureaucracy, and the undying faith in the role of the press—he can only speculate that the "years of silence" must have had a significant impact, perhaps even more of an impact than continued frenetic activity would have had. Perhaps less. This is not a satisfying answer to the student interested in exact correlations. But it is probably the only one possible.

Much less uncertain is the question of what was happening to the bakufu itself in these years. If 1862 had been a pivotal year in fully igniting the sparks of antiforeignism, the following year was important in signaling a shift of the *sonnō jōi* movement away from antiforeignism and toward "respect for the emperor"—a circumlocution (at least in the minds of cynics) for another key phrase of the period, *tōbatsu,* or "destroy the bakufu." Impressed with Western military might during encounters at Kagoshima and Shimonoseki during 1863 and disturbed with bakufu ineptitude, the extremists concluded that Japan's only salvation lay in changing regimes. Even more ominous for the Tokugawa was the fact that by 1866, the leadership in the *sonnō* movement had largely been taken over by establishment forces, many of which until then had worked with the government to control extremism. Especially problematic was the victory of a reformist, anti-Tokugawa government in Chōshū in 1865 and the obvious, if initially covert, decision of the large *han* of Satsuma to align itself with the Chōshū loyalists. It was, in fact, this alliance that spelled the final doom of a disastrous bakufu military expedition against Chōshū in the fall of 1866.

Maneuvering was intense throughout these years, with the bakufu belatedly undertaking active reforms and leaders of independent or pro-Tokugawa *han* such as Tosa working to effect reconciliation. But if inactivity was Fukuchi's curse in these years, too much activity was the curse of the government. For the preponderance of that activity, it seemed, was merely a response, an effort to counteract forces both at home and abroad bent on havoc, if not on total destruction of the bakufu. Few predicted an immediate Tokugawa fall by mid-1867. Even fewer expected that things could go on much longer as they were.

# CHAPTER II

# The Search for a Vocation: 1868–1874

> *You don't accept me. . . . I state my opinion of things frankly and win out by force of reason. You are incapable of trusting me because my knowledge is a threat.* [1]

On November 10, 1867, Fukuchi heard a rumor. Shogun Tokugawa Keiki, said a friend, had been so badly shaken by the decline of bakufu vitality and the growing strength of anti-Tokugawa forces that he had decided to resign and restore political power to the new boy-emperor, Meiji. Not so, replied Fukuchi, the story was beyond belief.[2] But Fukuchi, like most of his colleagues, was wrong, and on November 14, an official announcement confirmed the rumor: Keiki had indeed submitted his resignation on the previous Saturday, hoping apparently to avert a civil war and to facilitate the formation of an imperial council of *daimyō*, of which he would perhaps be the head. The anti-Tokugawa *han* of Satsuma and Chōshū had, at least for the moment, triumphed. Imperial rule had been restored, and Fukuchi's life was on the verge of a dramatic shift.

Government operations continued largely as usual in the weeks immediately following Keiki's startling resignation, with the Tokugawa foreign office handling most of the diplomatic affairs in the absence of any new government officials with the experience to do so. As a result, Fukuchi was called to Osaka in the middle of December to help arrange the peaceful opening of a commercial port in that area. Events occurred rapidly during his first six weeks there. On January 3, the anti-Tokugawa *han* carried off a coup d'etat in Kyoto, seizing control of the throne. The new "government," led by Satsuma and Chōshū men, then ordered Keiki to surrender all his landholdings. Late in January the Tokugawa forces commenced hostilities against the new government's army at Toba-Fushimi on the road to Kyoto.

Yet, Fukuchi remained convinced that the Tokugawa castle in Osaka would never be breached, that it would remain an impregnable fortress from which the Tokugawa would regain control of Japan. The final downfall of the 250-year-old regime had been too abrupt, he thought, to be credible. Indeed, in mid-January when Fukuchi had drawn up a proposed military strategy for shogunal resistance, he had been assured by a commissioner at the foreign office that secret allies in Kyoto would, at the last moment, forestall any final bakufu collapse.[3]

The commissioner's optimism was misplaced, however, and as Fukuchi prepared to retire on the night of January 30, a colleague in the foreign office rushed into his room with a warning to flee Osaka.

"Don't joke," Fukuchi retorted.

"Go over to the council room and have a look for yourself! Everyone has already fled!"

A quick survey proved the official right. The foreign commissioner's office had indeed been evacuated, left with nothing but a few scattered documents, a forgotten pistol in one corner, and a box lunch on the floor. So Fukuchi fled too (after eating the discarded lunch!), and as he sailed out of nearby Hyogo harbor a short time later he saw "black smoke leaping into the sky" from the overrun castle. "I could not," he said, "bear to look."[4]

Back in Edo, Fukuchi found the Tokugawa castle a scene of confusion. The shogun had returned from Osaka the previous day (February 5) and convened a conference on the course of action the fallen regime should take. Keiki himself favored submission to the new government; but numerous retainers, including Fukuchi's old superior, Mizuno, argued heatedly for intensified resistance. "There was much noisy discussion by everyone," reported Fukuchi, but in the end Keiki ordered his followers to submit peacefully to the new Meiji government.

It was not, however, a unanimous decision; for while a majority submitted to Keiki's will, some of them even entering the new Meiji government, others joined military resistance units. Some spent the early months of 1868 simply debating, uncertain about what action to take. A number of older officials took the course of Mizuno, who invited Fukuchi to "go for a drink" on the afternoon of February 10. "I thought that strange for this strict, austere man," recalled the protégé, "but I went along." Over sake, Mizuno told Fukuchi he had decided to retire for good. Disappointed in Tokugawa Keiki's unwillingness to resist, he would wash his hands of public life. Mizuno shed tears as he related the decision.[5]

For a time, Fukuchi joined those who simply debated. He remained aloof from the official discussions, and he spurned membership in a fighting unit.[6] But he was not interested in joining the new "talent-oriented" government either; for, though frustrated with his own bureaucratic experiences, his commitment to the Tokugawa family had never wavered. Instead, as passing weeks gave Fukuchi and his friends opportunity to stimulate each other's resentments ("to froth at the mouth in indignation," as he put it[7]), he thought again of his European experiences with the press and decided to bring a growing dream to fruition. Events seemed right; he knew he had the needed talents. So he would act. He would launch his own paper and fight the new regime with his pen.

### A Fighting Journalist

The first issue of Fukuchi's paper, which he named the *Kōko Shimbun* ("The World"), appeared on May 24, 1868, just nine days after his twenty-seventh birthday. From the first, it was both innovative and "popular,"[8] filled with news of the civil war, gossip about officials and samurai, "correspondence" columns, translations from foreign newspapers, and memorials to the government. It sold for one momme per issue, appeared once every two to four days and aimed to "make private, secret matters widely known."[9] It was, in short, one of Japan's earliest Western-style papers.

This is not to say that the *Kōko Shimbun* was among Japan's earliest attempts at journalism per se. For at least two and a half centuries, major incidents had been reported in broadsides called *kawaraban* (slate impression) and hawked or sold in the street several days after the event. These sheets frequently were referred to by readers as *yomiuri* ("read and sell"), and by

mid-1868 as many as three thousand of them had been issued
—all on a one-time-only basis.[10] Though they could hardly be
called newspapers, they did serve the important function of introducing the idea of printing and selling news.

Then, six years before the Restoration, the bakufu's Yōsho
Shirabe Dokoro (Office for the study of Western writings)[11] had
issued Japan's first "newspaper," the *Kanhan Batabia Shimbun*. Little more than a compilation of direct translations from
a Dutch paper in Batavia, Java, it lasted less than two months;
but as the first publication of news on a sustained basis, it broke
imporant new ground.[12] It was followed in 1864 by what has
been called "Japan's first daily newspaper," the *Shimbunshi*,[13]
a sheet that also died after a mere two months. Similar crude
publishing attempts continued from time to time until the Restoration—most of them coming out irregularly, none boasting
large circulations, their news tending to be more dramatic than
accurate, their delivery methods archaic. Some editors asked
subscribers to pick up their papers at the newspaper office;[14]
others hired "delivery boys" who wore dress coats and stopped
to smoke and drink tea at the home of each subscriber.[15] All fell
far short of the press standards Fukuchi had found in Europe.
Yet, despite their lack of sophistication or journalistic expertise,
the editors of these papers performed a significant function:
they introduced to a growing segment of educated Japanese the
concept of printing news and other information in a periodic,
commercial sheet.

With the Restoration of 1868 came Japan's first great leap
toward the development of a modern press, as well as Fukuchi's
first chance to become personally involved in the world of journalism. Numerous bakufu retainers, seething with indignation
over the fall of the Tokugawa yet hesitant (like Fukuchi) to take
up arms, sought outlets for their talents and fervor. Military
skirmishes provided abundant material for reportorial initiative. As a result, a host of new newspapers sprang up in the first
six months of 1868. The first of these, *Chūgai Shimbun*, was
begun in March by one of Fukuchi's close friends, Yanagawa
Shunsan. It styled itself the "father of Japanese journalism"

and claimed a circulation of fifteen hundred within a month after commencing publication. Two weeks later, the *Naigai Shimpō* came into existence, purportedly to supplement *Chūgai* by printing "the news from English papers in Yoko-hama and . . . all government orders and reports."[16] It would publish fifty issues in all, more than any other paper of the period.[17] These two were followed during the next three months by at least fifteen other such papers.[18]

The Restoration newspapers had much in common. They were, on the whole, products of former Tokugawa vassals who still opposed the new government. All were published on an ir-regular basis, most coming out every four to six days, depend-ing on the speed with which their staffs could write articles and prepare woodblocks. Their circulations were quite small, and the accuracy of their news stories was questionable. All of them appeared in pamphlet form (indeed, some scholars refer to them as "newsbooks" rather than as newspapers[19]); most issued from the pens of former English students; and by the end of the summer, all but one or two had died, victims of the declining interest of their readers and of government suppression.[20]

Conditions in the spring of 1868 seemed ideal, then, for Fu-kuchi to launch his own, rather innovative, newspaper. He was out of work; his new home across the street from Ueno's Shino-bazu Pond was large enough to house a wood-block printing press; several of his friends had begun papers, and—most im-portant—he needed both an income and an outlet for his pent-up fury. "I saw a chance to try out my pet theories on society," he said. "So I consulted secretly with Jōno Dempei, Hiraoka Kosuke and Nishida Densuke," all literary friends, and on May 24 the first number of *Kōko Shimbun* went on sale. Each of its twenty-two issues consisted of ten to twelve pages, each page a *hanshi* (about six by nine and one-half inches). Issues came out as often as Fukuchi and his assistants could get them ready. Fu-kuchi drafted nearly all the articles himself and later described his journalistic product as "a distant relative of today's news-papers."[21]

He attempted, quite successfully, to make his newspaper dis-

tinctive in at least two respects. First, its news coverage was
broader than that of other papers. Most editors relied heavily on
official proclamations or on translations from foreign-language
papers, showing little enterprise in the development of their
own news areas and sources. Fukuchi, on the other hand, determined to include many of the types of news that he had seen in
European papers. Hence his inclusion of detailed battle reports,
drama stories, official decrees, opinion columns, charts and pictures, as well as occasional items about actors, the Western
press, or European royalty. When he noticed items in other
papers that his own *Kōko Shimbun* had missed, he went so far
as to suggest to his readers that they consult, for example,
*"Chūgai Shimbun,* which has published this news as an ex-
tra."[22] The content of *Kōko Shimbun,* said one twentieth-
century observer in reference to this breadth, was "quite
newspaper-like for its time."[23]

Second, the *Kōko Shimbun* aimed at a wider readership. In
the hierarchical society of the Tokugawa era, only educated
male adults were regarded as worthy of attention by serious
writers or scholars. Yet Fukuchi, influenced again by what he
had seen in Europe, announced in his first issue that everyone
—"including women and children"—would be able to read his
paper.[24] It was for this reason that he included sketches of warriors and castles, pictures of Western maidens, numerous maps,
and more *furigana*[25] than did other editors. He also attempted
to write news more simply and understandably and called on
the assistance of his friend Jōno, a well-known writer of "cheap
fiction" *(gesaku),* to help give the newspaper a popular flavor.
Most other papers of the period were put out by elitist samurai
concerned more with impressive style than with simple communication. To them, Fukuchi's techniques were "hereti-
cal, . . . too frank, not inhibited by taboos."[26] Yet that style,
the most progressive of the day, "created quite an audience,"
making the *Kōko Shimbun* one of Japan's first newspapers to
deserve the label "modern."[27]

The primary characteristic of Fukuchi's paper, however, lay
not so much in its breadth or simplicity as in its political comment. The *Kōko Shimbun* opposed the government more regu-

larly, more completely, and more forcefully than any other paper. A brief consideration of that comment should, in fact, throw considerable light on the mind-set of the more enlightened men who held out against the new administration in this period.

Evidencing the sort of simplistic analysis so often reserved for "losers," most scholars have ascribed to the *Kōko Shimbun* an undiscriminating, unsophisticated probakufu, anti-imperial tone. Fukuchi was, after all, a man of deep emotions who despised the Satchō faction[28] that had led the Restoration. So such a position would seem only natural. Yet a careful study of the paper shows a much more carefully drawn point of view. While Fukuchi's articles did oppose the men who had set up the new regime and the method by which they had overthrown the Tokugawa, and while the articles evidenced unshaken loyalty to the Tokugawa family as Japan's rightful rulers, they held scant sympathy for the old administrative apparatus and indicated no opposition to the ascendancy of the imperial household. Fukuchi wrote that the bakufu administrative structure had become anachronistic, too cumbersome and "feudalistic" to propel Japan into a new age. At the same time, imperial rule was the historical constant that made Japan unique (a theme that would dominate his writing for the next twenty years). Thus, the best system would involve a complete overhaul of the bakufu system, with the Tokugawa family heading the administration and the emperor serving as sovereign.

Rather than simply longing for old ways or denouncing the imperial system, he focused his attacks merely—and specifically—on the new Satchō-led government that had established de facto rule, even while defending the Tokugawa family. The new government, he said, was not leading Japan toward a true restoration of imperial rule but toward another bakufu-type system with different people in control. As Fukuchi himself described his attitude:

From the first, I had not a particle of objection to reverence for the emperor; nor was I opposed to the shogun's restoration of the government to the emperor. But when I observed the actual situation, I saw that power had been returned not to the court but to Satsuma and Chōshū. In other words, the Tokugawa had fallen and Satsuma and Chōshū had formed a second bakufu. This not only ran contrary to my expectations but opposed the spirit of the Restoration.[29]

This conviction colored everything Fukuchi did at the *Kōko Shimbun*. He named his publishing company the Tori Naki Sato Zappōkyoku, a parody of an old Japanese saying that "a one-eyed man is king in the land of the blind" *(tori naki sato no kōmori)*.[30] The paper's factual reports emphasized the cruelty of government forces and the victories of the antigovernment, Aizu-Kuwana resisters. Well over four-fifths of the paper's civil war articles, in fact, reported rebel victories, while only one told of a clear-cut government triumph.[31] Most of the paper's memorials and petitions dealt with the faults of the new regime.

On July 9, for example, an exchange of correspondence between two members of the largely progovernment Kamei family in Tsuwano *han* spelled out the emotional attachments that inspired many resisters.[32] In the first letter, a family patriarch chided Kamei Yūnosuke, an iconoclast, for efforts he had been making against the Meiji government and urged him to return to Tsuwano. "You have held the head family in contempt and violated our will," he wrote; "there is no impropriety greater than this." Yūnosuke's reply, which consumed four times as much space, carefully detailed the rationale for his (and others') resistance. The Tokugawa, he said, were not enemies of the throne, even though they had temporarily lost their place of respect. If loyalty to this family, which had ruled Japan for over two hundred years, made "estrangement unavoidable, . . . I accept it." Moreover, he refused to admit to having shown impropriety: "I have had no lord but the Tokugawa, and I do not perceive that to be disloyalty. . . . Nor have I ever heard loyalty described as an impropriety." He pointedly reminded his elder that Chōshū, with which Tsuwano had sided, had also been called disloyal a few years earlier. "So if you think of me as being truly disloyal, injust or criminal, that fact can be attributed to nothing more than a difference of opinion." The views of both sides were presented in this exchange, but only those of the (antigovernment) son received a genuine, full hearing.

The most incisive, controversial expostulation of Fukuchi's point of view came on June 24 in an eight-page article called "Kyōjaku ron" ("On strength and weakness"), in which the editor explained why genuine peace could not be achieved by the existing government. As perhaps the sharpest rationale of the resistance ever printed, it became one of the pivotal articles in the history of Japanese journalism, leading to Fukuchi's arrest and goading the government into a policy of press control.[33] Its contents thus deserve examination.

Under an "author uncertain" signature, Fukuchi[34] opened the treatise with the query of an unidentified "guest": "Will there be peace now that the Tokugawa has fallen?" Then he proceeded to answer the query in negative fashion.

He maintained, first of all, that whereas there was no reason for an antigovernment *han* such as Aizu to oppose the imperial will per se, the despotic nature of the "southwestern clique" likely would make continued armed resistance a necessity. Unfortunately, this resistance could not be expected to bring immediate peace, but instead would probably lead Japan into another time of "confusion like that of the warring states period."[35]

And who, came the next question, "will be able to pacify the situation then?"

To which Fukuchi replied: "I do not know." He then proceeded to give an answer at great length.

It was clear, he maintained, that the western *han* could not do it, since "not one man from the West *[Kansai]* has controlled Japan . . . since ancient times. Think about it," he said, "Genji rose in Izu; Nitta and Ashikaga came from Jōshu; Oda and Toyotomi were from Owari. The Tokugawa hailed from Mikawa. Our land's tendency is to be strong in the East and weak in the West. By establishing the shogunate in the East *[Kantō]*, the Tokugawa were able to preserve peace forever—as if holding an entire country in check by grasping the area of the throat."

Did this mean that pacification of the country would come

from Aizu? Fukuchi did not think so. Recognizing the fait accompli of the Restoration, he argued that while the Aizu troops would easily be able to march as far as Kyoto, they would find it "difficult" to subdue all of Japan. Any such attempt on their part would split Japan and lead perhaps to another Sekigahara.[36] "And what a great military calamity that would create!" he added; for the situation was not the same as it had been a hundred years earlier when Aizu might easily have won a civil war.

Nor, in the third place, would it do for a restored shogunate —or any autocratic government, for that matter—to wield authority in the name of a titular emperor, since this would lead to "the kind of mis-government in which one country would have two rulers," a system that would bring disgrace to Japan. Even if such a government were to initiate a period of peace, he said, "power would merely pass into the hands of the strong *han,* leaving the emperor nothing to do but stand by, impotent." The result of this would again be a division of the country.

So what must be done? History dictated that the southwestern *han* (meaning the ruling Satchō faction) could not unify Japan. Time had weakened Aizu. A new shogunate would create only division. What possibilities remained?

"The day of peace will come," Fukuchi said briefly, "only after a great hero appears and abolishes feudalism—forsaking personal gain, unifying the country, assisting in imperial rule and setting up a representative government." It was, on the surface, a vague conclusion, lacking in specifics or concrete proposals, and strongly reminiscent of Yoshida Shōin's anti-Tokugawa calls for "a man like Napoleon . . . a leader to rise suddenly from among the people."[37] But given Fukuchi's precisely stated view that the current government's leaders met none of the conditions for his "great hero," it was clear that he saw absolutely no hope in the new regime (even as Yoshida had placed no hope in the *existing* regime a decade earlier). And to those who knew his feelings, it was equally evident that such a "hero" would likely be a Tokugawa, a member of that family for which he sought a new role as head of an evolving representative government.

Finally, "Kyōjaku ron" took up Japan's international role, asserting that commercial development demanded an administration led by forces in the northern and eastern parts of Japan. Foreign trade, he said, centered in the East. Export goods, such as tea and silk, were produced largely in the North and East. Therefore, leadership too should center there. Most important of all, however, economics demanded that unity must be achieved quickly, since civil war would only aid foreigners at the expense of Japan herself. "My hope," he concluded, "is that the entire country will work together, combining its forces and strengthening its prestige in the community of nations. All imperial servants must devote their primary efforts to this end."

"Kyōjaku ron" was, in many ways, an incisive treatise. The theory that only an eastern government could survive may have sounded contrived (though it must appear more so today than then, when the imperial capital had not yet been moved to Edo and when the regime still had not been secured). And his call for unity rings slightly hollow in light of his vehemently pro-Tokugawa sentiments. But the recognition of the key role that trade would play, the admission that rigid, old forms of government were no longer sufficient, the analysis of the weaknesses of the various factions vying for power, and the call for a representative form of government indicate a rather farsighted view, particularly for a former bakufu retainer who still genuinely hoped that the Tokugawa would regain power. The treatise pointed out, at the very least, that to resist was not necessarily to grasp blindly at time-worn ideas and ways.

It also illustrated vividly the tug Fukuchi experienced between the pragmatism demanded by a new age and the loyalty that bound him to traditions. "Goal orientation" is a phrase used often to describe the Meiji era.[38] And the prescient conclusions of "Kyōjaku ron" demanding international trade, national strength, unity, and new administrative structures show clearly that Fukuchi was not to be outdone by the Meiji ministers in his quest for a strong Japan. But, unlike some, he was not capable of easily sacrificing old loyalties on the altar of that strength. Therefore, even while arguing for renovation of the system, he would berate the new rulers and dream of the reemergence of the personnel who ran the old order. To integrate the emotional loyalty and cool pragmatism was difficult, but in a sense, that was what "Kyōjaku ron" was all about. Even its insistence on accuracy without full objectivity, a point to be discussed shortly, evidenced this struggle. Out of this struggle would grow Fukuchi's mature dedication to "progress and order."

From a professional standpoint, it has often been charged that the *Kōko Shimbun*'s strong biases precluded accuracy or reliability. Fukuchi himself said years later that he sometimes "made up false reports about the political and military situation and ran them in the paper."[39] Most subsequent scholarship has echoed that confession, claiming that "most of the news was his own creation"[40] or that the paper consisted "largely of rumors."[41] If such charges are true, one might justifiably question whether the *Kōko Shimbun* was truly a "news" paper.

Yet, a more recent, painstaking examination by Sugiura Tadashi, resident historian at *Mainichi Shimbun,* reveals a different picture. Studying the war reports in *Kōko Shimbun,* Sugiura has found that the paper, though biased, consistently eschewed opportunities to distort actual facts, reporting rebel victories only when such victories occurred. Of the thirteen battle reports that could be checked, eleven reported victories or defeats accurately, while just two were in error.[42] Given the handicaps under which Fukuchi operated—the crude reporting methods, the tendency of all papers to include rumors in many stories, the slowness of communication and resultant inability to check sources—*Kōko Shimbun*'s percentage of error hardly warrants the charge of "news fabrication."

A similar study of the paper's memorials and petitions[43] shows that while they too were full of antigovernment bias, they were at the same time consistently accurate on factual matters. Fukuchi told a government investigator in July 1868 that every effort had been made to check the accuracy of both news stories and memorials. "If some news was inaccurate," he said, "it was due to my own mistaken judgment. I did not mean to write the news inaccurately. The inclusion of any news without factual basis was unintentional."[44] He made the statement in a defense intended to secure his release from prison; so it could be charged that it lacked candor. The columns of the paper, however, would seem to support his assertion.

To say that *Kōko Shimbun* was objective would be grossly inaccurate. Antigovernment materials greatly exceeded progovernment reports; manufactured "correspondence" constantly pointed out the weaknesses and faults of the new government; the overall trends of the civil struggle were not correctly portrayed. At the same time, however, those facts that Fukuchi did choose to report appear, on the whole, to have been well founded and, to the degree that he could insure it, correct. That his sense of responsibility as a journalist had advanced even to that degree redounds to Fukuchi's credit, given the fervor of his sentiments and the times in which he lived.

The times also dictated that Fukuchi's newspaper would not live long. Meiji government officials became increasingly angered at the nature of his writing. Though they had warned him early in June to moderate his tone, successive issues became increasingly strident. What was more, Fukuchi's influence grew rapidly, and within six weeks he had issued some ten thousand copies of the paper.[45] As a result, on July 12, 1868, the young editor was arrested, jailed, and forced to discontinue his journalistic efforts. He became, on that day, a man of history, Japan's first major journalist jailed for writing.

The chain of events leading directly to the arrest began on July 4, with the defeat at Ueno of the pro-Tokugawa *shōgitai* fighting squad. The *shōgitai*, many of whose members had been responsible for policing Edo under the Tokugawa, had refused to submit to the new government, deciding instead to entrench itself at Ueno and fight to the end. On July 3, a Friday, friends had come to Fukuchi's home near the squad's barracks and urged him to flee. Government troops, they reported, were planning an attack on Saturday, and if Fukuchi did not flee he would be in danger. Fukuchi laughed off the warning, calculating either that the frightened, disorganized *shōgitai* would break up on its own or that the government was merely "trying to scare them with a threat." But his flippancy turned to embarrassment, then fear, the next morning when the whizzing sound of bullets roused him from a troubled sleep. Flinging aside the mask of courage, he awakened family members and "hurried them through the gunfire" to safety elsewhere in the city. On returning home that night after the collapse of all resistance, he found "bullet holes here and there in the four walls."[46]

The sight gave him pause. "Due to that single day's battle," he later recalled, "the Tokyo situation had changed completely. It convinced me that there was no chance for a restoration of the bakufu."[47] Nor were the prospects bright for his newspaper, which had published its nineteenth issue on the previous Thursday. That the government loathed the *Kōko Shimbun* Fukuchi knew well. Now, with even the protecting *shōgitai* gone, the government could work its will in freedom. Even so, he published three numbers of *Kōko Shimbun* the following week, continuing the ardor of his antigovernment editorials in a tone reminiscent of the pre-Restoration loquacity that had kept him incapacitated as an official for nearly half a decade. But on Sunday afternoon, July 12,[48] a government official came to inform Fukuchi that he was "under suspicion" of harboring resisters and would have to accompany him to the Wadakura Mon arraignment bureau *(kyūmonjo)* at Edo castle.[49] Asking only courteous treatment and time to change clothes, Fukuchi complied, offering no resistance even though the nervous officer had brought along "two platoons of troops, all carrying bayonets"—just in case.[50]

At the castle, Fukuchi found many other prisoners, most of them also jailed for resistance. There was no order, only confusion, he recalled. Everything was "very free," with prisoners "drinking sake, smoking and forwarding their bills to the jailer." The officials in charge allowed him to send home for underwear and tobacco.

It was not, however, a freedom from fear. For Japan was at

war and these men were regarded as traitors. Civil liberties were nonexistent, and punishment tended to follow individual pique. "If the official in charge heard that someone had committed a 'certain crime,' " noted Fukuchi, "that person often would be sentenced at once to death without a careful investigation of the real situation," a state of affairs that left him in genuine fear for his life.[51] As one Meiji writer observed, "There were just two kinds of treatment in the army camp then. . . . Either a man would be beheaded or he would be released. Since Ōchi Sensei was a defender of the bakufu, it was quite natural to expect that they would behead him."[52]

Fortunately, however, Fukuchi still had a number of well-placed friends and acquaintances, and when word of his arrest leaked out they began maneuvering for his release. Jōno, his *Kōko Shimbun* colleague, is known to have contacted key friends in the government. Kamei Yūnosuke wrote a petition for his release. And, according to most accounts, Sugiura Jō, a fellow traveler to Europe in 1865 and an intimate of the powerful Kido Kōin, worked with particular diligence to secure the release.[53] In the end, their efforts availed, and eight days after the arrest he was released.[54] Fukuchi stopped at a Ueno tea shop on the way home and celebrated the release. Then he went to Ike no Hata and dismantled the machinery used in printing the *Kōko Shimbun*—a condition of the release. It had been a trying week. His life had been in jeopardy. His future had lost all semblance of certainty. His first attempt at journalism, initially such a success, had been dashed.

But more important than the personal failures was the historic significance of the week. He had been forced during the prison interrogations to transcribe his view of journalism and in the process had articulated pathbreaking concepts for a profession yet in its national infancy.[55] The purpose of journalism, he said, was to "relate the news to an uninformed public" and to "spread culture and enlightenment, . . . making the times intelligible even to children."[56] Reporting must be accurate. And editors should be energetic, "gathering reports from all over the country."[57] His position was not yet fully developed; nor was it unique, since other editors such as Yanagawa at *Chūgai Shimbun* also had begun advocating a social role for the press. But he had formulated with unusual force and precision important ideas that would undergird the press' emergence as a powerful institution a few years later.

The week also had a marked (and historic) effect on the immediate development of the press at large. It directly prefigured the new government's first general attempt to muzzle the Japanese press. Following Fukuchi's release, the *Kōko Shimbun* was ordered to turn all woodblocks over to the government. A week later, on July 27, the Dajōkan, or Council of State, ordered all papers to close down and to secure a government license before resuming publication. And the first general press codes, issued half a year later, stated that ''anyone who promulgates his views, accuses others falsely, publishes political secrets, or makes statements which lead others into lewd practices, shall be punished.''[58] It was a dramatic series of acts. Only two of the early 1868 papers (both of them progovernment) ever resumed publication after that summer,[59] though many probably would have died anyway due to a fading interest in news as the war wound down. Not until after World War II did the Japanese press enjoy such total freedom to criticize the government as it had experienced for a while that spring. As Fukuchi, who would one day be damned by competitors as a ''kept editor,'' put it: ''The *Kōko Shimbun,* which I edited, was the first paper struck down by the general prohibition of printing. . . . It is a sad fact, but as a result of that general prohibition, the earth was swept clear of all those papers that had so suddenly sprouted, and the earliest shoots of the modern press were killed.''[60]

The long-range impact of this week was thus immense. For Japan's press it meant that the old Tokugawa attitudes toward the control of communication would be continued under the new Meiji administration; for Fukuchi it meant an end to public life as a supporter of the Tokugawa, a temporary suspension of the philosophical evolution that to date had brought him to admire the progress of the West, love the old values, and loathe the usurpation of prerogatives by upstarts from western Japan.

Yet the long-range significance meant far less to him at the time than the short-range problem of what to do about sustaining existence. His old benefactors had all fallen or fled; the *shōgitai* had been crushed, and members of his own social class, the elevated samurai, were to be seen selling vegetables, running restaurants, and operating brothels. As Kido Kōin described Edo in August: "The great castle of the shōgun lay in charred ruins, the mansions of the feudal lords were in disrepair, and even the common people lacked spirit. Their eyes had in them the look of men 'in famine years.' "[61] Now, with the demise of the paper, Fukuchi too would have to come to grips in a personal way with the Restoration's "fearful cost in cultural dislocation and psychological strain."[62]

I "gnashed my teeth in frustration," he said of the sad state of the fallen Tokugawa vassals at this time. "Then when I would really look at the situation, at how they had gone from the peak of the mountain to the bottom of the valley in one day. . . . I would feel my anger vanishing. I would become convulsed with unending laughter; it was so absurd." He might have felt differently had he been able to reconcile himself to entering the new government, which desperately needed men of his talent. But he could not. He was ordered to join the government in August, but his anti-Meiji feeling had only intensified during his days at *Kōko Shimbun* and his subsequent imprisonment; so, feigning sickness, he refused to answer the summons.[63]

Instead, entrusting his family to the care of a friend in Yokohama, Fukuchi left Edo for the Shizuoka home of the deposed Tokugawa, expecting to find some sort of profitable employment there. Unfortunately, however, too many Tokugawa followers had had the same idea, and shortly after arrival he found himself writing to his wife: "Things are most confused. . . . Inns are extremely dirty and cramped, just like small beggars' lodgings. The people here . . . make a pitiable sight."[64] After a month of living "like a homeless pup," the twenty-seven-year-old former editor returned again to Tokyo,[65] ignored another order to report to the new government, and rented a tiny two-room apartment in Asakusa; he was determined to bury himself as a commoner, free of the ways and connections of public life. One of the pseudonyms he now chose for himself was Dream Hut (Yumenoya).[66]

The next two years were important for Japan, years in which the new government struggled to revive an administrative structure that had disintegrated badly, in the process setting in motion changes that would win the label "revolutionary" for the Meiji Restoration and its five-year aftermath.[67] For Fukuchi, however, they merely meant a return of the frustrations and isolation he had known at the end of the Tokugawa era. Only this time the isolation was worse because now the separation from power was complete, the routes to recovering personal influence seemingly obliterated. He spent some time translating and writing cheap fiction;[68] opened another language school, Nisshinsha;[69] and read a great deal. But mostly the ambitious young man merely writhed in the sense of being unfulfilled.

A talent like his could not go unrecognized forever, however, particularly in a society so much in need of expertise to direct and fuel its drive toward economic and military strength. Still an ebullient personality, Fukuchi often met—and impressed— junior officials in his visits to the Yoshiwara's "nightless quarters"; one of these, a former aide of Tokugawa Keiki named Shibusawa Eiichi, eventually recommended him to higher officials, who in turn persuaded him to rejoin the official world. The specific lure was a request in 1870 that Fukuchi study Western scholarship and prepare a treatise on Western banking. Needing money and weary of isolation, Fukuchi agreed, producing Japan's first detailed description of a banking system, the *Kaisha ben* ("Treatise on banking").[70] It was an elementary, concise description of the functions and operations of such a system. But that was just what Japan needed. Much impressed, Itō Hirobumi, the assistant finance minister, urged Fukuchi in mid-1870 to accept appointment in the Ōkurashō (Finance Ministry).[71] And he did.

That Fukuchi should have accepted has been described as surprising, even shocking, in light of his earlier defiance of the new government. Yet such surprise would seem to overlook the effect two years of bitter frustration were likely to produce on a man who had known a degree of power and influence. In the most thorough consideration of his change, Shimane Kyoshi of Tokyo Gaigo University has noted that it was more "natural" than "unusual" for Fukuchi to shift. He was, after all, a man still in his twenties and without high rank when the Tokugawa fell. He had done "his best" at *Kōko Shimbun* for the fallen regime. Prison had taught him the psychological and physical difficulties that could be provoked by undue resistance. Life as a commoner had been bitter. Other former bakufu retainers had switched much more easily and quickly. So the surprise was not that he switched but that he held out so long. Besides, adds Shimane, Fukuchi and Itō had much in common: a love of talk, an energetic approach to problems, and a shared affection for brothels.[72] Thus, at the end of 1870, two and a half years after the collapse of *Kōko Shimbun*, Fukuchi became a Meiji official.

## A Peripatetic Official

It was a pragmatic, innovative government—and a particularly energetic ministry—that the twenty-nine-year-old Fukuchi now entered. The Satchō "rebels" might have mouthed idealistic slogans prior to 1868, but pragmatic utilitarianism had become their guiding principle once in power. A "charter oath" early in 1868 had pledged the new government to such concepts as "deliberative assemblies" and the seeking of knowledge "throughout the world."[73] Movements had been initiated to abolish the *han* and weaken the status of samurai. Commerce, long regarded as a necessary evil, was now accepted as a key building block in national progress. Kido, who only a few years earlier had taken a blood oath to destroy supporters of Western learning, now championed the "promotion of men of talent," regardless of their former allegiance.[74]

Few of the former bakufu vassals found themselves more sought after in this talent search than those acquainted with the West. A study of "fifty of the most prominent Japanese leaders in the early Meiji period" shows that of eleven former bakufu vassals who became Meiji leaders, nine had traveled abroad and all had learned a Western language, while fewer than one-fourth of the nonbakufu men had had such encounters with the West.[75] Obviously, the new Satchō leaders experienced little difficulty in finding men from their own ranks who were simply "talented"; what they could not find was the man who was both bright and acquainted with the West. Hence, while the typical Tokugawa retainer fell from personal power right along with his lord, those vassals with a knowledge of the once despised West soon found their talents in great demand.

After all, the government was now considering such momentous problems as revision of the educational system, establishment of a central bureaucracy, replacement of the *han* with prefectures, eradication of the old samurai class, erection of a modern monetary system, development of a national army, revision of the tax system, and a host of other measures—all of them dependent to a greater or lesser degree on a knowledge of "modern" institutions in the West. A man like Fukuchi, who not only could speak English and French but had been abroad twice, seemed indispensable.

One wonders, in fact, whether Fukuchi might not have been lured partly by the offer of yet another chance to go abroad, this time to the United States. For no sooner had he gone to work than he was named one of four officials who would accompany Itō to the New World for a much-needed study of the U.S. banking and currency systems. He plunged immediately into trip preparations, and within three weeks of his entry was off for the United States with Itō. It would be, he said, one of the "most enjoyable and best" experiences of his life.[76]

The trip was dictated by the economic situation at home. The changes now under way demanded massive amounts of money and, as soon as possible, governmental solvency. Yet, ever since 1868, the government had been forced to struggle with meager resources and constant financial pressures. Notes had been issued from time to time to meet current expenses, but their effectiveness had been hampered by a lack of popular confidence in the government's ability to pay debts. Widespread use of counterfeit coins had led early in 1869 to a prohibition on the use of specie, which in turn had created a flood of paper currency and an instability in prices. In reaction to both of these problems the government had decreed in the spring of that year that all outstanding notes not redeemed with specie or silver coins by the end of 1872 would subsequently earn 6 percent interest annually. Also, officials had come to the conclusion that a modern banking system must be established quickly if the chaotic currency situation ever were to be regularized. Hence the decision to include the English-speaking translator of *Kaisha ben* on the U.S. study trip.

The five-man mission arrived in San Francisco on the evening of January 17, 1871, and after a two-week overland trip through Salt Lake City and Chicago, reached Washington, D.C., on Monday, January 30. Like most Japanese groups that went abroad during this period, it was a serious, no-nonsense mission. The proposed stay was short: just three and a half months. The goal was awesome: to become familiar with the intricacies of a nation's banking and monetary systems. The group's diary[77] makes it clear that from the day after arrival in Washington each member of the mission plunged into his tasks with something approaching feverish abandon. As an illustration of both the way in which Japanese missions tackled the problems of foreign study and Fukuchi's own eclectic, enthusiastic approach to learning, it deserves more than cursory note here.

At 9:00 A.M. Tuesday, January 31, a letter was sent to Secretary of State Hamilton Fish requesting an interview "at your earliest convenience,"[78] a reply being received the same evening. On Wednesday, Itō, Fukuchi, and one other member braved a downpour and went to the secretary's office for the stated interview, then were granted audiences with President Ulysses S. Grant and members of the cabinet. Each official assured the group that they would be given "fullest cooperation" in their investigations, and on Thursday they settled down to their studies with a visit to the Treasury Department. From that day on, each week was filled with six or seven days of constant investigation. A summary of the diary's record for a typical

week illustrates both the nature and the intensity of their
work.[79]

March 6. Monday. Clear. Guided by Mr. Fish to the Internal Revenue Bureau. Studied methods of its establishment.

March 7. Tuesday. Clear. Inspection trip to the office that issues national bonds. Also went to see the documents bureau. Fish took us
to both places. A letter for [Itō] arrived from the head of the nickel
mint in Philadelphia concerning the circulation of nickel coins. . . .

March 8. Wednesday. Clear. Went to the Treasury Department.
Visited receipts and disbursements office, receipts branch, documents branch, bonds office, etc. Guided by Fish. At 6:30 in the
evening, Mr. Stewart, the manager of a New York paper currency
engraving firm, called. . . . He gave us a box of diagrams for
Japan's engraving. He also showed us samples of various denomina-
tions of paper currency, etc.

March 9. Thursday. Clear, with violent rain at night. Learned about
the drafting of national bonds and securities.

March 10. Friday. Clear. Gave Stewart of the New York paper currency engraving firm drafts of the Japanese government's national
bonds and securities and of paper money issued by private companies.

March 11. Saturday. Clear. Went to the Treasury Department to see
the activities of the public bonds department and of the branch office in charge of receipts and disbursements.

During this particular week, the entire mission stayed in
Washington, studying primarily government securities and currency. Other weeks, certain members went to Philadelphia to
study banking and minting, or to New York to investigate engraving techniques. During the week of February 12, for example, Itō and Fukuchi traveled to Philadelphia on Sunday, secured a room at the Continental Hotel, then spent three days
wading through deep snow and studying the operation of the
local mint. They encountered the head of the Sydney, Australia, mint, who was there to learn how U.S. plants analyzed gold
and silver content; lunched with thirty officials—''all of them

college graduates''—and visited the Philadelphia National Bank, the local library, and the "famous Lippincott Bookstore," where Itō was given a series of biographical dictionaries and Fukuchi a geographical dictionary.[80]

Actually, the bulk of the mission's time was devoted to investigating four matters: the printing of currency, the minting of coins, the flotation of national bonds, and the development of a banking system. They visited at least five different banks, made a dozen trips to the Treasury Department, went to the Philadelphia mint no fewer than five times, studied bonds specifically on fifteen different days, and spent nearly three weeks (not on consecutive days) in offices and factories dealing with paper currency. They also visited Wall Street, the Department of Internal Revenue, the U.S. Post Office, and the government's printing office. At each place they studied manufacturing techniques; lunched with and interrogated officials; translated pertinent documents; and/or gathered samples of currency, bonds, and promissory notes. They also sent one colleague to London early in April to study English banking practices. In short, they developed for themselves a demanding, effective crash course on the U.S. banking and monetary system.

Of particular significance to Fukuchi's career was the intimate relationship he developed during the trip with Itō, the man who one day would be Japan's most eminent "great man." The official diary shows the two men working in almost constant tandem: they went together on study trips to Philadelphia and New York; they made side excursions to museums; they alone undertook the round of farewell visits. And during these months together they spent many hours discussing Japan's political and economic future. Fukuchi argued repeatedly that Japan must have an "imperially-granted form of democracy," that it must abolish all institutions that "still smack of feudalism." Itō called Fukuchi's views extreme at times, arguing that Japan must transform, but more slowly.[81] They were not really far apart; both wanted to abolish the old institutions; neither desired a European-style republicanism for Japan; both would become members of the soon-to-evolve "gradualist" faction, calling for orderly (as opposed to radical or immediate) reform. So the arguments, though heated and prolonged, were "warm and affectionate."[82] The trip and discussions played an important role in solidifying Fukuchi's commitment to the new regime. They provided an exhilarating introduction to the official world of Meiji Japan, and though he would again come to despise bureaucratic life, his enduring identification with several of the men who led the government (especially those from Chōshū) may be traced to this initial encounter.

By the time the mission returned to Tokyo on July 8, Itō and his assistants were ready to propose three reforms: first, that Japan adopt a gold standard; second, that the government begin issuing public bonds; third, that companies be established to issue paper notes. They felt certain that their recommendations would be promptly enacted. Itō had exerted a powerful influence in the ministry from the first; now he also knew more about Western economics than any other leading official; why should his suggestions not be followed? The Ōkurashō response was not, however, quite that simple. Two of the ministry's leading officials, Inoue Kaoru and Ōkuma Shigenobu, were skeptical, fearful that Japan was too backward for immediate implementation of the three proposals. Another group, led by Yoshida Kiyonari, argued for further study of England's banking methods, fearing that the U.S. system would just add more money without solving the problem of inconvertible government notes.

Itō's general plan eventually was adopted, early in August, but even then he and his mission colleagues were not allowed to carry out their own suggestions. Due as much to factional infighting as to philosophical differences, Shibusawa was given responsibility for the plan's implementation,[83] while Itō was sent to Osaka to care for local currency problems, then called back to Tokyo in mid-October to head the new Ministry of Industry (Kōbushō).[84] His economic ideas, it was alleged, leaned too much to the West.[85]

If the shifts were frustrating to Itō (and they were), they were more so to Fukuchi. He too had strong commitments to the U.S. banking system; and he too was shifted, ordered to assist Itō in Osaka. When Itō was recalled to Tokyo, however, Fukuchi was left behind to continue the work there—and to ponder the possibility of a repetition of his earlier bureaucratic experiences, when each foreign trip was followed by workless isolation. A repetition was not to be, however, for within the month Itō had sent word that he should return to Tokyo "at once, on urgent business."[86] He had been appointed a first secretary *(ittō shokikan)* in the Finance Ministry and was about to be sent abroad again, this time on Japan's first imperially commissioned embassy to the West, the Iwakura mission.[87]

The Iwakura mission must rank among the most auspicious foreign trips of world history. It was led by five of Japan's highest officials and included forty-three other luminaries, ranging from department heads and court nobles to bureau chiefs and talented linguists. Its goals included the study of Western institutions and the making of preparations for eventual revision of the unequal treaties with which Japan had been plagued since the coming of the West. Its itinerary included no fewer than fourteen countries, from the United States on the west to Russia on the east. As Marlene Mayo has noted, the mission was "unique in world history, for no country had ever before sent a group of its foremost leaders and ablest administrators to journey abroad for an extended length of time, sacrificing a large proportion of its leadership when there were pressing economic, political and social problems at home."[88] To have been a member was—for Fukuchi—exhilarating.

The actual experiences and outcome equaled (and perhaps exceeded) the goals and expectations. Sailing from Yokohama late in December 1871, the group spent more than seven months in the United States, carrying on instructive though unsuccessful treaty negotiations in Washington and winning an abundance of goodwill through such acts as the donation of a $5,000 check for relief of victims of the great Chicago fire. Another ten or eleven months in Europe taught mission members an exceptional amount in areas as diverse as constitutional law

and industrial techniques, education and carpet manufacturing. A rather ominous lecture by Bismarck in March 1873 con-
fronted them squarely with the frightful notion that "international law was usually insisted upon by those who found it to be
to their advantage," whereas "when it was clearly not to their
advantage they ignored it and resorted to arms."[89] As Fukuchi
later said of the mission:

> They brought back to Japan abundant and valuable fruits of their
> observations abroad, the first and most important of which was . . .
> the seed of Western civilization. . . . The enactment of the na-
> tion's constitution and the establishment of a Diet are fruits of the
> mission's world trip. . . . I believe it might not be too much to say
> that the orderly and systematic cultural development of the country
> thereafter owes much to the influence of the ambassadorial party.[90]

Fukuchi's role in the Iwakura mission, unfortunately, has not
been recorded in much detail. He himself wrote only sparingly
about it; others wrote even less. He did spend considerable time
again with his close friend Itō, going with him on several side
tours to study economics and industrial development. He is also
known to have worked, in his role as a first secretary, with several of the other main luminaries. It was on this mission, while
studying constitutions, that he first became intimate with
Kido,[91] and it was here that he developed an antipathy for
Japan's finance minister and leading oligarch, Ōkubo Toshimichi, as a man who was "all politician," "without discernable
personality," like a "North Sea iceberg." During one conversation in the statesman's hotel room in London, Fukuchi chal-
lenged: "You don't accept me. . . . I state my opinion of
things frankly and win out by force of reason. You are incapable
of trusting me because my knowledge is a threat." Ōkubo reportedly laughed and agreed, somewhat sardonically: "As you
said, if you know a secret, you cannot keep it. You're a talented
person in the prime of life, with great plans for the future.
Henceforth, you should correct your habit of bragging about
what you know and practice earnestly the trait of prudence and
mature reflection. Otherwise . . . you will suffer the misfor-

tune of being cut off from society, even while yearning to serve your nation."[92] It was incisive advice, not necessarily aimed at cultivating Fukuchi's friendship. But the effusive Fukuchi did not—could not—take it, a fact that helps explain why he eventually left the government to become a journalist.

The young first secretary's most significant contribution to the mission came in its latter months when he was selected to leave the main group to go to Egypt to conduct a study of diplomacy and court systems. Japanese leaders, struggling with the knotty, treaty-induced problem of extraterritoriality, had heard that the Egyptians were in the process of setting up a "mixed court" *(konsei saiban)* system to deal with similar legal difficulties. So it was decided that Fukuchi, experienced as he was both in language and in the study of Western institutions, should go there to study the Egyptian courts. He left the group in Paris on February 25, traveled through Italy, Greece, and Turkey, stopping in Jerusalem,[93] and spent some two months in Egypt. At the end of the study, he returned to Japan by way of Bombay, Calcutta, Singapore, and Hong Kong, reaching home early in July.

On arrival back in Japan, he prepared a lengthy report on the mixed courts for the Gaimushō (Foreign Ministry), describing his studies, outlining the newly adopted Egyptian system, and, finally, proposing a treaty under which Japan might set up similar judicial procedures.[94] He explained that the "mixed court" system, adopted on the basis of a proposal by Egyptian diplomat Nubar Pasha, provided that resident foreigners would be tried, in civil cases, by a court made up of both Egyptians and foreigners. The Egyptians had made the suggestion after suffering for years under the "evils" and injustice of extraterritoriality treaties first imposed on Egypt by Turkey. Representatives of the foreign powers had conceded that the idea was a good one. Fukuchi felt that under such a plan, especially if it were extended to criminal as well as civil cases, the worst abuses of extraterritoriality would be removed even while the fears of resident foreigners about receiving a fair trial would be assuaged.[95] He said it would also hasten the total abrogation of extraterritoriality by giving Japan a chance to prove its ability to conduct legal affairs in acceptable fashion.

The report was delivered to Japan's foreign minister, Soejima Taneomi, on July 17. But Soejima, like the *rōjū* who had read Fukuchi's report on Europe in 1863, either laid it aside or lost it, and the suggestions soon disappeared in the ministry's files, not to resurface until uncovered by the scholar Inō Tentarō in recent years. Fukuchi and others kept "mixed court" suggestions alive for the next few years, but that was about all. Unlike Egypt, the Japanese would keep pressing until they achieved the complete abrogation of extraterritoriality, an eventuality that finally occurred in 1894.[96]

### An Unfulfilled Official

A vivid illustration of the rapidity of change in Japanese politics during the quarter century after Perry's arrival in Japan can be seen in the events that transpired during Fukuchi's trips to the West. Twice—in 1862 and 1872—he stayed away for more than eight months, and during both of these trips the political mood at home changed almost beyond recognition. In 1862, he returned from Europe to find antiforeign extremism sweeping the ranks of the samurai. Now, in 1873, he found conservative, expansionist administrators—many of them the most ardent *jōi* zealots a decade before—threatening to change the direction of national reform completely.

When most of the progressive, pragmatic leaders—men like Kido, Ōkubo, and Itō—opted to accompany the Iwakura mission in 1871, conservatives like Saigō Takamori and Soejima were left in virtual control of the government, checked only by an agreement that they would make no major changes without Iwakura's written approval. Most of these men had already harbored serious misgivings about the direction in which the new government was heading. They had seen the growth of the movement for the commutation of hereditary samurai stipends, had felt the suffering of their fellow *bushi* (warriors) in the loss of social status. And, increasingly, they had begun turning a sympathetic ear to the clamor of numerous samurai for a

Korean war that would stir Japan's martial spirit and punish the Korean government for its refusal to open trade relations with Japan.

The result was that on August 17, 1873, the Council of State (Dajōkan) approved a plan whereby Saigō would go to Korea as envoy, with the understanding that if he were ill-treated Japan would attack Korea. The policy could not, however, be carried out until Iwakura's approval was secured, and most members of his mission had become convinced during their travels that internal reform must precede external aggression. Accordingly, when the embassy returned on September 12, Ōkubo and Kido set about trying to reverse the Dajōkan decision, and when they finally succeeded on October 23, Saigō's war faction resigned from the government en masse.

It was a traumatic, government-wrenching series of affairs, and Fukuchi's own ministry, the Ōkurashō, was in some ways at the center of the storm. Its leaders during most of Iwakura's absence had been Inoue Kaoru and Shibusawa, men committed to a belief that Japan must increase its wealth before setting out on foreign exploits. As a result, early in 1873, when the prowar minister of justice, Etō Shimpei, requested a budget increase, they refused it. When the Dajōkan overruled them in May, both resigned, claiming in a controversial letter that the government would go into debt by ten million yen in the coming year.[97] The result had been a power struggle within the ministry equal in intensity, if not in scale, to the Korean crisis itself. When Fukuchi returned in July, his clique in the ministry had largely lost power; so the demand for his services was limited.

After completing the report on the Egyptian courts, he set up several interviews with Saigō, hoping to enlighten the "elder" statesman on the advanced state of Western civilization. But Saigō was not interested in such "exotic" matters. He seemed to "pay no attention to complicated details" of foreign culture, Fukuchi noted; instead, he grilled the returnee on just three topics: postwar relations between France and Germany, the way "people felt about each other" in those countries, and the policies of Western governments toward Korea and China.[98] Beyond these interviews, Fukuchi had little to do but "await the return of the mission," and even when it did arrive he found himself outside the councils of power. Those who wielded most of the influence concentrated on the Korea problem, while men on the second level were forced to look on in frustrated impotence. Fukuchi occasionally discussed the exploding crisis with his new mentor, Kido, but beyond that he remained an uninvolved bystander.

With the conclusion of the Korean crisis, work returned to a more nearly normal state in the Ōkurashō. Yet Fukuchi remained unfulfilled. Ōkuma, the new finance minister, was not among his favorites, though the youthful minister deigned to make a place for Fukuchi now that his friends Itō, Inoue, and Shibusawa were gone.[99] Moreover, in the United States his pursuits had been far broader than the rather mundane work now assigned to him. Hence, he began to branch out again. He started writing anonymous opinion pieces for several Tokyo newspapers. He began studying and collecting ancient drama texts *(marubon)* as a foundation for the writing of his own plays someday. He began participating actively in Tokyo's drama reform groups. He and Numa Morikazu, a fellow employee in the Ōkurashō and one of his later opponents in the press, founded the Hōritsu Kōgikai, a lecture society aimed at stimulating public awareness of Japanese culture.[100] As these outside interests grew, Fukuchi's emotional ties to the bureaucracy weakened.

Then in the spring of 1874 Kido, the "man with more moral influence on me than any other,"[101] withdrew from office over the government's decision to placate Saigō's supporters by sending a military expedition to Taiwan,[102] and Fukuchi decided to follow suit. The hour had come, he said, to stop marking time. Late in the summer he announced his resignation. Numerous friends, including "several cabinet ministers," tried to dissuade him, arguing that his greatest contribution to Japanese history would come through official service.[103] But Fukuchi was adamant. His bureaucratic career had been nothing but stormy. Whether under the inert, inept Tokugawa or the innovative but faction-ridden Meiji regime, he had found that bureaucratic decisions and assignments related as often to personal politics as to rational ideas. When his knowledge and expertise were needed, as on foreign trips, he had been fully employed. When his faction fell or his talkativeness offended, he quickly found himself on the outside. It was the fate of many a bureaucratic third-runger. But he was not a proper bureaucrat. He had neither the patience nor the tact to work smoothly under superiors he did not respect or like. His decision was quickly and firmly made. The government might be engineering sweeping social and institutional reforms. But he would map out and evaluate those reforms from a position more to his liking *outside* the government.

The next chapter of Fukuchi's life would bring his talents and contributions into full flower; it would make him a pathbreaker, one of his country's genuine opinion leaders. For now, however, the thirty-three-year-old graduate of the bakufu foreign office knew only that the preparatory years had brought him further than he might realistically have expected, yet left him frustrated beyond what he had dreamed possible. They had been important years, but in ways that he could hardly have evaluated at the time.

One of the first things they had done was to give Fukuchi an unusually insightful understanding of the inner workings of the bureaucracy and of the things that needed to be done to propel Japan into the world community. Government service, Fukuchi had found, was not necessarily the most satisfying work, especially for idealistic or frank men. Too many bureaucrats still reminded him of the bakufu's "wooden monkeys."[104] Factionalism had repeatedly dashed his own hopes—and with them, faith in the rule of merit. At the same time, the bureaucratic years had taught him that real progress must stem from the policies and actions of the government itself, and that certain specific policies would need to be carried out if that progress were to be genuine. Like Kido, he had come to feel that the government should patronize a mass-circulation newspaper to facilitate the development of public opinion. He saw more clearly than most that government instruction and aid would be necessary in the establishment of secure economic foundations. He had become a firm believer in the necessity of an enlightened approach to international diplomacy. And he had developed a solid source of power through his personal friendships inside the government. Each of these factors and principles would strengthen his influence in the next ten years.

A second product of the early years, not unique to Fukuchi but unusually characteristic of him and of his times, was the growth of a personal tendency to eclecticism. His father and the Osagawa family of Nagasaki gave him a lifelong love of both Confucian ethics and history. Interpreters Namura and Moriyama introduced him to the West. Service in the bakufu stimulated an abiding interest in the workings of power and politics. The Yokohama coinage and trade negotiations stirred interests in economics and diplomacy. On his first trip to the West, he was fascinated by the press and the world of drama. His second trip to Europe encouraged a curiosity about law and government, while his last two Western journeys deepened his involvement with economics and legal systems. Throughout the remainder of life, Fukuchi would play significant, at times pathbreaking, roles in the fields of journalism, politics, economics, literature, drama—and, to a lesser degree, law and diplomacy. Only Fukuzawa Yukichi would equal or surpass him in breadth of intellectual contribution to his society. While one might lament the lack of a singular focus in his interests and contributions, the observer could just as easily see the diversity as a significant, fortunate springboard to a renaissancelike life of unique contribution.

And then, in a third area, the preparatory years also had moved Fukuchi well along the road to becoming a political "gradualist" or moderate. He had not yet used that phrase. But its outlines showed up in the tendency, described several times previously, to struggle with the tension between emotional attachment to old traditions and pragmatic insistence on workable new solutions. Early Confucian studies had taught him the importance of traditional values, of strong governmental institutions, of loyalty both to established structures and to human superiors, of highly structured human relationships; while the first trips to the West had convinced him of the necessity of change. They had shown him that Japan must be strong and shrewd to stand up to Western nations, that it must be willing to innovate. Yet it is worth noting that Fukuchi's demands for innovation sprang, not from a belief in the inherent "rightness" of Western philosophical underpinnings, but rather from the pragmatism that seemed to say: The old order cannot be defended unless it is changed enough to make it workable in a "modern" world. In other words, the reason for progress or liberalization was not an ideological concern with "human rights" or "modernity" per se. Rather, it was a conviction that it was necessary to "strengthen our national prestige in the community of nations."[105] Fukuchi's most intimate patron of the Tokugawa period, Mizuno Tadanori, had, he said later, taught him to "hate extremism and love gradualism, to value order and loathe recklessness."[106] Years later he would support a political platform calling for the nation to "move forward within the bounds of gradualism," to "seek the parallels of progress and order."[107] His ideas were not that well articulated in 1874, but the two sides already were much in evidence, the foundations well laid to make him famous eventually as the "champion of gradualism." All he really needed now was a platform from which to speak. And that would soon be available.

# CHAPTER III

# Years of Power at *Nichi Nichi:*
# 1874–1881

> *When I think over the vicissitudes of my life,*
> *I feel like an old man dreaming. Ah! One*
> *should never go into government or political*
> *service; nor should one ever become a jour-*
> *nalist!*[1]

Photographs of Fukuchi Gen'ichirō in the mid-1870s show two different men. One is a short-statured, brooding young scholar with penetrating eyes and stiffly disciplined bearing. The other is a dilettante, with an elegant wardrobe, a full, well-trained mustache above a dimpled chin, and a carefully styled Western haircut. The photographs suggest an enigma. Which man is Fukuchi—the conservative-looking student or the stylish dandy? Those who knew him best probably would have answered, "Both." While few personalities can ever be described as simple, fewer still so completely resist simple, consistent characterization as Fukuchi at midpassage.

He was acknowledged to be one of the most talented, brilliant men of his age. Iwakura suggested that he could do the work of four average men.[2] Miyake Setsurei, noted journalist and critic, said he was "rich in talent, . . . capable of anything."[3] Yet, the effect of that talent was all too often dissipated by an undisciplined, undisguised overconfidence that made enemies as easily as friends and led him into an unwise diffusion of effort. Because he felt himself capable in all areas —whether writing, politics, or business—he spread himself thin and failed to completely fulfill his potential in any. As Miyake put it: "If he had concentrated on politics he probably would have ranked with Inoue and Itō. . . . If he had emphasized business, he likely could have equalled Shibusawa." But he did not, because he failed to concentrate.[4]

There was also a constant tension between cool ambition and warm sentiment. The thirty-three-year-old Fukuchi who quit the Foreign Ministry in 1874 was as ambitious as anyone alive. He left Nagasaki in 1859 because chances for success seemed better in Edo. He resented his omission from the first embassy to the United States most of all because it cost him a chance for immortality. He went with Iwakura to the West in 1871 primarily to enhance his personal prospects. Yet his ambition, like his talent, frequently melted under the heat of sentiment or withered before a blast of impulsiveness. More famous officials, men like Itō and Ōkubo, sacrificed friendships and emotions to coolheaded calculation and ambition. Not so Fukuchi. He could not keep a secret; nor could he remain quiet when he disagreed with an official, even when the expression of his opinion might cost him influence or connections. He loved children and provided graves in his own family plot for favored rickshaw men.[5] As Itō once said of his emotional loyalty to old ways and friends: "If you would just give up being like a feudal retainer, you would win the post of foreign minister."[6]

Then there was the austere, sternly disciplined side of Fukuchi, balanced by the playboy philandering. He won fame as a teetotaler, worked harder in the office than any of his colleagues, demanded absolute loyalty as a supervisor. Said a colleague: "He was stern and decorous to the point of severity."[7] Yet again, if Fukuchi at work was "most diligent," Fukuchi off work had long since gained a reputation as one of the "fastest livers" in the city. Rarely a night passed that failed to find him at an Asakusa or Shinagawa brothel. An often repeated story found him sitting at the deathbed of a favorite geisha, flipping the lid of a gold watch open and shut. The girl, it seemed, loved no sound so much as the *pa-chin, pa-chin* of watch covers. So until she stopped breathing he opened and closed covers, ruining more than twenty gold watches in the process.[8] He also lived, dressed, and ate extravagantly. His lavish home became known as the Palace of Ike no Hata, a favorite spot among officials for viewing Ueno's cherry blossoms each spring. He owned, in his best years, no fewer than thirty-five fine-patterned kimonos.[9] Even his underwear was so fine that a Parisian servant once placed a pair on the dining table, mistaking them for a cloth napkin.[10]

Fukuchi's two sides showed themselves, finally, in a curious combination of cynicism and idealism. On the negative side, the years already had held more disappointment than most men might expect in two lives—disappointments that would later in life make him a philosophical nihilist, scornful of such terms as "fairness" and "justice." Yet, on the positive side, there is no ignoring the idealism that keenly motivated him during his peak years. For if despair and cynicism helped force him out of government service in 1874, so did an idealistic belief that individual men could shape their times. He still believed in the validity of reform, still believed that there were ways for individuals to influence that reform. Hence the decision to get out and use other vehicles. His cynicism regarding specific aspects of internal bureaucratic politics was not directed at the overall system or at the government's general policies. It was his idealism that told him that "if one could not be prime minister," one could exert nearly as much influence as a journalist, the "uncrowned king" of modern society.[11]

Fukuchi was, in short, a complex man; and it was this very complexity that made him, in so many ways, a complete journalist even before he became one. The overconfidence that sometimes obscured his talent within the bureaucracy would give authority and precision to his editorials. The ambition would provide motivation and stimulus, while the sentimentality and impulsiveness would give his articles warmth and directness. The disciplined severity would enable him to write both adeptly and prolifically, while the dandyism would keep him from losing either the human touch or the flare for pithy, colorful prose. Finally, the cynicism (he would have called it realism) usually would enable Fukuchi to keep a certain critical distance, even while the idealism helped him to write with the moral fervor that sways readers. The blend was not, of course, quite that simple; nor was it always positive. Any one of these traits grown out of proportion might damage his journalistic contributions. But at age thirty-three, just out of the government, his personality clearly was better fitted to the role of a journalist than to that of a bureaucrat. A call from the *Tokyo Nichi Nichi Shimbun* that fall would give him a chance to prove that fact.

*The Maelstrom of the Press*

The Japanese newspaper press to which Fukuchi turned his attention in mid-1874 could hardly have been called robust. Newspapers had been slow to take hold after the government's regulatory laws of 1868 and 1869, and it was not until February 1871 that Japan's first genuine daily newspaper, the *Yokohama Mainichi Shimbun,* was established.[12] It was followed over a year later (March 22, 1872) by Tokyo's first daily, the *Nichi Nichi.* Yet, by the time Fukuchi left the Ōkurashō in 1874, the Tokyo-Yokohama area still could boast only a handful of daily news publications.

These papers were, moreover, far from modern. Their editors were haughty and inexperienced, their writers often mediocre persons who showed little talent or insight in the area of political discussion. Fukuchi thought the papers looked like "relics,"[13] and a Western observer noted that "their columns were always defaced with such filthy paragraphs as to render them worse than contemptible."[14] What was even more damaging to their quality and journalistic independence was that each of them had developed exceedingly close ties to men in the government. Indeed, all of Japan's first genuine newspapers had appeared at the instigation of leading officials, and they had managed to attain stability only through political patronage. The *Shimbun Zasshi,* for example had been patronized by Kido Kōin as a tool for educating citizens in the modes of civilization. Maejima Hisoka had arranged a subsidy to launch *Yūbin Hōchi Shimbun.* And by 1872, various officials had created similar government-oriented papers in nearly all of Japan's present-day prefectures.[15]

Relationships between the government and these papers were not always smooth, however. As a leading student of the Meiji press, Albert Altman, has noted, these papers were "caught in the cross-current of two conflicting demands." On the one hand, the Meiji leaders who backed them sought to control their content, sometimes even to the point of engaging in Tokugawa-style censorship of any news deemed sensitive. On the other hand, those same leaders talked idealistically about the need for widespread dissemination of news "to encourage identification with national goals."[16] The result was a sharp tension over the amounts and kinds of news that should be made available. The arbiters of these disputes, however, were the official patrons rather than the editors. Japan's traditions included nothing of the concept of journalistic freedom—and, until at least 1873, her editors showed little inclination to change that fact.

Following the governmental split over the Korea issue in October 1873, however, the close ties between press and state began to loosen. Inspired by the disgruntled followers of Saigō, more and more individuals took to expressing open opposition to official policies. And when, in January 1874, Itagaki Taisuke and several others issued a memorial calling for the establishment of a popular assembly,[17] the government's ability to control the expression of opinion all but disappeared. The general populace of Tokyo began to debate the issue of a popular assembly, dividing between a progovernment, "gradualist" *(zenshinshugi)* faction that maintained that the people were not yet ready for "representative" government and an antigovernment, "radical" *(kyūshinshugi)* faction that demanded an assembly at once. During the debate, which consumed most of 1874 and part of 1875, the papers themselves turned to a new brand of partisanship, many of them severing their ties to the government and creating for themselves an important new role as opinion molders.

It was in this changing environment that the *Tokyo Nichi Nichi Shimbun* really came into its own as Japan's leading gradualist paper. Established, like its early counterparts, as a voice for certain officials (in this case, Ōkuma Shigenobu and Minister of Justice Etō Shimpei[18]) who desired to "contribute to the advance of culture,"[19] it had from the first endeavored to introduce the kinds of features that would make it a cultural and financial leader. The paper's editors[20] used a better grade of paper than was then common; they employed the finest available quality of lead type, and they hired several of the country's most energetic reporters, sending one of them, Kishida Ginkō, abroad in the spring of 1874 to cover Japan's military expedition to Taiwan. The result was that by mid-1874 the newspaper's circulation had reached several thousand, and its offices had been moved from editor Jōno Dempei's home to expensive quarters in the Ginza. One of the more popular plays of the day was entitled *Tokyo Nichi Nichi Shimbun*.[21]

Despite this modicum of success, the paper found itself in a rather tenuous position during the early months of the debate over a popular assembly. Its ties to the government had precluded it from branching out into any genuinely innovative directions. And, like the other papers, it had no staff members capable of writing incisive political comment on a sustained basis. Kishida may have been recognized as the country's foremost reporter, but he was only that—a reporter and not an effective editorialist or polemicist. Thus, the *Nichi Nichi* editors found themselves dependent on outside contributors for their preparation of the opinion pieces that the public was coming to demand.

To their credit, the editors recognized the potential of the new climate and began to seek means of capitalizing on it. If *Nichi Nichi* could hire a writer of political stature, Jōno suggested to his colleagues, it might score a coup. And the rewards would be financial as well as journalistic. They agreed, and as a result the *Nichi Nichi* invited Fukuchi in the summer of 1874 to become its chief editor and writer *(shuhitsu)*.[22] It was not an invitation that Jōno necessarily expected his friend to accept, given Fukuchi's relative prominence in official and intellectual circles. But he surprised them and late in October took the leap into that tantalizing world of which he had dreamed years before in Europe.[23]

Fukuchi's decision to enter *Nichi Nichi* was not an easy one. For one thing, he had received a prior offer from *Hōchi Shimbun,* the paper that would become his fiercest competitor, and he had turned that offer down largely because he would have been forced to work under another leading talent, Kurimoto Jōun, not an appealing idea to the self-assertive side of Fukuchi.[24] For another thing, nearly all his government friends scoffed at the idea of a ranking official becoming a newspaper-man. The press had not yet become respectable. Few of Fuku-chi's official colleagues had even dreamed of the "hidden power lurking in the press or of the way reporters' opinions might come to influence public opinion." They regarded the newspaper as a "form of amusement." But, on reflection, Fukuchi concluded that their evaluations of the press were wrong. He decided that, more than hurting his own reputation, such a move might actually raise the reputation of the press. He came to the conclusion that "if I were to take up writing with the brush, using the newspaper as my medium, I might even-tually see my ideas realized in society."[25] He accepted Jōno's offer.

Within weeks, Fukuchi had taken complete command of the editorial content at *Nichi Nichi*. The names of Jōno and Kishida continued to be listed as technical "editors" *(henshū-chō)*, but theirs was a figurehead title; Fukuchi had accepted the *Nichi Nichi* offer only on the condition that he receive the title chief editor and be given control.[26] Even his salary spelled out his preeminence. Editorial writers normally received some-where from 50 to 80 yen a month, with an unusually talented man occasionally earning as much as 100 yen.[27] Yet Fukuchi went to work for 150 yen a month, plus two personal shares of the monthly profits. The paper's managers reportedly offered him 50 yen less than that, with a promise that the salary would be increased if his entry caused the circulation to rise three hun-dred—to which he laughingly suggested that he be given the higher sum at once, with a promise to take a fifty yen cut if the circulation gains were not forthcoming. Significantly, the circu-lation lists grew by far more than three hundred very soon after his entry.[28] It was a propitious beginning. *"The Tokyo Nichi Nichi Shimbun* is already well founded," said one observer. "Now its self-confidence grows even stronger."[29]

### The Innovative Editor

It goes without saying that Fukuchi entered *Nichi Nichi* with a well-developed set of ideas about the nature and role of the press. Like Kido, he considered newspapers indispensable in contributing to the "enlightenment" of the people and felt that articles should be "as easy as possible for our people to read."[30] He believed in keeping a relatively critical eye on government policies, yet, somewhat paradoxically, saw no value in the kind of independence that might cut off government sources or invite punishment. He saw a need for broader coverage and greater emphasis on reportorial skills. He considered journalism a "respectable" profession that demanded not only competence but dedication. Most of all, he saw the press as a tool for "shaping the thinking of the day and controlling the fundamental political thought of the public."[31] As a *Nichi Nichi* editorial put it several months after Fukuchi took over: "Newspapers are the eyes and ears of the world, the movers of mankind."[32]

Out of this philosophy flowed a new, precedent-setting editorial style that contributed several innovations to the world of Meiji journalism. Until the advent of Fukuchi, most papers had been managed without any abiding philosophy, without coming to terms with the nature of the more advanced Western press. Fukuchi, on the other hand, knew rather clearly what aspects of Western journalism he wanted to introduce into Japan and, as a result, began at once to make transformations in the areas of management, editorial publication, news reporting, and government-press relationships.

The problems most papers then faced in the field of management, though perhaps not the most crucial, were numerous. Friction between business managers and writers *(kisha),* for example, created a constant and serious economic problem, since writers tended to be arrogant types ("with self-respect higher than Mt. Fuji"[33]) who demanded absolute autonomy in their areas and completely ignored economic realities. The lack of advertising deprived Japan's press of one of modern journalism's major revenue sources. Inadequate presses forced *Nichi Nichi* to make two separate press runs daily after the doubling of the paper's size to four pages at the end of 1874. And the unavailability of skilled labor caused papers to hire inexperienced, poorly motivated youths for jobs as difficult as typesetting.[34]

The new *Nichi Nichi* editor handled most of these areas with

東京第弐所銀坐通名瓦
石煉坐所弐第京東

These stately brick buildings of the downtown Ginza were among
Tokyo's leading tourist attractions in the mid-1870s—ostentatious
symbols of the nation's headlong rush of modernization. Of particular
interest to the artist, Hiroshige III, were the *Nichi Nichi* publishing offices, which he not only pictured but labeled, on the far right. The in-

dividual about to step through the front doorway represents Fukuchi, while his chief reporter, Kishida Ginko, follows him up the steps and *Nichi Nichi* founder Jōno Dempei peers out the window directly overhead. *(Photo courtesy of Mainichi Shimbunsha Shi Henshūshitsu)*

characteristic forcefulness. For the first time in Meiji journalism, he unified the business and editorial sides of a paper under a single person's control, thus eliminating many wasteful editorial practices. He attempted to educate businessmen to the value of advertising, even running some ads in the margins of the paper to make them more conspicuous and conserve space. He gave hours of his own time to training the troublesome typesetters to become capable professionals. The result, by his own exaggerated claim, was fourteen years of management "without dissension."[35] Though specific figures are, unhappily, unknown, it is clear that these new practices did indeed manage to create a steady and "sizeable" profit during these early years at *Nichi Nichi.*[36]

Fukuchi's second major innovation, the institution of a daily editorial column, came on December 2, 1874, the day the *Nichi Nichi* format was changed to include more (and larger) pages at a higher price.[37] It became, in many ways, one of his most significant journalistic contributions, the medium through which he ruled the press for a decade.[38] The paper's editorials began on page one under the simple but authoritative title "Tokyo Nichi Nichi Shimbun" and consumed, on the average, one-third of the paper's total space. Fukuchi wrote most of them himself and controlled the content of those he did not write. The column was, in the words of one historian, "a phenomenal success."[39]

Fukuchi's editorials broke ground, first, in the breadth of material with which they dealt. On February 12, 1875, he articulated his theory that a paper was not a "news" paper unless it discussed all areas of public life, "whether commerce, scholarship, society or politics."[40] During that year he followed his own maxim, running not only one hundred editorials on politics and government (there was nothing unusual about that in the press of the 1870s!) but nearly sixty on economics, with heavy emphasis on trade, shipping, and taxation. Three dozen more dealt with government-press problems; another thirty-seven treated general East Asian affairs; nine discussed the Western world; and some eighty-one others treated everything from religion and law to education and culture (see Table 1).[41] By mid-twentieth-century standards, it was not an unusual degree of versatility or breadth. In the Japan of 1875, however, when major newspapers *(daishimbun)* had heretofore largely limited themselves to official matters, it was an innovation.[42]

At the same time, Fukuchi's editorial columns set new patterns in journalistic writing styles. Though unsigned, those written by Fukuchi himself were generally recognizable by the idiosyncratic use of the term *Gosō* or *Gosōshi,* roughly translatable as "We."[43] It was a new word to the Japanese, borrowed by Fukuchi from ancient Chinese, and before long colleagues were referring to Fukuchi as Gosō Sensei (Professor Gosō) and to the term itself as a symbol of *"Nichi Nichi,* gradualism, excellent style and extraordinary use of words."[44] Fukuchi's style embodied a rather terse simplicity—refined yet short sentences incorporating a colorful but understandable vocabulary. The "secret of writing," he maintained, was to shun "ostentatious glibness" and to simply "make people understand."[45] Or, as

TABLE I
Nichi Nichi *editorials, 1874–1887, by year and subject matter*

| Year | Government | Economics | The West | The Far East | General | The World | Law | Education | Literature-Culture | Religion | Journalism | The Military |
|---|---|---|---|---|---|---|---|---|---|---|---|---|
| Avg. | 70 | 48 | 13 | 30 | 32 | 9 | 9 | 6 | 8 | 3 | 11 | 6 |
| 1874 | 11 | 6 | 0 | 4 | 5 | 4 | 0 | 0 | 2 | 0 | 0 | 0 |
| 1875 | 118 | 58 | 9 | 37 | 34 | 4 | 8 | 5 | 16 | 7 | 35 | 7 |
| 1876* | 79 | 73 | 18 | 22 | 39 | 5 | 15 | 1 | 16 | 2 | 23 | 2 |
| 1877* | 37 | 63 | 5 | 6 | 19 | 17 | 6 | 0 | 6 | 0 | 13 | 5 |
| 1878 | 35 | 87 | 19 | 9 | 34 | 5 | 13 | 3 | 4 | 4 | 1 | 2 |
| 1879 | 65 | 13 | 5 | 13 | 18 | 21 | 1 | 1 | 6 | 0 | 2 | 3 |
| 1880 | 122 | 29 | 1 | 23 | 32 | 26 | 9 | 0 | 0 | 1 | 0 | 0 |
| 1881 | 119 | 40 | 0 | 17 | 36 | 5 | 19 | 5 | 2 | 7 | 20 | 3 |
| 1882 | 113 | 39 | 1 | 53 | 28 | 0 | 5 | 21 | 3 | 1 | 4 | 6 |
| 1883 | 51 | 52 | 12 | 43 | 44 | 3 | 24 | 12 | 8 | 4 | 27 | 16 |
| 1884 | 53 | 52 | 26 | 75 | 32 | 14 | 11 | 8 | 9 | 10 | 4 | 13 |
| 1885 | 35 | 46 | 19 | 61 | 33 | 4 | 7 | 8 | 5 | 1 | 2 | 10 |
| 1886 | 68 | 41 | 19 | 30 | 56 | 6 | 5 | 6 | 11 | 0 | 10 | 10 |
| 1887 | 76 | 79 | 44 | 28 | 33 | 7 | 6 | 10 | 22 | 1 | 7 | 9 |

*There were an additional 30 editorials on samurai uprisings in 1876 and 114 in 1877.

he admonished a competing editor who loved elaborate prose, "Embellishment is vain. . . . If writing simply penetrates what you want to say, your work is done."[46] A classic example came in one of Fukuchi's better-known editorials on political gradualism: "What is gradualism?" he asked. "It is the philosophy of carrying out reforms gradually."[47] That, to him, was effective writing—sentences that were brief, catchy, and artless. He worked hard at incorporating that style in his *Nichi Nichi* editorials and in the process influenced many an aspiring (or competing) young journalist.

How much influence the editorial columns exerted may be seen in the fact that they were soon imitated in other major papers. Until Fukuchi entered *Nichi Nichi* all the *daishimbun* had run frequent opinion pieces or essays *(ronsetsu)*, sometimes assigning staff writers to compose them, usually inviting contributions by scholars or bureaucrats. But they had printed such essays irregularly, often confining them to the correspondence *(tōsho)* columns. And none had attempted to maintain anything resembling editorial consistency. One writer might call for the immediate opening of an assembly, while the next day another might urge the Tokyo government to tighten its grip. But spurred by Fukuchi's innovation and by the growing politicization of the times, the Tokyo press quickly followed suit and by the spring of 1875 most *daishimbun* were publishing editorials with at least relative regularity and general consistency,[48] although most never did develop the breadth or diversity of *Nichi Nichi.*

The third *Nichi Nichi* innovation stemmed from Fukuchi's new view of reporting. Reporting had previously been deemphasized at most papers because editors and writers thought the gathering of news beneath their dignity. Under the traditional system, poorly paid menials called *tambōsha* (news gatherers) were almost solely responsible for collecting news items, while highly paid writers *(kisha)* took these items and composed stories. Since most *tambōsha* came from the lower classes and were despised by officials, the news items they gathered were often spotty and full of errors. The result was that "news," according to the understatement of one early journalist, "was lightly treated."[49]

Fukuchi, though by no means the possessor of a contemporary Western view of reporting, decided to exert greater efforts in this area. As he wrote shortly after entering *Nichi Nichi:*

> When there is a major event . . . in foreign countries, the newspapers report it in detail. This is a newspaper reporter's duty. But Japan's reporters do not do this at all. What can we call this but a sign of weakness?[50]

*Nichi Nichi* already was known for the most lively news coverage among the major papers, thanks to Kishida's writing. Fukuchi resolved to strengthen that reputation by recruiting more writers of talent and by insisting that *kisha,* as well as *tambōsha,* go out regularly to search for news.[51]

He led the way in this change by working as a reporter himself. His ties inside the government were, of course, numerous, and his curiosity was unbounded. So although he did not include a specific time for developing news sources in his daily schedule, he made it a constant task, cultivating official contacts assiduously, using business friends to garner inside stories, probing for leads during lunches with prominent friends, even asking acquaintances at brothels to pursue news items.[52]

He drove his staff like a drill sergeant. His newsroom snapped with rules, some related to writing, some to Fukuchi's whims: beards were taboo, as were woolen waistbands and dark blue *tabi* (socks); tardiness was not allowed. The odor of sake usually drew a blast: "Hey! Somebody is drinking! If you want to booze it up, do it on leisure time, after you get home!" When an article or comment unveiled a failure to keep abreast of the times, he would erupt: "That's stupid! You can't do it because you don't read." He made an effort, furthermore, to inspect all articles before they went to press. If he liked one, he would write "excellent" *(myō)* in red ink, an inscription his employees regarded as "our greatest honor." If, on the other hand, ¹ ²

found the story unacceptable he might spend thirty minutes in-
structing the writer on grammar or style. Writing, he would tell
them, "is like marshalling an army. If you don't plan, what can
you expect? My articles are nothing but a copying down on
paper of compositions in my mind. . . . I begin my scheme in
the toilet, then work on it in the *jinrikisha*."[53]

The result of this diligence was that reportorial writing became, by contemporary standards, even more of a *Nichi Nichi*
forte. Kishida, able to concentrate solely on reportorial writing,
blossomed. Other talented writers, such as Kubota Kan'itsu
and Suematsu Kenchō, were hired. Even scoops became important. Typical was *Nichi Nichi*'s coup in the reporting of the collapse of the Ono group, one of Japan's most powerful financial
blocs, about a month after Fukuchi joined the paper. The decision to declare bankruptcy was confirmed on November 21,
1874, a Saturday, and by Monday morning (a press holiday, due
to the Shinto Harvest Festival), *Nichi Nichi* was out with an ex-
tra, describing the facts of the failure with surprising accuracy
and detail. Other leading papers, by contrast, failed to mention
the collapse before their Tuesday editions, and even then reported it superficially or incorrectly.[54]

Fukuchi never halted the use of uneducated *tambōsha;* perhaps the economics and thinking of the times required their
use. Nor did he ever regard news columns as being as important
as editorials; he would, in fact, have been scandalized by the
willingness of contemporary U.S. editors such as Joseph Pulitzer, Adolph Ochs, and Melville Stone to run sensational news.
But Japan's press was operating within a different political context than was that of the United States, a politically charged
context that probably precluded a full-fledged news orientation. By the mere fact of abandoning the old idea that it was
"disgraceful" for writers *(kisha)* to gather news themselves, he
had raised the level of Japanese news reporting markedly.

Fukuchi's fourth innovation at *Nichi Nichi* involved a new
approach to government-press relations, an approach that
rocked the press world of his day more than had his institution
of editorials, even while illustrating the undeveloped state of

journalism philosophy in Japan. As soon as Fukuchi joined *Nichi Nichi*, the paper began running on page one the label: "For use in the printing of Dajōkan [Council of State] articles."[55] Then on December 2, the day Fukuchi changed the paper's format, an editorial announced:

> This *Nichi Nichi Shimbun*, which for several years has been painstakingly managed with a view to spreading enlightenment, has in name and reality been appointed to the service of printing Dajōkan articles and will from this day forward change its format accordingly.[56]

At the same time Nippōsha (the corporate name of the *Nichi Nichi* publishing company) hoisted a long white banner in its front hallway stating that the paper had been designated for "the service of Dajōkan items,"[57] thus formally initiating an era in which *Nichi Nichi* proudly proclaimed itself to be the nation's foremost "patronage paper," or *goyō shimbun.*

The meaning of the term *goyō shimbun* was not, however, quite as clear at *Nichi Nichi* as the translation, "patronage paper," might today suggest. Before entering Nippōsha, Fukuchi had admittedly advocated the use of the paper as "an organ through which I would express the cabinet's policies," an intermediary between government and people.[58] But government officials had not bought that suggestion. They "disliked the idea of disclosing their ideas to the public through a newspaper" and feared the ideological straitjacket into which publication of a party-line, official gazette might put them.[59] Fukuchi, moreover, would never have been content to have given up editorial independence. It was important to him that being a "patronage paper" did not mean "receiving prior knowledge of the government's policy."[60] And he frequently invoked the right to criticize government policies, calling at one point for the abolition of a ministry that was itself patronizing *Nichi Nichi*,[61] and at another for modification of harsh government press laws. During 1876, in fact, some of his reporters were jailed for breaking such laws.[62]

So it was with a peculiarly early Meiji, non-Western definition in mind that Fukuchi began to proclaim the official receipt of *goyō* status. Legally, the term meant simply that *Nichi Nichi* had been granted the right, as of October 27, 1874, to "carry out the official business of publishing yet-unprinted government notices," a right shared with several other papers. *Nichi Nichi* also had been designated two years earlier for purchase by all prefectural and city governments, but that right too was shared with other journals.[63] So the technical meaning of the word *goyō* was hardly an exceptional one. Unofficially, however, the printing of the *goyō* label itself served at least two much more important functions: it gave an air of prestige and authority to *Nichi Nichi*'s articles; and it called attention to the fact that *Nichi Nichi* had become, in an informal sense, a "platform" for the views of leading members of the government's Chōshū faction.

Though the term *goyō* came to be despised in later years when the idea of press freedom had taken deeper root, and though competing papers frequently used it as a damning epithet, the word connoted power and prestige in 1874. People tended to respect the government more than other institutions and hence regarded receipt of its sanction as a sign of reliability. To be officially accorded a *goyō* status (even if the advertisement of that label had more publicity value than unique meaning) was seen as an indication that a paper had more dependable sources and wrote more carefully and more accurately. As one scholar analyzed it: "When *Tokyo Nichi Nichi* got a jump on the other newspapers by claiming the Dajōkan patronage, the other papers had to attack it in order to keep their own readers."[64]

Actually, *Nichi Nichi* probably would have become a "Chōshū platform" even without the *goyō* label, given Fukuchi's close ties to men like Kido, Itō, Inoue, and Yamagata Aritomo;[65] but the *goyō* designation spotlighted those ties. After entering *Nichi Nichi,* Fukuchi continued to foster close relationships with key oligarchs, seeking their opinions, sharing his, and frequently relating their views anonymously in the *Nichi Nichi.* But these opinions were always, he emphasized, "those of a single minister rather than of the entire cabinet.''[66] And, despite a popular view that Itō used *Nichi Nichi* most often, Fukuchi claimed to have collaborated primarily with Kido Kōin. "I would discuss my views with Kido," he reported, "and the matters on which we generally agreed were numerous." Fukuchi's most candid discussion of the *goyō* matter suggested that as Kido became increasingly disgruntled over the direction of government affairs, he desired a mouthpiece to express his views anonymously. The friendship with Fukuchi made *Nichi Nichi* ideal.[67]

To say then that Fukuchi allowed *Nichi Nichi* to become a "kept paper" would be to grossly exaggerate the case. To say, on the other hand, that he kept the paper free from government influence would be an equal exaggeration. The truth seems to lie between: he used the official *goyō* label to raise the prestige of his paper; he maintained unofficial ties with certain friends within the government, frequently writing editorials or columns that coincided with their views; yet he maintained, at least during his years of greatest influence, a personal independence from both the government at large and the Chōshū faction in particular, insisting on the right to support or criticize freely. He was, in short, a man whose basic sympathies lay with the gradualists or moderates inside the government, a man who often used the government and was at the same time willing to be used by it—so long as that use was in the service of a cause with which he agreed. It was a complex arrangement, one that fit the political atmosphere of the early Meiji era peculiarly well, and one that would someday bring Fukuchi a great deal of grief. In the early years at *Nichi Nichi*, it helped make his name influential.

### The Political Gradualist

If Fukuchi quickly set his imprint on the institutional nature of the press during late 1874 and early 1875, his blossoming commitment to "progress and order" also began at once to exert a profound influence on the public discussions carried on in that press. In fact, his participation in the 1875 discussion of the establishment of a national assembly proved pivotal in inspiring an era of unprecedented politicization of the Meiji newspapers. And an exciting era it was, one that Fukuchi would call Japan's "most prosperous period" for "freedom of discussion and publication of lively debate,"[68] because, ironically, even though concepts of journalistic freedom had not yet matured, neither had the government's more stringent methods of controlling the press. As the period, moreover, in which Fukuchi first came to be known as "the great gradualist," it demands rather careful attention.

After Itagaki Taisuke and a number of Saigō's followers petitioned for a popular assembly early in 1874, officials, scholars, and journalists alike had begun debating heatedly the question of when such a body should be opened. Former samurai in various areas formed rudimentary political clubs such as the Risshisha and the Aikokusha to push, among other things, for immediate establishment of an elected assembly.[69] Leading oligarchs countered with the contention that the time was not yet ripe. Both officials and intellectuals debated every aspect of the issue in *Meiroku Zasshi,* the journal of the influential Meirokusha (Meiji Six Society).[70] By the end of 1874 the controversy had spread, full gale, to the press, focusing public attention as never before on Tokyo's growing newspapers. As Fukuchi described it: "The discussion about a popular assembly has become like *Chūshingura* [The Forty-seven Rōnin] at the theater; whatever the date or the weather, there is always a full house."[71]

Most of the major papers, including *Hōchi, Chōya Shimbun,* and *Akebono Shimbun,* joined the call for an early assembly, characterizing opponents as "feudal" or devious. Fukuchi's editorials, on the other hand, held out for slower, more gradual movement in that direction, with the result that *Nichi Nichi,* already Japan's largest newspaper, strengthened its influence with the government and with nonofficial gradualists, even while earning the epithet "conservative" from competing newspapers. While other papers tended to lose individual identities during this "war," due to the similarity of their arguments, *Nichi Nichi* heightened its own identity.

The opposition press articulated three basic themes. First, they described the ruling faction as a group of self-seeking autocrats, men who were moving Japan toward authoritarian misgovernment "like captains of a pleasure boat running their craft full-speed into a mountain."[72] Some minor publications went so far as to urge that state ministers be "executed by the sword."[73] Second, they demanded that an assembly be convened immediately to counter this government tyranny, claiming that only those "former lords and councillors" who demanded assembly government "could be called true statesmen."[74] Third, they argued that the assembly should be made up exclusively of the elite nobility, or *shizoku*, since "the people of our land called *heimin* [commoners] are essentially unlearned, powerless fools who live in the realm of servitude."[75]

Fukuchi's response to these three criticisms constituted one of the more incisive political attacks of his life, blending aspects of both conservatism and progressivism. Beginning with a discussion of "moral enlightenment" on December 2, 1874, he ran no fewer than forty editorials in six months on political gradualism, or *zenshinshugi,* as it related to popular rights and the establishment of an assembly. In his first considered attack on radicalism, four days after inaugurating the *Nichi Nichi* editorial column, Fukuchi outlined his general understanding of gradualism, laying a foundation for later consideration of his opponents' specific contentions. He maintained that *kyūshin* (radical) arguments were not consistent with "the tranquility of a nation."

> Historically, no nation tending to radicalism has long been able to maintain national tranquility—regardless of its political system. . . . It is true that there are radical factions in Western nations today, factions such as the Democrats in America, the radicals in England and the commune movement in France. But a logical consideration of these groups convinces one that the realization of their aims would be much more harmful than beneficial. Nor is this my view alone. It is the opinion of wise statesmen in both England and the United States. If our aims are similar to theirs, we too should pursue the course of gradualism.

Fukuchi said Japan's most urgent need was to shift away from extremism, a course he considered responsible for the 1874 military incursion into Taiwan, and to "move more resolutely toward a gradualist approach which would introduce enlightened ways to our people in practical affairs." The populace, he said, needed to be taught modern methods at the local level, in everyday life, before being called upon to govern itself nationally.[76]

Having thus outlined the essence of *zenshinshugi,* Fukuchi proceeded in the following months to meet the specific arguments of his opponents, point by point.

He refused, first of all, to accept the opposition view of the existing government as autocratic or tyrannical. His hero, Kido, had indeed left the government, as had Itagaki, the champion of the radical press. But Kido never rejected the power structure per se. Neither would Fukuchi. The *Nichi Nichi* editor, moreover, remained sufficiently intimate with leading officials to be convinced that they intended to support oligarchic rule only until representative government became practicable. "If I had not known the officials' intentions, I too likely would have fervently urged fundamental reforms," he said, "but for three or four years I had had close, intimate contact with various officials and knew that they were not themselves comfortable with clique [*hambatsu*] government. I knew they hoped gradually to institute a constitutional system."[77] The result was that one finds in Fukuchi's columns no castigation of the existing regime. He did not spend much time actually defending the rulers. Rather, he made that defense implicit in his carefully reasoned support of their policies.

There was nothing veiled or implicit, however, in his editorials about the establishment of an assembly—the second line of opposition attack. Fukuchi made it clear from the outset that he agreed with the *minken,* or "popular rights," movement's call for an assembly: a nation did indeed have a responsibility to "redeem the basic national rights" of "all the people" by establishing representative government.[78] But on the matter of when that assembly should be established he attacked the *kyū-*

*shin* faction vigorously. "People who have been reared under oppression have little incentive to assume their rights," he warned. Hence, advances in popular wisdom, in education, in enlightenment, must precede nation-wide self-government.[79] "I have bitterly criticized . . . the vice of undue rapidity," he wrote again. "We must move gradually toward a popular assembly, opening ward assemblies first, then prefectural assemblies and, finally, a national assembly."[80]

The reason, he explained more fully late in 1875, lay in the nature of the recently ended Tokugawa period. "It is doubtful how much the people (excepting those at the top of society) really knew about the basis of self-government at the beginning of Meiji," he said. And if they were to govern themselves, principles of self-government would have to be taught first.

> The farmers, artisans and merchants have lived under oppression for many years. How can they be expected to understand the fluctuations and struggles of society when they are not even capable of managing their own economic affairs? To hurriedly establish a national assembly for these people, weak as they are in the spirit of self-government, would not be advantageous. . . . Let us oppose feudalism; but let us recognize the present situation as it is. We must move toward such a representative assembly gradually.[81]

Closely tied to this evolutionary view was Fukuchi's rather progressive definition of popular rights, a definition that spoke to his opponents' third line of attack. Whereas *Hōchi* and *Chōya* insisted on a democracy of the elite and demanded that the government continue to pay Tokugawa-initiated stipends to the old samurai class, Fukuchi denounced the stipends as "unmerited" and called for the inclusion of Japan's thirty-two million *heimin,* or commoners, in cultural and popular developments—thus bearing out an assertion by Maruyama Masao to the effect that the "thinking of those in the government up to 1877 was clearly more progressive than that of most of the opponents."[82]

Discussions of popular assemblies and samurai stipends were integrally related, Fukuchi argued first of all, because stipend-bearing *shizoku,* or former samurai, could claim no more inherent right to self-government than the farmers or *heimin* who paid those stipends through land taxes. He ran a particularly incisive series of editorials on this point in March 1875. The elite *shizoku,* he said, were "parasites sustained by the people, men who . . . logically must be regarded as residents of orphanages or poor houses" and therefore had no grounds for claiming "greater rights than rich or good commoners."[83] Indeed, he suggested, the *heimin* actually deserved not just equal, but greater, legal consideration, since propertyless *shizoku* had "absolutely no reason to call for the same parliamentary electoral rights as good commoners who possess their own family property."[84]

In another installment of the series, he answered *Hōchi*'s charge that commoners were "weakminded":[85] "If you ask why these *heimin* are now without spirit and power, it is because they have had to live in servitude under an oppressive governmental system, an oppression that . . . resulted from powerful *shizoku* pressure on the government." He asserted that "*shizoku* power had become all the stronger since the Restoration," with nobles and former samurai taking almost complete charge of official affairs and with the government "straining its ears to hear the will of the *shizoku.*"

> Yet one can hardly regard the kind of power that springs merely from hereditary wealth and position as "splendid in spirit." . . . The *heimin* were not born without spirit and power. They merely have been oppressed by the so-called spirit and power of the *shizoku.* It is for this reason alone that they have not been able to make a show of their strength and vitality.[86]

The answer to the commoners' problem, Fukuchi said, harking back to the question of how self-government should be introduced, was to encourage them to "snatch their rights" by forming local legislative and commercial bodies and thus giving them practice in self-government. It would not be a simple task; the commoners had been "unjustly discarded" for centuries. And "vitality is definitely not a quality that develops in an instant. But as we increase the rate of the restoration of popular rights, their spirit will increase commensurately."[87]

Much of the heat left this early editorial war after April 12, 1875, when an imperial decree was issued, announcing that an assembly of "representatives from the various provinces of the empire" would be convened so that the "public mind will be best known, . . . the public interest best consulted, and . . . the wisest system of administration . . . determined."[88] The decree also set up a Senate (Genrōin), in response to demands that the oligarchs' personal rule be checked, and it established a Daishin'in, or Supreme Court, to act as Japan's judiciary. The opposition press hailed the move as a victory for democratic government,[89] while Fukuchi, perhaps understanding the government's intent more clearly than did his competitors, approvingly called it a "light on the road of progress." It provided for an assembly, but a sharply limited one, thus avoiding "the vice of undue rapidity."[90] And the Senate was made up of "safe" nobles and officials—all appointed—who had little authority.

It was thus clear by mid-1875 that Fukuchi's view of gradualism involved at least three basics: faith in the existing government's intentions; popular rights for *heimin* as well as *shizoku;* and the following of a gradual, step-by-step approach to the creation of popular assemblies. It could be argued, of course, that he merely sought to stave off representative government until the oligarchs had had time to consolidate personal, autocratic rule. But the fervor of his editorials and the consistency of his views on these matters would tend to discount such a theory, as would his sustained opposition in later years to all forms of oligarchic absolutism—a point to be detailed later in this study. "Though attacked from a hundred directions," he hyperbolized, "I never bent the slightest."[91] Even his opponents called that a fair analysis.[92]

Perhaps the most fascinating aspect of Fukuchi's position was its elevation of the *heimin* to a level equal to that of the former samurai. Polemical or not, it was in line with the most innovative political writing of the day. As has often been noted, even the more advanced late Tokugawa bakufu thinkers had limited their political visions largely to the elite. Aizawa Seishisai's *Shinron* ("New proposals"), described by Maruyama as the "bible of the *sonnō jōi* movement," called commoners "stupid."[93] Yoshida Shōin, the proponent of new ideas about "everyone" participating in government, still found it the "function of the samurai to stand above the three [common] classes."[94] Itagaki's limitation of "popular rights" to the upper classes already has been noted. Even Fukuzawa Yukichi, long hailed as the era's most influential advocate of rights for the common man, has increasingly come to be recognized as essentially "a politically conservative ideologue of the samurai class," one who addressed himself almost solely "to the aspirations of that class."[95] Thus, for Fukuchi to have argued so forcefully for the *heimin* places him in the vanguard of the political thought of his day.

Equally fascinating and, in the long run, even more significant is what the debate over representative government showed about Fukuchi's evolving mind-set, about his maturing general approach to the nature of the Japanese state. It was this editorial campaign that finally stamped him as the nation's foremost private advocate of "progress and order," or gradualism. We have, of course, already seen the implicit rudiments of this approach, both at *Kōko Shimbun* and in his role in the bureaucracy. But now the implicit became explicit. For while his view of the commoners was very much on the "progress" side of the ledger, the fact that he made the existing regime the initiator and object of such progress showed steadily growing concern about tradition or "order." In other words, it was above all national, not individual power that Fukuchi sought. It was the government that was to "train" the commoners. Tranquility was essential to national progress—so essential in fact that notions of popular sovereignty could not be allowed to advance to a point of threatening it. Thus, the great merit of the government's decision to set up an "assembly of representatives" in 1875 was the fact that this privilege would be "given by the emperor" rather than forced on him by the people.[96] Fukuchi's position may have been—indeed was—more forward-looking than that of *jiyū minken,* or popular rights, advocates, but he defined progress largely in national or state terms, solely within the framework of national ''order.'' As that framework became increasingly important in Fukuchi's thinking, it would eventually make him look more and more conservative. For now though, it was very much in keeping with, if not ahead of, the times.

One thing that neither Fukuchi nor his opponents knew at the time of the emperor's decree was that it would in certain ways affect him quite personally. When the Conference of Local Officials (Chihōkan Kaigi) convened at Asakusa's Honganji on June 20 to hear a welcoming speech by the emperor, Fukuchi was in attendance as secretary. The conference's reluctant president, Kido Kōin,[97] noting Fukuchi's kindred viewpoint and his unique acquaintanceship with Western parliamentary ways, had summoned him to help draw up conference rules and record the activities of each session. Thus, during the conference he aided Kido as a sort of de facto parliamentarian,[98] even while filling several colorful conference reports with acid evaluations of ''such and such a governor who was yawning,''[99] or ''those absurd arguments.''[100]

Despite this intimate involvement, however, Fukuchi's enthusiasm for the conference itself quickly soured. He was not really upset by the fact that it was an extremely ''timid step'' along the road to representative government,[101] convened and tightly controlled by the oligarchs. But he objected strongly to the caliber of the delegates, most of whom were prefectural governors *(chikenji)* under appointment by the Home Ministry. They made up, he said, an ''assembly of fools,'' hardly a good omen for the future of popular government.[102] He also objected to the central government's assumption of two-thirds of the conference's total cost, as a needless expense on the taxpayers ''from whose blood the money must come.''[103] Most of all, he castigated the government for excluding the press from the sessions. Perhaps the purpose was to ''screen the inexperience'' of officials who might invite ''the nation's ridicule,'' he wrote sarcastically. But the end result was merely to place the government in an even more unfavorable light, especially since several foreigners (who were admitted) reported the sessions fully in the English-language press.[104] It would appear, in other words, that while Fukuchi dreaded pitfalls along the path of "undue haste," and although he supported the government's general approach, he remained capable of dissatisfaction with the concrete ways in which policies were administered. It was an attitude reminiscent of his old frustration over the maladministration of a Tokugawa government that he abstractly and generally defended, a skepticism about specific execution of official policy that would appear again and again.

One area of recurring discontent was the government's tendency to delay in holding a second Chihōkan Kaigi, a tendency that held off the second conference until 1878.[105] Another was the government's attitude toward the press. He had always advocated press freedom, despite his professed willingness to work voluntarily with members of the government. In fact, it was this independence that had shipwrecked *Kōko Shimbun.* Now, on June 9, 1875, he reiterated that view with an assertion that government interference with the press in a modern nation constituted "an obstacle on the road of popular progress." Therefore his reactions were strong when, just three weeks later, on June 28, the government began a policy of serious interference, issuing harsh new press laws that forbade the publication of anything intended to "revile existing laws or confuse the sense of duty of the people to observe them," and threatening offenders with prison terms of up to three years.[106]

The effects of these new laws were, in many ways, extraordinary. Suehiro Tetchō of *Akebono Shimbun* was jailed and fined for boldly assailing the new laws. At Fukuzawa's urging, the influential *Meiroku Zasshi* stopped publishing altogether; and the antigovernment *Hōchi,* cowering in fear, called the new laws a necessary "omen of cultural progress."[107] Most of the editors, however, led by *Nichi Nichi*'s "champion of gradualism," drew together in a surprising new display of press unity, meeting together in Japan's "first journalistic guild meeting"[108] and agreeing that the country's leading writers should test the new laws by composing anonymous articles for presentation to the government under the heading: "If I wrote thus, would it constitute slander or libel?"

More than a dozen editors carried through with the assignment and wrote essays variously demanding that the government resign or that unskillful "plaintiffs who make a nuisance of themselves be dismissed."[109] The anonymous article apparently prepared by Fukuchi attacked the government's favoritism toward the *shizoku* as a special sort of treatment that "might have been alright in ancient times . . . but is definitely improper in these days when impartiality has become the imperial will." It called favoritism "a disgrace that bodes ill for the future of the great imperial Japan."[110]

The government refused to comment directly on the articles, replying late in September that it had "neither a responsibility to make refutations in regard to the newspaper laws nor any instructions to give."[111] Instead it merely acted. Beginning early in August the Home Ministry instituted a severe new policy of repression, and by the end of the next year's "reign of terror," more than sixty journalists from all the major papers (including *Nichi Nichi*) had gone to jail or been fined.[112] As Fukuchi described the period: "It was like a gush of water. . . . As soon as a reporter spoke, he was summoned. Many respectable reporters and gentlemen were fined or jailed."[113] Not that it was a totally impossible situation. Newspapers continued to publish, and editors continued to discuss the issues of the day, but no longer with the same freedom.

One significant aspect of the entire episode for Fukuchi was the role it played in proving that he would not be a kept man, that he would allow his own reporters to go to jail rather than involuntarily giving in to the government. He was a dedicated gradualist; but his gradualism included a higher respect for the press than did that of many of his official friends. Pressed thus in a personally significant area, he did not bend.

During the next few years, however, as the shock of the press laws wore off, Fukuchi turned to a new political topic, which was increasingly becoming central to the debates of the official world: constitutionalism. From the year of the Restoration, the more enlightened in the government, aware of the absence of any kind of legal or normative basis to rationalize their ad hoc control, had given at least lip service to the necessity of governing by the rule of law. And the Iwakura mission had turned that lip service into conviction for men like Kido and Itō. Yet during the first decade of Meiji they had taken little concrete action in that direction. The first five years of the era had been dominated by the immediate, often frantic, necessity of devising structures that would simply assure continuation of their de facto power. Then, after the return of the Iwakura mission, the Korean and Taiwan issues had sparked four years of samurai unrest, marked first by several localized revolts in western Honshu and northern Kyushu, and finally, in 1877, by a full-scale rebellion centered in the old area of Satsuma *han*. When one adds to these the presence of excruciating financial difficulties, sharp factional divisions within the administration, the humiliating struggle over unequal treaties, and a massive invasion of Western culture, it becomes understandable that the more abstract, legal issues like the creation of a fundamental law of state were postponed.

From the end of 1877, however, the constitutional issue became more pressing. With the superficial control structures quite securely in the hands of a few oligarchs from the Satsuma and Chōshū areas, there was at last time to plan for the basic foundations of the state. It may have seemed like a cart-before-the-horse approach (and it would be a mistake to ascribe delays solely to the demands of time, since personal power maintenance was always a basic priority); yet, given the sudden nature in which control had shifted at the time of the Restoration, it was probably the only approach possible. So from early 1878 on, feeling the combined pressures of political logic, of campaigns by "popular rights" advocates and of demands by foreign diplomats that the government be rationalized before they would seriously consider treaty revision, the oligarchs turned more actively to the constitutional issue. By June 1878, the Genrōin (Senate) had drawn up a draft constitution. And by the end of the 1870s, the junior councillors had been asked to submit personal opinions to the emperor on the kind of constitution Japan needed. Few favored a truly democratic document. In fact, as those opinions came in, all but the one prepared by Ōkuma supported imperial sovereignty, with a strong executive and a highly limited legislature. And all except Ōkuma called for very deliberate movement in the constitutional direction.[114] But at least the constitutional issue had been actively broached.

Fukuchi generally kept pace with this trend, and although he did not stop writing about the need for local and prefectural "assemblies," the vanguard of his political editorials had shifted to the constitutional issue by the beginning of the second Meiji decade. By the year 1880 the issue of constitutionalism—what it meant, what kind of constitution Japan needed, how it should be adopted—had become the central focus of his evolving gradualist position.

His discussion of constitutionalism was initiated, in a sense, by a series of editorials early in 1879 entitled simply, "Zenshinshugi." In them, he broadly defined gradualism as a position that "reverently accepts imperial authority at the top with a trillion people enjoying freedom beneath to participate in government and develop culturally," a view "based on real situations," not on mere theories.[115] Then, after minutely dissecting the views and motives of his opponents on the right and the left, he proclaimed the specific goal of *zenshinshugi* to be "the gradual establishment of a constitutional system" to replace today's "personal autocracy *[dokusai seiji]*." He admitted that the pace was tortuous at times and that "we have not yet reached the hour for offering a song of victory." But he expressed faith that the day was indeed coming "when we will attain the merits of *a constitutional system that encompasses the joint rule of people and sovereign [kumin kyōchi] . . . , the goal of gradualism.*"[116]

One of the most significant aspects of this series was that it highlighted a drift in Fukuchi's own thought. Disturbed with a number of specific government acts, cut off by the death of Kido in 1877 from his most intimate Chōshū tie, and concerned that Satchō men might be intent on establishing a permanent autocracy, he had begun showing subtle but clear signs of increasing liberalism or popular-mindedness by 1878 and 1879. More editorials began calling for "popular rights" or the "protection of human rights."[117] He made stinging attacks on Ōkuma's fiscal policies, thus creating a permanent breach between the two that would never heal.[118] Openness in government increasingly concerned him,[119] and more and more he began looking toward the creation of new vehicles that would give expression to the popular will. As biographer Yanagida Izumi has noted: "The very constitutional system planned in the days of Kido and Itagaki seemed threatened. So Fukuchi decided to abandon his close ties and take a more even-handed approach. Increasingly, he began wielding his brush in criticism of government policy."[120]

Before turning to the specifics of this shift, a word of caution seems essential. One should not assume that this was the kind of drift that might seriously endanger Fukuchi's basic "progress and order" approach to gradualism. For his liberal tendencies, as we shall see, still focused largely on the maintenance of national order. As one reads his editorials in these years, it becomes clear that he found the main source of popular rights not in a concept of inherent or contractual human rights below but in the imperial way that shaped Japanese tradition from above. Thus, representative government and constitutionalism might be seen as "modern" and essential to "order," but they were not inherent popular rights in and of themselves. Always the focus was "above" rather than "below." A constitutional system, he said, "aims first of all at carrying out the will of the imperial line."[121] "A constitution is the key, the passageway, to national tranquility."[122] So though Fukuchi shifted leftward, it should be kept in mind that he never departed from the essential view that liberal gains would serve above all to guarantee the strength of the state and the prosperity of the imperial way.

Now, to look at the specifics of his political shift. One of the clearest signs of Fukuchi's new concern with "rights" came early in 1880 when he began proposing concrete steps to hasten the day of *kumin kyōchi,* or joint rule of sovereign and subject. In the early spring of that year, he wrote a series of editorials contending that the time had come to "call together representatives from across the country to open a constitutional convention and draw up a constitution."[123] There was, he conceded, a degree of danger in allowing a popular assembly to approve a constitution, a danger that the people might "extend their rights too far and even attempt to select and dethrone emperors," an eventuality he genuinely abhorred. But he thought that the advantages overbalanced any dangers. Draft constitutions and constitutional opinions already had been prepared by the Genrōin (Senate) and several junior councillors to guide the people. An imperial decree would be issued stating that "the purpose of the constitution will be to revere the succession of the imperial line and . . . to grant all administrative rights to the emperor." Since "our people possess a depth of respect for their sovereign, a fervency of loyalty to the ruler unparalleled under heaven, I have no doubt that those who participate . . . will uphold and respect the emperor."

Moreover, he feared that unless the people were thus allowed to adopt a constitution, they would raise a clamor of dissatisfaction that would endanger national tranquility or force the eventual adoption of an unduly liberal constitution, a constitution that might violate imperial prerogatives. Illustrating the "universal rule" that "if you give people an inch they will want a foot and if you give them a foot, they will want a yard," he pointed to widespread dissatisfaction with limits on prefectural assemblies that had been created in 1878 "by arbitrary imperial decree." The grumbling, he noted, had arisen even though the people "should have been satisfied" with the imperial beneficence in setting up such bodies. It would be the same with a constitution. If the people were "given" a constitution rather than being allowed to adopt it themselves, they would only complain and clamor for "more rights," regardless of the magnanimity with which they had been treated. The preservation of order called for a constitution adopted at least in form by the people themselves, a "national contract" *(kokuyaku)* constitution rather than the social contract constitution demanded by men like Ueki Emori.[124] As Fukuchi said that same spring: "The orderly movement of the past has been awaiting this day. . . . It is time to open a convention and adopt a constitution."[125]

Equally important, it was also at this time that Fukuchi began discussing in some detail the actual nature of a constitution. A constitution, he wrote in March, must "exalt the way of the emperor."[126] It should establish the ruler's "responsibility to the people through a prime minister, divide legislative rights between emperor and people, . . . establish an independent judiciary."[127] And it must encourage progress, support Japan's historical polity, or *kokutai,* and assure a two-house legislature.[128]

*Nichi Nichi*'s most significant contribution to Japan's constitutional debate came in March and April 1881, the same months in which the junior councillors were finishing the delivery of their own constitutional opinions to the emperor. In a detailed series of fourteen editorials that sparked almost as much debate as the 1875 struggle over an assembly, Fukuchi stated his view of what constitutionalism should mean. Entitling the series "Kokken iken" ("An opinion on the national constitution"),[129] he made it clear that the government had no monopoly on astute political insight, drawing much attention in the process. As the first private constitutional draft, the series took a place among the important documents of the period.

Following a rather progressive introduction that explained the merits of constitutional government and called for joint promulgation by the emperor and the people, the editorials offered, and commented on, a total of eight ideal chapters. The first, most conservative and most controversial of them, established the imperial institution as the foundation of all Japanese government.[130] "The emperor is divine in nature; only descendants of Amaterasu Ōmikami may occupy our imperial Japanese throne," it said. Heirs were to be selected by the reigning sovereign, with the upper house of the assembly asked to choose the successor if a ruler died before making his selection. The emperor's powers of administration, deliberation, and law were in no way to be restrained.

Japan was, in other words, an imperial country, and while Fukuchi would limit that power by the very fact of stating the emperor's rights in a constitution, he intended to maintain the inviolable, supreme, and divine nature of the emperor forever. It was a point of view that drew heavy fire from other Tokyo newspapers, most of which claimed that assertions of imperial divinity in the modern era were both absurd and dangerous. But it was also a profoundly significant chapter; for it posited a position (and an emotion) regarding the emperor that had faded during the first dozen years of Meiji but would soon reemerge as the solid-rock foundation of Japan's domestic nationalism and foreign expansion.

The second chapter, by contrast, was rather "liberal."[131] It dealt with public law, maintaining that "the Japanese people shall possess equal rights before the law, regardless of rank or social status." All men were to pay taxes according to the value of their possessions, to enjoy equal opportunity in military or government posts, and to be responsible for military service. Legal punishments were to be meted out "without respect of persons." Freedom of faith, speech, and press would be insured "within the limits of the law." And the right to own property would not be disturbed. The chapter showed, in short, that the same Fukuchi who believed deeply in the conservative tenet of imperial sovereignty also believed in a fairly broad definition of civil liberties. That he would limit those liberties if they threatened tranquility was consistent with his "progress and order" approach. On the whole, however, chapter II was as progressive as one could have expected given the times in which he lived and the associations that had formed his thinking.

Succeeding chapters generally continued this moderate to progressive tone, patterning Japan's envisioned government largely on the English system. Administration (chap. III) was to rest in the hands of the emperor, with a cabinet responsible for carrying out his administrative will. That cabinet (chap. VI), in turn, was responsible to the legislature; ministers could belong to the assembly and could be impeached by assembly vote. The popularly elected legislature (chaps. IV and V) would be bicameral, with the lower house maintaining the greater legislative power and the emperor holding final authority for the sanction of all laws. Judges, described in chapter VII, were to be appointed for life, thus assuring the independence of the judiciary. And a miscellany of "Special Laws" in chapter VIII provided for such varying matters as the right of petitioning within legal limits, military pensions, and the administration of Okinawa and Hokkaido. A concluding statement added that such a constitution would achieve a "balance between the majesty of the emperor and the rights of the people," serving as a foundation for the true way of righteousness. Anyone who used the label "imperial sovereignty" to hinder the progress of popular rights, Fukuchi explained, was a "traitor," just as anyone who abused the imperial prerogative in the name of popular rights could be called disloyal.[132]

And that, to Fukuchi, represented the continuing essence, the balance, of gradualism in 1881: imperial sovereignty above smiling on popular rights beneath. It was hardly, for its time, a thoroughgoing conservative position, though it could not be called fully progressive either. It included numerous halfway points: the spirited defense of imperial sovereignty balanced by clauses pledging the emperor to uphold the constitution; the provision of suffrage circumscribed by sharp limits; the curbing of popular rights by the clause "within the limits of the law." Yet, more than his friends within the government, Fukuchi supported basic popular freedoms and rights. His definition of suffrage was more liberal than that eventually included in the first Meiji election law.[133] The emperor's powers were curbed by the very fact of legislating them. His view of the judiciary was relatively liberal, assuring free and independent courts. Civil liberties were extended rather broadly. And a procedure was provided for the impeachment and conviction of cabinet ministers. He was bitterly attacked by *Tokyo-Yokohama Mainichi* for his chapter on imperial sovereignty and his restrictions on civil liberties.[134] Yet it would appear that, on the whole, Fukuchi in

1880 had found a position much more concerned than the oligarchs with popular progress, yet very much mindful of the maintenance of order and tradition. The constitutional draft, says a leading political scientist, was "a brilliant work."[135] How much it influenced the simultaneous moves being made within the government in the direction of constitutionalism is a problem to be considered in the next chapter. What is clear is that Fukuchi had now found his center as a gradualist, a center highly influential in the circles of public opinion.

"Gradualism," wrote the *Nichi Nichi* editor in 1880, "is the philosophy of carrying out reforms gradually."[136] Looking back over the "golden years" from 1875 to early 1881, that definition generally involved two specific political themes: the *eventual* convening of a national, popular assembly and the adoption, *at the right time,* of a constitution. He differed from radical opponents on the assembly issue by pressing for commoner as well as elite suffrage and urging the prior establishment of local and prefectural assemblies as training grounds in self-government. On the issue of constitutionalism, he placed far greater emphasis on imperial sovereignty than did other newspaper editors, even while calling for more guarantees of personal liberty than might have suited his government allies. "I have never changed my philosophy," he asserted in 1880.[137] It was an assertion open to interpretation; yet it approximated the truth. The specifics of timing and the concrete incarnations of broad policies might vary for Fukuchi, but always the channels of the stream had remained consistent: progress and order assured by measured movement toward constitutionalism and representative government.

### The Influential Citizen

During the summer of Fukuchi's third year at *Nichi Nichi*, several dozen prominent newspapermen met beneath the massive old red pillars and flickering ancestral candles of Tokyo's leading Buddhist temple, the Asakusa Kannon, for a strangely curious service. As onlookers packed the hall, Buddhist priests chanted sutras, musicians played ancient court music, and a

representative from each of Tokyo's three leading papers—
*Nichi Nichi, Chōya,* and *Hōchi*—read Shinto funeral prayers.
Then twenty-six journalists from more than a dozen papers read
speeches calling for divine aid in their newspaper ventures. The
stated purpose was to petition the *kami* or divine spirits for
journalistic success, to confess reportorial sins, to mourn for colleagues who had died, to honor imprisoned writers, and, all the
while, to "answer the clamorous opinion that newspaper men
were completely mad."[138]

It was a strange meeting, called for fanciful reasons, joining
competitors and allies alike, hinting at the sentimentality that
ever seethes beneath the self-confident masks of hard-bitten reporters. It was at the same time both symbolic and illustrative of
the state of the profession, showing the collective pride journalists had come to feel and suggesting the distance the profession
had traveled in just two years both in attracting talented young
writers and in creating a powerful role in Japanese society. It
symbolized, as well, the troubled times in which the press now
found itself, days of open rebellion by disgruntled ex-samurai
and press oppression by a beleaguered government. And it
highlighted Fukuchi's role in the press. His newspaper helped
sponsor the event; he was on the four-man committee that
planned it; and his speech was chosen to conclude the service.
He had, by now, become the acknowledged "leader of the profession,"[139] and throughout the late 1870s, even as he was writing his forceful editorials on political gradualism, he enjoyed
the fruits of power in a myriad of areas.

Even more symbolic of Fukuchi's success as *Nichi Nichi* editor was the transfer of the Nippōsha offices in 1877 to a new
building in the heart of Tokyo's business and financial district.
The building was impressive, reflecting annual gross profits of
nearly 100,000 yen,[140] and it came to be cited widely as a sign of
the arrival of the press as an influence-wielding institution.
Wrote competitor Narushima Ryūhoku in *Chōya Shimbun:*

> Whose edifice is this, standing on the corner, thrusting itself high
> into the beautiful clouds, glistening in the light of the sun? It could

be the home of a nobleman, or the abode of a general. But no, it is the newly completed office of our comrade, the Nippōsha. . . . It is amazing in its grandeur and splendor. It reminds one of the golden cavern of a heavenly hermit.[141]

A widely circulated cartoon of the period showed rural pilgrims praying in front of the building, mistaking the gaslights that etched it on feast days for those of a temple or shrine.[142] *Nichi Nichi* had become the first of Japan's powerful "national" papers.

One area that caught public attention in these years was the continuing innovativeness of the *Nichi Nichi* reporting. In 1876, for example, the newspaper inaugurated Japan's first book reviews and medical articles. It hired stringers in such far-away places as Australia. In 1877, it launched the press into the field of foreign correspondence.[143] That same year it engineered the most dramatic reportorial scoop of Fukuchi's career with the editor's own front-line reporting from the battlefields of the Southwest (Satsuma) Rebellion.

The rebellion, often seen as the dying gasp of Tokugawa Japan and of the old samurai class, had been building ever since the Restoration and particularly since Saigō and his followers had left the government during the Korean crisis of 1873. Distraught with a series of government moves that had stripped them of power, income, and prestige, ex-samurai in parts of southwestern Japan had risen in scattered, relatively localized rebellions during the years 1874 to 1876. Their comrades at the center of discontent in Satsuma, meanwhile, had congregated by the thousands in a network of private, peaceful military schools and Confucian academies founded by the almost legendary Saigō. Unfortunately, however, many of the Satsuma malcontents had deeper interests than mere academic learning, and when a rumor spread early in 1877 that government agents were going to assassinate Saigō, they rose in general rebellion.

Back in Tokyo, Fukuchi saw the uprising as a genuine threat to the existing government, as well as to national order, and advocated a swift and sizable military response. On February 20,

*Nichi Nichi* offices in 1877, described by *Chōya Shimbun* as ''amazing in its grandeur and splendor.'' The man in the middle on the balcony is thought to be Fukuchi. *(Photo courtesy of Mainichi Shimbunsha Shi Henshūshitsu)*

when he heard the imperial order to attack the rebels, he left for Osaka to discuss developments with Itō, who was in that city formulating strategy. When Itō suggested jokingly that the *Nichi Nichi* editor might himself go to the front, Fukuchi seized the idea, secured official permission and suitable clothing from Itō, and headed for Kyushu without so much as returning to Tokyo to inform his staff. There, he called on Yamagata, the field commander, and asked permission to accompany the troops. Yamagata explained that reporters were not allowed among the troops but suggested that he needed someone to write reports and draft official documents, a job he thought might appeal to Fukuchi. Fukuchi agreed that it would—as long as he was allowed to write articles in spare time for *Nichi Nichi*—and thus began a life as a war correspondent.

Fukuchi's news reports became a sensation in Tokyo and boosted *Nichi Nichi*'s circulation well above ten thousand, a record for Japanese journalism.[144] They also illustrated in a new, concrete way Fukuchi's genius as a journalist. His forte to date had been editorials, almost to the exclusion of personal reportorial writing. Now, faced for the first time with the necessity of composing regular, factual reports, he produced a series of brilliant stories equal to the best standards of war correspondence.

Written in the first person, the stories tended to be long, full of poignant detail, and crisply written. They described the terrain, the condition of the troops, the strategies of commanders, the weather—everything in precise, yet rarely tedious, detail. Excerpts from his March 23 article, describing a trip south from Fukuoka toward Kumamoto over terrain the imperial troops had just crossed, illustrate these stylistic qualities:

At one o'clock I arrived at Setaka, a relatively large post town sandwiched between rivers. Most of the people seemed to have been evacuated. All the doors were shut, the canopies down; inside one saw the *tatami* folded up. A company of troops had erected a fortress here.

Laborers were gathering from each post town. Most of those who came from the direction of Minami no Seki were carrying wounded soldiers (on rain shutters with ropes attached to the hooks). Others were carrying ammunition. Or bearing loads on their shoulders. Or riding horseback. The coming and going was impossibly confusing. . . .

The morning of the eleventh: It had been raining softly since the previous evening, and the sky still had not cleared off. The rain turned to light snow, then cleared up about eleven o'clock. The troops under General Yamagata had now vacated the Minami no

Seki barracks and headed toward Takase, almost five *ri* away.[145] Most of the first two *ri* were mountain roads and, the way being muddy, extremely difficult to traverse; but from there on the road became easier, though still a bit uneven. We arrived in Takase at 2 P.M. . . .

For eleven days the company that I joined had lived in the mountains, enduring the rain and dew without so much as a barracks. They could neither sleep nor eat. Consider, my reader, how bitterly they fought by day and by night, even while enduring three days of continuous rain. It is impossible to imagine their hardships. This company's blood speaks the glory of patriotism. Its deaths speak the righteousness of national service. . . .[146]

Life in a soldier's barracks, where everyone "had to bear infestation by lice,"[147] must have been difficult for the luxury-loving lord of Ike no Hata. Nothing in his past had prepared him for insects or spoiled food, for mud or foul-smelling latrines; but the sacrifices were apparently worth it. During the first weeks of war, he alone among Japan's journalists was able to report from the front, and even after the popularity of his reports had been established, *Hōchi* was the only other paper equipped to send a correspondent to the scene of battle.[148] *Nichi Nichi*'s reports were, consequently, far more factual than those of others, especially after Fukuchi sent two more reporters to Kyushu later in the rebellion. The increased circulation showed that, in many respects, Fukuchi more than his fellow Japanese editors "genuinely understood the role of newspapers and newspapermen."[149]

The prestige of the press was further highlighted when the emperor invited Fukuchi to repeat his observations personally during a two-hour conference at the imperial palace on April 6—an unprecedented honor for a newspaperman. As Fukuchi, the loyal imperialist, wrote his wife: "I suppose you know that . . . I was received by the emperor and given fifty *yen* and two rolls of crepe silk. This is the greatest honor I have ever had."[150] He described the audience in the *Nichi Nichi* of April 12, concluding:

This honor was not mine alone; actually the glory belongs to Nippōsha. Nor would it be inappropriate to call it an honor for all newspaper reporters—or for society in general. When I actually ponder the reason for which I was so honored, I am awestruck. . . . The opportunity resulted from the magnificent benevolence of our imperial sovereign, a man who grieved so deeply over the troops' casualties and the people's war sacrifices that he deigned to listen to the report of a man who knew the war situation intimately. And he did this even though I was but a journalist, a common man![151]

Fukuchi had never been one to err on the side of underestimating his own accomplishments. He was right, however, in assuming an honor for the press at large. In a country of growing emperor orientation, the mere granting of such an audience indicated to the world that journalists had gained respect as interpreters and reporters of significant information.

The emperor also appears to have given Fukuchi a secret assignment; for though he had planned to return to Tokyo after the audience, he instead went back to Kyushu. And although his battle reports continued for another two months, Fukuchi's most significant task this time seems to have been the drafting of a letter from Yamagata to Saigō. Yamagata's intimate friendship with the rebel general had made the prosecution of the war exceedingly difficult for him. So, drawing on that friendship, he decided to send Saigō a (now famous) plea that might end hostilities. To draft the plea he called on Fukuchi, whose literary talent he admired.[152]

The letter recalled old friendships and stated Yamagata's conviction that Saigō was not personally responsible for the fighting. It concluded with an eloquent plea to end the resistance: "Several months of fighting have already passed; hundreds of casualties on both sides occur daily; friends kill one another, kinsmen are pitted against each other . . . yet the soldiers bear no hatred. The Imperial troops are fulfilling their military obligation while Satsuma men say they are fighting for Saigō. . . . I entreat you to take measures to end the fighting both to prove that the present situation is not of your doing and to eliminate casualties on both sides as quickly as possible.''[153] It was, unfortunately, an ineffective plea; Saigō continued fighting until the collapse of the rebellion and his own death that autumn. But it illustrated movingly the respect in which most officials continued to hold Saigō and the hopes they held for a negotiated peace.

After writing the letter, Fukuchi stayed with the troops for another month, journeying from one battle site to another and continuing his war reports, then returned to Tokyo early in June. Two and a half years earlier, he had helped establish the press's role as an opinion maker by inaugurating Tokyo's first daily editorial column. Now he had illustrated the potential influence of solid reporting. It was not undignified, he showed, for respected men to leave their offices and search out facts, even in the mire and blood of a battlefield. Prima donna writers who relied solely on *tambōsha* (news gatherers) to gather their facts would in time become an anachronism. Fukuchi's reportorial role in Kyushu helped point Japanese journalism in that direction.

Even so, it remained the editorial sphere for which he enjoyed his primary reputation during the late 1870s. One of his colleagues, looking back to the editorials of these years, wrote that Fukuchi was "the only man among Meiji writers who genuinely epitomized the journalist's ideal." He called him "a superior, civilized man, a leader of public opinion."[154] A scholar described his editorials from 1876 to 1880 as "the law of the editorial world each morning."[155] And a prominent editor of the next generation, Tokutomi Sohō, copied Fukuchi's editorials as a lad in Kumamoto to "learn how to write."[156]

The most distinctive quality of those editorials, beyond the style of their prose and the logic of their argument, was the breadth of subject matter about which Fukuchi wrote. While editorialists at most papers continued to concentrate on politics and, to a much lesser degree, on economics, Fukuchi consciously gave his editorial columns over to discussing whatever issue seemed newsworthy. This point is clear from even a glance at the overall subjects on which he wrote. Of 1,230 *Nichi Nichi*

editorials during the years from 1876 to 1880,[157] some 338, or
27.4 percent, did indeed deal specifically with domestic politics
and government. But another 265 (21.5 percent) discussed economic issues; 195 (16 percent) dealt with international affairs;
and some 430 treated such diverse topics as civil rebellion (11.7
percent), law (3.6 percent), journalism (3.2 percent), literature
and culture (2.6 percent), the military (1 percent), education
(0.8 percent), religion (0.5 percent), and miscellaneous matters
(11.7 percent).

A study of the key events of the period—and the paper's handling of them—makes the point even more clearly. A list of
Japan's most important developments during these years would
likely center on: (1) extension of Japanese influence in Asia, inaugurated by the treaty with Korea in February 1876; (2) constant efforts to revise the unequal treaties with Western powers;
and (3) economic growth, especially as seen in inflation, currency policies, and the expansion of trade. These are certainly not
inclusive; nor can they be treated exhaustively. Yet even a cursory survey shows just how completely Fukuchi's *Nichi Nichi*
kept abreast of every important topic throughout the period.

The 1876 treaty, providing for Japanese recognition of
Korea's independence from China and for Japanese commercial
and extraterritorial rights, was signed in Inchon on February 26.
As early as January 16 Fukuchi began discussing the attitudes of
China and Russia toward Korea, and on January 24, five days
after the receipt in Japan of a request for troops to back up Kuroda in his negotiations, *Nichi Nichi* ran the first of two editorials discussing the need for restraint, even if it was necessary to
send the troops.[158] Early in March, a *Nichi Nichi* editorial
reported at length on Kuroda's return from Korea,[159] and during the next month the paper ran no fewer than six editorials ex-
pounding on the importance of both military preparedness and
restraint in treaty negotiations, on the efficacy of the treaty
itself, and on the inadvisability of making Korea apologize
publicly for the bombardment of two small Japanese vessels off
Inchon the previous September.[160]

*Nichi Nichi* covered other East Asian developments too. In

1879, it handled the conversion of the Ryukyu Islands into Okinawa Prefecture in half a dozen editorials, claiming that the islands were, historically, "part of our country" and not vassal states of China, as some had claimed.[161] In all, Fukuchi ran an average of fifteen editorials a year on East Asia during this period. And like most gradualists in the government, he took a relatively moderate stand toward Japan's northern neighbors—especially toward Russia and Sakhalin—but remained expansionist in his attitudes toward southern areas such as the Ryukyus and China.

*Nichi Nichi* did an even better job in keeping abreast of the treaty revision movement. From early 1874 on, the Foreign Ministry had begun actively to seek revision, with a view to gaining tariff autonomy and, if possible, relief from extraterritorial provisions. Negotiations in Washington led in mid-1878 to a restoration of that autonomy, with a proviso that the other powers must approve the revision before it could take effect. The British refused, however, and the plan failed. Negotiations continued, with Inoue and Ōkuma completing a new draft treaty in July 1880; but this plan also died, from premature exposure by the foreign press and subsequent British objections—setting a frustrating, decade-long pattern in which each time Japan would appear on the verge of success, an obstacle (often in the guise of Great Britain) would arise.

From 1876 to 1880, *Nichi Nichi* ran some seventy editorials on revision, an average of fourteen a year. Early in 1876, for example, Fukuchi spent three days discussing ways to lessen the curse of extraterritoriality. Foreigners could not be expected to give up that right until they felt absolutely certain of fair treatment in Japanese courts, he maintained in a typically pragmatic tone. Since that would be a long time in coming, he recommended that a series of "mixed courts"—of the kind explained in his 1873 report to Soejima—be adopted, allowing Japanese and foreigners to sit together in trials of foreign cases.[162] More than a year later, when negotiations with the U.S. representatives were reaching a climax, Fukuchi ran a series of five editorials stating that the public equated treaty revision with both extraterritoriality and tariff autonomy, even though the government had for the present reduced its demands to the latter. The editorials ran excerpts of an 1875 letter from Townsend Harris to Edward H. House, U.S. editor of the *Tokio Times,* describing the extraterritoriality provisions as "an unjust interference with the municipal law of a country," thus supporting *Nichi Nichi*'s claim that the original treaties were indeed unfair and oppressive.[163]

One of Fukuchi's favorite topics in this area was the *techniques* of diplomacy. Negotiations, he frequently maintained, should be handled secretly and negotiators should keep a constant and sharp eye for the treachery of foreign countries. "If the treaty gives them three concessions to our one," he said in August 1878, "we would still probably gain more than they, as long as we received the rights of legal jurisdiction and tariff autonomy."[164] Beginning late in 1879 and extending into February 1880, he discussed the entire treaty revision matter—its history, Japan's rights, its prospects—in great detail in a series of more than two dozen editorials. The series is not only detailed but perceptive, a clear indication that diplomacy was among Fukuchi's fortes.[165]

The late 1870s were also years of economic trial and expansion. A new banking act in mid-1876, which allowed national banks to issue notes whether they had specie reserves or not, helped create a serious inflationary problem during and following the Satsuma Rebellion. National banks proliferated in these years, so that by the end of 1879, 153 of them had been chartered.[166] The government continued to encourage private industry. Trade, particularly the export of silk, grew rapidly, though the tariff restrictions seriously damaged Japan's balance of payments, resulting in a drain of gold and silver of some 71 million yen between 1872 and 1881.[167]

In no other area did Fukuchi's editorials so surpass the rest of the press as in covering these economic issues. Economics were then (as now) complicated—the more so since the whole field of modern commerce was new to the Japanese. Hence the complaint of Fukuchi's competitor, Yano Fumio cf *Hōchi,* that "we always felt . . . inferior in writing about economics."[168] Fukuchi, on the other hand, was not so timorous. His earliest work in the Tokugawa bureaucracy had been with problems related to currency and customs regulations; he had introduced Western banking concepts to Japan, had worked in the Finance Ministry, and had accompanied Itō on a trip to America to study banking and currency. As a result, he regularly wrote influential editorials on every economic issue of the time—an average, in fact, of some forty-four a year.

No major economic issue escaped his pen. In April and May 1876, for example, he did a series on monetary policy; the same year he wrote nearly two dozen editorials on shipping and trade, another half dozen on stock exchanges. The year 1878 saw major series on the development of national resources, on currency, and on the use of foreign capital. Other topics ran the gamut from banking and agricultural development to industrial growth and general analyses of the state of the economy. In other words, he was the complete journalist in the area of economics.

Most of Fukuchi's specific economic policies continued the pragmatic "progress and order" approach seen in his political editorials. For example, he came out solidly in favor of public education regarding the value of once despised commercial exchanges. When a rice exchange was set up in Tokyo in August 1876, *Hōchi* ran a Confucian-based series of editorials opposing market speculation as a form of gambling and a threat to national morality.[169] Countered Fukuchi: "Where should we contract together on large sales if not in a public market? What would these theorists use in place of markets or exchanges?" He claimed that his opponents failed to understand the true nature of such exchanges—or to comprehend how much they would facilitate commerce.[170]

His view was equally practical on tariffs. Though friends might label him a "conservative" in politics, they would never have dared to do so on matters of trade; for he argued consistently (and in a considerably more liberal vein than the "protectionist" Fukuzawa) that the best policy was not one that would repel foreign merchants by taxing them heavily but a course that would win goodwill and attract as much foreign trade as possible. The idea of high protectionist tariffs, even when treaties made them possible, should be thought through with great care, he admonished. Protectionism could not be called evil per se; the United States and England had grown rich on protectionist policies. Yet duties should be levied with caution, after first making certain that they were indeed limited to items that Japan already possessed in plenty. Since the Japanese government still could not be certain "what imports it should decrease or what areas should be protected," it had best exercise restraint in considering duties.[171]

Closely tied to this view of protection was his opinion that the government should aid—but not interfere with—fledgling domestic industries. It had initially been necessary, he felt, for the Meiji government to show the way in the development of industry. Commerce had too long been the exclusive domain of hidebound *chōnin,* or city dwellers, who were "excellent at recording daily transactions" or at "using the abacus" but slow at adopting Western economic practices. So the government had initially found it necessary to "wake up" the merchants and point the way to a "new age" by establishing its own model bank and industrial plants.[172] Yet, Fukuchi contended, the government must be cautious in this policy of aiding industry. It must take care not to "shield or protect a certain industry or a certain person" above others, and it must gradually curtail its ties to industry as entrepreneurs became better able to stand on their own feet.[173]

Most incisive of all, at least compared with the writings of other papers, were Fukuchi's editorials on currency. Unlike Ōkuma, who headed the Ōkurasho during these years, he believed firmly that the best way to check inflation and stabilize the national economy was to decrease the "excessive" circulation of paper money. The nation needed, he said in July 1877, a "healthy currency," which meant that the government should refuse to issue any more currency than was presently in circulation, even though fiscal pressures were intense.[174] His most comprehensive statement in this area came in a series of twenty-two editorials on the "handling of government bonds" during June and July 1880.[175] Financial conditions had, by that time, reached a crisis, with inflation skyrocketing, interest rates hitting an all-time high, imports causing a serious deficit in the balance of payments, gold and silver draining out of the country rapidly. In an impressive—almost overwhelming—marshaling of statistics, Fukuchi detailed for days on end the exact nature of government expenditures since the Restoration, the amounts and types of national debts, and the various currency issues.

He divided Meiji economic history into four periods: the "money-issuing years" (1868–1871), the years in which the government tried to reduce the currency in circulation (1871–1873), the stable period (1874–1876), and the years in which national debts had soared (1877–1879). The theme woven throughout this history was that the government, particularly since 1877, had constantly issued too much inconvertible currency through its "indulgent money principles," thus bringing the current crisis on itself.[176] Fukuchi admitted that the constant expansion of currency and bonds had contributed to consolidation of the government and to the growth of industry. But "on the other hand," he insisted, "this reckless issue of currency spurred the increase in imports, the drainage of gold and silver, the rise in consumer prices. It transformed the people's thrift and kindness into haughtiness and flippancy, into a habit of concerning one's self always with today and never with tomorrow. It created today's serious difficulties."[177] He did not ask that Japan try to change directions immediately; that would be dangerous and inconsistent with his gradualist insistence on order. Instead, he called for the nation's leaders to "solve our problems skillfully *and gradually* by adopting a rigid money policy."[178]

The series quite naturally angered Ōkuma; for it was an unusually sharp attack on his policy of frequently meeting crises by issuing new currency or notes. But it could not be flippantly refuted, filled as it was with solid research and detailed descriptions and analyses of Meiji monetary history. One might disagree with the conclusions; but one could not question the sharpness of the presentation. Fukuchi, said one historian, "was a power in economics," a man whose name "must be added to the ranks of Meiji economic scholars."[179] The economic editorials of his "golden era" support such a conclusion.

To analyze the editorials in these various areas is, unfortunately, outside the purview of this study. Fukuchi's overriding concerns were journalism and domestic politics. Their significance, for our purposes, is the evidence they bear of the versatility and breadth of Fukuchi's knowledge and interests. If the private Fukuchi knew the Yoshiwara quarters better than did any of his contemporaries, the public Fukuchi knew the nooks and crannies of national life—of culture, of economics, of diplomacy, even of the arts—with a perceptivity and detail that frequently left fellow editors distressed. He was known as the most versatile Japanese editor: there was "nothing, but nothing, about which he did not write."[180]

Fukuchi's influence in the late 1870s was enhanced, finally, by a host of nonnewspaper activities, even a glance at which suggests a man known for power broking. His official roles in the first Conference of Local Officials and the Satsuma Rebellion already have been mentioned. In 1878, he served as secretary of the second Conference of Local Officials, this time under Itō. And late that same year he ran—and won—in Tokyo's first city council *(fu kai)* election,[181] an election that gave him great satisfaction both because it represented a practical involvement in the gradualist process he so often advocated and because of the sense of history involved in being a member of the first such council. He was even more pleased the following January when the council elected him its first president in a close race over Fukuzawa Yukichi,[182] an honor that the critic Miyake Setsurei described as similar to "being the first head of the House of Commons."[183]

Fukuchi also took an unusually active part in Tokyo's financial world. In 1875, for example, he was appointed a custodian, along with Shibusawa and others, of the Tokyo *kaigisho,* a citizens' organization aimed at spending or investing public money for the promotion of public works.[184] A year later, he also helped Shibusawa and another leading businessman, Masuda Takashi, launch Tokyo's first economic newspaper, the *Chūgai Bukka Shimpō* ("Price News at Home and Abroad"), a sheet that eventually became the *Nihon Keizai Shimbun,* one of today's leading economic publications.[185] And Fukuchi served as a founding director of both the Tokyo Trade Association (Shōhō Kaigisho), an organization much like a Western chamber of commerce, [186] and the Tokyo Stock Exchange (Kabushiki Torihikisho).[187] His name connoted influence in the late 1870s. Hence, when contemporary Japanese sought to launch public, commercial projects they frequently approached the *Nichi Nichi* editor for support or leadership.

Fukuchi's ready acceptance of many of these positions might not have been acceptable by the standards of twentieth-century journalism; they would have been seen as compromising journalistic independence. That philosophical problem, however, seems never to have crossed Fukuchi's mind. The day of the fully independent press had not yet arrived. Journalists—including Fukuchi's more liberal opponents—worried more about political influence than about abstruse relationships related to independence. While Fukuchi did insist on the freedom to write as he pleased, he based his independence on personal strength of character rather than on the erection of impersonal, external "fences" to prevent outside pressure.

We have already seen that what Fukuchi wanted most was the orderly progress of his homeland. What he wanted second was the success of *Nichi Nichi;* and, to him, the two were inseparable. If the accumulation of outside responsibilities would aid in his nation's development and at the same time enhance the influence of *Nichi Nichi* (both by giving it greater access to news sources and by giving its articles greater authority), he saw no reason to avoid entanglements. The years from 1876 to 1880 were probably his best, certainly his most powerful. *Nichi Nichi* had become his personal vehicle for transforming the nation's press and articulating a rationale for political gradualism. His reporting, particularly on the Satsuma Rebellion, had become legendary. His editorials, versatile to an unprecedented degree, were required reading by competitors and officials alike. So the acceptance of outside responsibilities and offices seemed at the time but a simple outgrowth of power, as well as an indispensable ingredient in the accumulation of more of it. His viewpoint was national and institutional, not popular and grass roots. From that perspective, formal and informal ties with established interests seemed natural indeed. After mid-1881, this approach would cause him troubles, both professionally and philosophically, but when he laid down the brush after finishing the "constitutional opinion" series in May of that year, the potential conflict between independence and vested interest had not yet crossed his mind.

# CHAPTER IV

# Years of Struggle at *Nichi Nichi:* 1881–1888

> *I felt most keenly that I was misunder-*
> *stood. . . . The loneliness of those theorists*
> *who believed in gradualism was not unlike*
> *that of the morning star at dawn.* [1]

## The Troubled Loyalist

No time in Fukuchi's journalistic life was more turbulent, no succession of months more pivotal, than middle and late 1881 —the period in which he turned forty. For six years he had dominated the Meiji press with a vigor that suggested invincibility. Yet, within a few months of his birthday on May 13, he would find himself embroiled in the most intense, eventually the most damaging, fight of his career.

Some hints of a shift had begun to show up as early as 1879. He had, of course, always been the target of competitors' attacks, but those attacks became particularly virulent after Fukuchi, as president of the Tokyo city council, helped entertain the United States' former president, Ulysses S. Grant, during a visit to Tokyo on his round-the-world trip that year. A farewell address arranged by Fukuchi and several colleagues "in the name of the people of the city" was charged with being ostentatiously elaborate. Numa Morikazu, a former official in the Justice Ministry, joined the staff of the *Yokohama Mainichi* primarily so he could launch a public attack on the *Nichi Nichi* editor for self-serving use of "the name of the people." He said Fukuchi and his colleagues had acted on their own, not as appointed or elected representatives of the council.[2] It was basically a political attack, born more of personal animosity than of true indignation, since Fukuchi and his colleagues were indeed leaders of the council, even if that body had not actually elected them as an official entertainment committee. Fukuchi said as much in his refutation, suggesting that Numa "was simply ignorant of the true situation,"[3] and the controversy soon subsided as such matters do. But the nature of the attack, aimed not only at refuting *Nichi Nichi*'s positions but at undermining its editor's personal reputation, boded ill for Fukuchi's future.

As has been seen, Fukuchi's relationship with the government also had begun undergoing somewhat of an evolution during the last year or two of the 1870s. Perhaps nothing highlighted this drift more than the attempts of Itō, Ōkuma, and Inoue to form a government newspaper. Alarmed at the growing strength of antigovernment sentiment, as evidenced in the constitutional discussions being conducted in both the press and numerous lecture societies, they met at Atami near the end of 1880 to discuss Fukuchi's old theory that the government should use its own newspaper to lead the public directly. On reaching a consensus, they offered the editorship to Fukuzawa, who agreed to undertake the project after some hesitation.[4] A number of political crises in 1881 eventually wrecked the scheme, but for Fukuchi the effect was disheartening. No one had so often urged the government to use the press in leading the public; no other major journalist had as regularly supported the government's general course; nor had any editor apparently maintained closer ties to Itō and Inoue. Yet when a decision was made to adopt his plan, he was overlooked by his own close friends. It may have been a pragmatic move on the oligarchs' part; Fukuzawa's voice likely would have carried more weight, while Fukuchi's political views had been publicly aired too regularly in a daily editorial column to claim freshness. Perhaps Fukuchi's growing signs of journalistic independence or (from a reverse point of view) lack of dependability also played a role. Certainly his opposition to Ōkuma's monetary policies weakened any chances for such an appointment. At any rate, he was bypassed, and the result, for Fukuchi, was keen disappointment. As he rather bitterly commented about the entire episode: "I wanted to convert my own paper into a channel for informing the public about the government's views, to make it a government paper. But the government would not go along. . . . So I finally discarded that notion and saw to it that *Nichi Nichi* would be completely independent."[5]

With the coming of spring, one might have expected his spirits to rise, since no one enjoyed the season of resurrection and rebirth more than the cherry-blossom-viewing lord of Ike no Hata. Yet the irony of the early spring in 1881, the period in which his "constitutional opinion" was exerting such influence, was that it simply brought more troubles. In March he became involved in a legal battle with another powerful segment of the Meiji establishment, a battle that was to set off the incredible string of frustrations and controversies that marked the year so indelibly in his personal career.

In a strident editorial on March 14, he accused Japan's attorneys of "earning personal profits by promoting disputes among men" and called for legal action to end the abuse. He noted the steady increase in the number of civil suits being brought into Japan's courts and said the increase indicated not so much that the public had learned to exercise its rights as that attorneys *(daigensha)* were taking advantage of the populace. He accused them even of provoking arguments between "flesh and blood" and thus perverting the Japanese customs of "humility and subservience." To remedy this "leprosy," he said, Japan needed new regulations that would consolidate civil law and provide for inspection and control of legal practices.[6]

The attorneys' response was predictable. Stung bitterly, they demanded a retraction and apology, but when Fukuchi answered with an editorial repeating the charges, the Tokyo attorneys' association decided to sue. On May 18 two association representatives began litigation at the Tsukuji ward court, accusing the Nipposha president of causing economic injury by "damaging our honor, the most priceless possession we have." They demanded that a written apology be published in *Nichi Nichi,* displayed in the Nipposha offices, and run in other leading papers throughout Japan.[7]

Fukuchi's response was to countersue, and during the summer the Tokyo press (rather gleefully, one suspects) recorded a succession of legal moves in which neither side made much headway. As one of Fukuchi's successors at *Nichi Nichi,* Asahina Chisen, wrote: "A power struggle between Japan's attorneys and Tokyo's leading newspaper was not likely to end with the simple victory of one side. So they piled appeal upon appeal."[8] Both sides eventually reached an out-of-court settlement,[9] which dropped the demands for Fukuchi's apology. But despite the agreement, the entire episode won for Fukuchi the lasting enmity of one of the Tokyo establishment's increasingly important groups.[10]

Most important of all in the development of Fukuchi's career, however, were the 1881 upheavals within the government itself. In accordance with the call (noted in the previous chapter) for the junior councillors to draw up suggestions regarding the path Japan should follow in the establishment of a constitution, most ministers had by early 1881 submitted proposals advocating gradual, orderly progress toward the creation of a constitutional monarchy, with sovereignty posited clearly in the emperor. Ōkuma, by contrast, had failed to submit his written opinion until March, and he then had shocked most of his colleagues by calling for a constitution to be adopted immediately and advocating that the assembly, to be convened in 1883, be given a great deal of power. His fellow councillors had been infuriated by this break in ranks.

Then, a few months later, news leaked to the press of the government's plan to abolish its Hokkaido Colonization Office, which had been developing large areas of land on the northern island over the past twelve years, and of a supposed agreement whereby several of the commission's members and business allies would be permitted to purchase the Hokkaido lands at a tiny fraction of the government's investment. The public reacted with a show of anger, condemning especially Kuroda Kiyotaka, the opportunistic councillor who had headed the commission. Before long rumors spread that Ōkuma, with a personal design on power, had been instrumental in leaking news of the scandal. The result was a cabinet "compromise" the night of October 11 whereby progressives were to be placated by the dropping of the land sale and by the issuing of a promise of a concrete date by which a constitution would be granted, while the more conservative oligarchic side won the ouster of Ōkuma and the long-term postponement of constitutional government. An imperial rescript the next day promised a constitution within nine years.[11]

Although Fukuchi took no direct part in the government's decision, his writings and actions played a significant role in the unfolding of events. That he had already become somewhat disenchanted with the cliquelike nature of power is by now clear. On becoming convinced that the rumors about Hokkaido were true, Fukuchi gave vent to the most heated public outburst of his life. "I had never been so angry as I was at the government's slipshod ways in the Hokkaido land deal," he said.[12] He expressed his views, as usual, in *Nichi Nichi* editorials—on August 10 and 11 and again from August 27 to 31. "Thinking it all to be a false rumor, I did not at first believe it," he wrote, explaining an initial silence on the issue; "when I saw how the accusations diverged off into thirty-one different directions I doubted their truth." Once convinced, however, he "could not" remain silent. He likened the councillors' actions to the English government's patronage of the hated East India Company and said that no "discussion of the profits and losses, advantages and disadvantages" was even necessary to show the devious nature of the deal.[13]

This time he did not, however, limit his attack to the specific misdeed. The time had come, he argued in a momentous departure from his consistent support of the existing institutional structure, to change the whole system. "It is natural that scandalous things will occur in an oligarchy," he wrote. "We must set up a constitutional system as soon as possible, with government carried out jointly by both rulers and subjects [*kumin dōchi*]." The situation was so pernicious, he intoned, that nothing short of radical change could quiet the populace: "I am firmly convinced that even if my own tongue should fail me and my brush be broken, public clamor still would not die down."[14] His subsequent editorials, written after he had had time to more carefully research the situation, analyzed the facts of the Hokkaido land deal in great detail, arguing meticulously the evils inherent in an oligarchy that would thus deceive its citizenry. On September 6, *Nichi Nichi* ran excerpts from the Hokkaido commission's petition and from Kuroda's supporting statement to the Dajōkan (Council of State). On September 30 an editorial written by Fukuchi declared that *Nichi Nichi,* "though not having changed its basic philosophy at all," was no longer obligated to publish official government decrees and statements. The break appeared complete.

Nor did Fukuchi limit his expression of outrage to the *Nichi Nichi* columns. One of the more colorful aspects of the public outcry over the Hokkaido scheme was the organization of numerous lecture-protest meetings throughout Japan. Fukuchi quickly became one of the celebrities of these assemblages. It was as if in the United States in 1860 Stephen Douglas had abruptly become a vocal antislavery Republican. The enemy— the very articulate, powerful enemy—had become an ally. Little matter that his general political philosophy had not shifted much; he was now willing to speak on a "liberal" platform; that meant overnight popularity. The most famous of the lectures was held the night of August 27 at Tokyo's Shintomiza. Some five thousand tickets were sold, and the audience so packed the theater that many had to sit on the platform[15] and speakers reportedly "strained their voices" trying to speak loud enough that all could hear.[16] Fukuchi entitled his speech, "A discussion of public finances in the disposal of the government's reclaimed lands." He said the current *hambatsu* (clique) government was managing Japan in a fashion that called to mind what it might have been like had the old Fujiwara family left the court and gathered forces to topple the government.[17]

The reasons for Fukuchi's sudden switch, though much debated by scholars, were probably not especially complex. He himself explained it by denying that he had switched at all, claiming that he had always evaluated issues objectively and supported or opposed the government at will.[18] To a degree, he was right. He had always supported constitutional government, and from the day he joined *Nichi Nichi* he had clearly opposed the permanent existence of a *hambatsu* government; even now he set no dates for the promulgation of a constitution, though he did put greater emphasis on its "early" adoption. Yet, no number of denials could obscure the strange fact that Fukuchi was suddenly the hero of those liberals he had earlier labeled "extremists." His emphasis had shifted, even if not his basic direction.

The most likely explanation would seem to be twofold. First, he honestly and rationally disagreed with what the rulers had done. From the outset he had argued that an oligarchy was acceptable only temporarily. Hearing of the Hokkaido scandal, it seems he genuinely feared that its current strongmen were now moving toward permanent consolidation of personal power, a development he could never accept. Second, the events of the past year had increasingly alienated him from the government. The offer to Fukuzawa of the editorship of a government paper had given him a feeling of isolation. The fight with the attorneys had heightened his disillusionment and left him psychologically fatigued, if not emotionally alienated, from the establishment. Now the Hokkaido scandal finally convinced him that his future lay outside the power structure. "The government had become a temporizing, vacillating entity; so I lost my interest in serving it," he wrote.[19] It was the rationalization of a disappointed, disillusioned man; but it approximated the truth.

The furor, including Fukuchi's protests, did (as has been noted) have its effect. It showed the councillors, in dramatic fashion, just how intent the opposition had become in its pursuit of constitutional government. The presence of Fukuchi in that camp gave special urgency and conviction to the clamor, which in turn helped to precipitate the imperial decree on October 12 declaring "that We shall, in the twenty-third year of Meiji [1890], establish a Parliament, in order to carry into full effect the determination We have announced."[20]

But Fukuchi's cooperation with the "liberals" was short-lived; for at the end of October, after the assurance of a constitution and an assembly, he switched again. On October 14, he published the imperial decree, with the statement that *Nichi Nichi* was not yet ready to comment on it. Then he requested from Itō an explanation of the government's true intent. When Itō asked if he was satisfied with the decree, Fukuchi replied that 1890 seemed too late. "Although I am not a radical who hopes for the opening by 1883 like Ōkuma," he said, "I feel the preparations should certainly be completed by 1887." He added, however, that the important thing was that the opening had been promised: "Since I have heard of the august imperial decision, I will respectfully, happily and fearfully submit." After further talks, Itō replied, "If that is really the way you feel, we are of one and the same mind."[21] Fukuchi also made calls on Inoue and Yamagata, who expressed similar views and, thus satisfied, plunged back into the "gradualist" mainstream. It was, said one scholar, his "second *tenkō* [conversion]."[22]

This time public reaction to his switch was different. The liberals who had so enthusiastically welcomed him in August now denounced his instability, accusing him of deceit, fraud, and disloyalty. One might question whether he was in truth much more unpopular than if he had never joined the anti-*hambatsu* camp in the first place. But the immediate reaction to his second switch was dramatically vocal and vigorous.[23] Contrasted with the acclaim of the last two months, it seemed like the outcry against a traitor.

Actually, his return to the establishment camp should not have seemed much more surprising than his desertion two months earlier. That earlier move had resulted from anger over a series of specific government acts, not from a philosophical rejection of the gradualist way. Indeed, it had been consistent with the "pillars" of his gradualist definition. Even when cooperating with the liberals, he had not felt genuinely at ease among them.[24] Moreover, his old friends Itō and Inoue exerted considerable pressure early in October, chiding him for abandoning old allies, arguing that the government had not forsaken gradualism, apparently even hinting at official patronage or use of *Nichi Nichi* as an unofficial mouthpiece (a move designed to assuage Fukuchi's pique over the earlier offer to Fukuzawa of the editorship of the proposed government news-paper).[25] At any rate, one can hardly conceive of Fukuchi remaining long outside the establishment camp once the emperor had announced the government's intention to move toward the adoption of a constitution and representative government. This was, after all, the policy he had advocated since the Restoration; constitutionalism and popular representation had often been declared the pillars of his gradualism. Moreover, it was "order" consistent with imperial sovereignty that he most demanded, an order that would have been endangered either by oligarchic tyranny or by full popular sovereignty. Any suggestion of *Nichi Nichi* being used as a government voice would only have added incentive, since government use of the press (as long as the editor consented of his free will) was a policy he had long advocated.

Accordingly, on November 14, a *Nichi Nichi* editorial declared the paper's intent to again "place itself at the service of the government," meaning that it would henceforth give its columns over to a defense of general government policies and actions—probably in a more consistent way than ever before. A related editorial a week and a half later discussed the government's need of a paper to publicize its views. It still warned against the danger of unduly harsh press laws, but in a tone reminiscent of the middle 1870s, it said the use of a *goyō* paper would "enable the government to educate the people without necessitating the suppression of competing newspapers."[26] Fukuchi was ready to fill that role, although the failure to insist on press independence would this time bring him grief—partly because his envisioned government ties were much closer than even the oligarchs themselves had in mind.

To remove any potential internal obstructions to *Nichi Nichi*'s assumption of the new *goyō* role, Fukuchi reorganized Nippōsha in December—bringing the paper under more complete personal control than ever, making every department an extension of his own personality. The first step in countering radicalism, he declared, was to "gain complete freedom in using *Tokyo Nichi Nichi* as I felt best."[27] Accordingly, the officers of the paper were formally released, making it possible for Fukuchi to buy up all company stock and resell it to thirteen carefully chosen men for a total of 62,500 yen.[28] The list of new stockholders was made up entirely of old friends or solid supporters of his plan to now make *Nichi Nichi* a solid party-line publication *(shugi shimbun).* The company's economic position might possibly be hurt by such a shift in the paper's editorial policy, Fukuchi admitted prophetically, but he thought the times demanded a paper that would support the imperial intent and fight liberalism regardless of economic consequences.[29]

Popular rumors, not surprisingly, tied the reorganization to a secret deal whereby the government had paid Fukuchi as much as 100,000 yen for his support.[30] Fukuchi denied these reports, and the most likely explanation of the reorganization is that Itō and others encouraged certain sympathizers to buy stock in the reorganized company and thus carry out an early version of Japan's traditional style of *kinmyaku* or "money-vein" politics,[31] a policy that would have been legally defensible even if ethically questionable.[32] Whatever the reasons, Fukuchi clearly set his paper on a new course during that December. Until now he had been a "true journalist," devoted to most government policies but equally devoted to the development of a professional press. For the next year and a half, by contrast, the *Nichi Nichi* would become something approaching a true *goyō* newspaper, a seldom swerving defender of the government and its policies. The lip service to "independence" would continue, but the reality would not.[33] The result, as we shall see in the following pages, would be bitter.

### The Partisan "Conservative"

Symbolic of the shift in Fukuchi's professional orientation was the public promulgation on January 4, 1882, of the highly conservative "Imperial precepts to soldiers and sailors" *(Gunjin chokuyu),* a brilliant, influential, and markedly traditional document that Fukuchi helped shape. The Precepts, issued as an imperial decree at the urging of Yamagata,[34] blended "the traditional samurai ethic and imperial nationalism" in what a leading scholar has labeled a personification of the "Meiji spirit."[35] It asserted, unequivocally, the eternal supremacy of the emperor over all Japanese military forces, then urged the troops to practice five precepts: *loyalty* ("duty is weightier than a mountain, while death is lighter than a feather"); *propriety* ("always pay due respect"); *valor* ("never despise an inferior or fear a superior"); *righteousness* ("the fulfillment of one's duty"); and *simplicity* (lest you "become effeminate and frivolous").[36] It urged military men not to interfere in politics and encouraged them to value the nation's interests above personal freedom or rights. Though aimed directly at the military, it "helped to form the basis of the official popular ideology: duty and loyalty to the emperor, the spirit of courage and sacrifice."[37] And coming, as it did, less than three months after the imperial promise of an assembly and a constitution, it was seen by many as an effective counterweight to the "popular rights" sentiments unleased by that earlier promise.

The significance of the document for our present study lies in the fact that Fukuchi was partly responsible for its conservative ideological tone and its literary elegance. The original draft, prepared by Yamagata's right-hand man in the Army Ministry, Nishi Amane, had inculcated similar principles but in milder prose and with only a weak assertion of the emperor's supremacy. Thus Yamagata, not totally satisfied, called on several others to rework the draft.[38] Fukuchi's main contribution was to give it a ringing admonitory tone and to strengthen its emphasis on the emperor's divinity and inviolability. He also added the warning against military interference in politics. It was not a difficult task, given Fukuchi's skill as a writer and his deep commitment to the concept of imperial sovereignty. But the additions took on "important historical meaning" in helping provide key underpinnings for the imperialism that would characterize later Meiji Japan.[39] He wrote the draft, ironically, in 1880 when his gradualism had begun more and more to emphasize the importance of popular rights, but even then his "progressive" tendencies had been balanced by an unshakable faith in imperial supremacy and in the centrality of the state. The fact that the Precepts were announced in the early weeks after Fukuchi had declared his fervent rededication to government gradualism seemed an ironic coincidence.

It was this view of the emperor, moreover, that sparked the sharpest political debate of early 1882, a debate over the locus of sovereignty that would eventually draw Fukuchi actively into the partisan political arena. The sovereignty issue actually had been introduced to the public in the fall of 1881, sparked by the government crises described above. Newspapers across the political spectrum began publishing discussions of the question, with some positing sovereignty in an abstract quality of "justice,"[40] some declaring that it rested in the people,[41] and others finding it in the imperial institution.[42] But what was at first a mild, rather theoretical, discussion evolved into a full-scale war, reminiscent of the 1875 battle over a popular assembly, after the publication by *Nichi Nichi* in January of a series of three editorials[43] outlining in great detail the basis of Fukuchi's belief that sovereignty resided exclusively in the emperor. The *Tokyo-Yokohama Mainichi* answered the next week with the assertion that it was shared by both the people and the emperor;[44] thus was born a stimulating, acrimonious editorial war, the fierceness of which has best been described by Fukuchi himself:

> The Tokyo editors took up their brushes and wrote article after article about the issue. I attacked their views, and before long it seemed that everyone had become my enemy. . . . As the attacks on my view of sovereignty increased in both number and intensity, however, it began to get frightening. I had really not thought that a controversy like this on the nature of sovereignty was even possible in the Japanese empire. Its occurrence caught me totally off guard. . . . It reached a point that I saw but two alternatives: either I could doff my helmet and surrender or I could die fighting. . . . I believed so deeply in my cause, however, that there really was no alternative. I could never quit. As long as I had a tongue or a brush, I would have to continue the battle, even if it meant that *Tokyo Nichi Nichi* would lose its readers and have to stop publishing. So I just fought harder.[45]

The heart of Fukuchi's position lay in his defense of absolute imperial sovereignty as the only system suitable to Japanese tradition. He defined sovereignty as "the nation's chief power, which represents the highest, the supreme, independent authority of the country." "From the international perspective," he said, "sovereignty expresses the nation's independence and defends its honor. In domestic politics, sovereignty refers to the center of the supreme legislative, executive and judiciary power."[46] And that "center," he reiterated in some thirty editorials during late 1881 and 1882, could neither legally nor practically be attributed to any but the ruler himself. Since states functioned "organically," since the political community was like a "great body which must have a head to govern it,"[47] the emperor, or locus of sovereignty, must be seen as the "head and brains" of the state.

To support this view, Fukuchi raised an issue previously unmentioned in the sovereignty debate: *kokutai,* or maintenance of a philosophy consistent with "the unique essence of the historic Japanese system." The word *kokutai* was not new itself; it had been coined by the Mito school early in the nineteenth century and had been a pivotal phrase undergirding anti-Tokugawa rhetoric in the 1860s, a code word for men like Yoshida Shōin and Aizawa Seishisai.[48] Yet, like the emperor himself, its place in the rhetoric of Restoration leaders had diminished once the new government had been consolidated. Now, in the heat of battle, Fukuchi once again made the emotion-laden term the chief weapon in the arsenal of the proemperor forces. It was ironic, of course, that he had been a Tokugawa retainer, a loyal supporter of the side attacked by the *kokutai* theorists in the 1860s, while now he was an attacker. But, as we have seen, defense of imperial prerogatives, which he saw as the key to Japan's unique essence, had occupied him increasingly since entry into *Nichi Nichi.* That he should dust off the term now was both natural and significant for the future of his land.

Sovereignty, Fukuchi maintained, must be determined by a nation's individual heritage rather than by any sort of universal law. To rely on the abstract ideas of Western theoreticians like Jean Jacques Rousseau or Charles de Secondat Montesquieu was inadequate, as was undue reference to the present state systems of the West. Rousseau's "social contract" might be novel, but in the final analysis it must be admitted that it lead to the French Revolution and would be a threat to Japanese tranquility and order.[49] Moreover, those who espoused such theories did so without considering the fact that Japan's *kokutai,* or historical essence, differed markedly from that of Europe, where popular rights sentiments could be traced back for centuries. "To delight recklessly in the systems and customs of Europe, to embrace arbitrarily the social contract theory and to say that we must snatch sovereignty from the hands of the emperor in order to achieve the essence of a consitututional monarchy is to do violence to the shining spirit of our *kokutai.*"[50]

The heart of *kokutai,* for Fukuchi, was the manifestation of loyalty to a sovereign and divine emperor. "It is not of our own choosing that all government be carried out by imperial will," he wrote. "It has been decreed by the gods from the time of the first ascension to the throne that state affairs should be decided without bias." Imperial sovereignty might be another word for tyranny in Europe where rulers had so often been despotic, but in Japan imperial rule had been benign and heaven-sent, as well as immutable.[51] It was important, he added, to make a distinction between a nation's political systems and its *kokutai.* "Though political systems should indeed advance with the movement of the times, *kokutai* is fixed, something that never changes."[52] To maintain a fixed principle on which Japan's political systems could evolve peacefully, a sovereign imperial institution was a necessity.

It is possible that Fukuchi disparaged undue reliance on the West at least partly as a result of an inability to locate Western scholars who supported his view of sovereignty. Seki Naohiko, his assistant at the time, recalled that Fukuchi became ecstatic to the point of "pounding his desk" one day when he found a Western work that offered some support for his views.[53] Fukuchi himself expressed "complete discouragement" over a failure to find much assistance in Western writings.[54] But, whatever his motive for raising the issue of *kokutai,* it was a forceful and significant argument, one that would become basic to all of Fukuchi's later articles on national development and central to the nationalistic spirit that began to grip Japan from the 1890s onward. The intellectual historian H. D. Harootunian has found the "rhetoric of Japanese jingoism . . . in the prewar period" to be "little more than a restatement of the intellectual spirit of the Restoration."[55] If that is true, Fukuchi's role in reviving the *kokutai* theme probably formed at least a link in the chain leading toward that restatement.

This is not to suggest that Fukuchi completely discontinued his advocacy of the more progressive aspects of gradualism after the beginning of 1882. If he was now placing more emphasis on imperial sovereignty, he continued at the same time to discuss the need to go forward with preparations for opening the assembly,[56] to write editorials on popular freedom and liberalism,[57] and to call for a constitution that would make a place for political parties.[58] It was just that whereas the need for a constitution had dominated his editorials before 1881, imperial sovereignty now became dominant. The national assembly's power was to be granted by the emperor; the people were not to "insist on the popular will in defiance of the imperial will."[59] Even the question of whether Japan needed party cabinets was to be "left completely to the emperor."[60] It seems never to have occurred to Fukuchi—at least in print—that a ruler might someday be despotic, that the advocacy of both true freedom and absolute imperial sovereignty could be regarded as a contradiction. That, to him, was what was unique about Japan's *kokutai*: Japanese rulers were benevolent; imperial violation of the public's best interests was unthinkable, a contradiction in terms. Hence, the simultaneous maintenance of popular rights and imperial sovereignty became not only possible but natural. It was a concept that would become increasingly important with the passage of years.

A key question here is, of course, why Fukuchi's series on sovereignty took on a more conservative tone than had the constitutional articles he had written the preceding year. Though the superficial observer might write the change off to political expediency, careful analysis seems to reveal at least two more significant explanations. First, both constitutional government and the national assembly had now been promised by imperial decree, thus giving him an entirely new framework in which to write editorials. This promise assured the realization of those goals that until then had meant most to him in the stream of gradualism. Now, in order to keep either the constitution or the assembly from being influenced too much by liberal or extreme ideas, ideas that still might introduce disruption or revolution, it seemed necessary to call for restraint, to bolster the foundations of imperial rule, which he thought would prove Japan's savior. Second, Fukuchi had always been given to the instinctive weakness of overreacting. Hence, when liberals began attacking his articles on sovereignty, he defended his position even more vigorously than his original viewpoint might have warranted, perhaps creating an unconscious shift in his own attitudes in the process and letting the conservative facets of his overall philosophy take on an importance he might not have given them in calmer times. This is not to say that the conversations with Itō and Inoue in October 1881 had not helped bring him back to the government side. It merely suggests that the emphasis on sovereignty was quite sincere and within the perimeters of Fukuchi's lifelong conception of gradualism. Satisfied with the direction of "progress," he began to place more emphasis on "order."

The year 1882 was not marked, however, merely by theoretical discourses and intellectual sparring. In that year Fukuchi became involved in a more practical way than at any other time in his life in the confused world of politics, both in writing editorials and in founding one of Japan's first three political parties, the Rikken Teiseitō (Constitutional Imperial Party).

His view of political parties, as it showed up in the *Nichi Nichi* editorial columns, went through a vague evolution during the first five months of the year, an evolution that attempted to balance his own basic support of such parties with the government's increasingly negative view of them. At the beginning, he favored a system similar to that found in England, as did most other papers, arguing the merits of a constitution that would allow the establishment of party cabinets.[61] During the week following the launching of the Teiseitō in mid-March, he stated publicly that the current government leadership group might justifiably be called a "party cabinet" since its views coincided with those of his new party.[62] That opinion drew direct and heated fire, however, from key oligarchs like Yamagata who insisted that the only connection between parties and the government should be indirect assistance and protection of groups that chose to support official positions.[63] So Fukuchi began to modify his stand. He called his labeling of the existing government as a Teiseitō cabinet a "snap judgment on my part," admitting that political party cabinets had the inherent danger of becoming "the haunts of party hacks" and of bringing government into such subservience to the assembly's majority party that "the emperor would possess glory in name only."[64]

Yet he refused to concede that Japan should forever revoke the possibility of party cabinets. The final decision on the nature of cabinets, he maintained (with a bit of waffling sophistry), would have to be left until the promulgation of the constitution in 1889, since it had already been determined that all cabinet ministers would be imperial appointees until then anyway.[65] His paper added later in May that someday in the future, in times of tranquility and peace, Japan might enjoy the possibility of occasional party cabinets to insure governmental harmony and honesty—as long as those cabinets unselfishly observed the "national spirit."[66] In other words, though he would not defy the oligarchs' insistence on separation of politics and administration for the time being, he refused, even as a *goyō* editor, to simply parrot their positions.

Fukuchi's belief in the validity of party politics showed up most clearly—and most practically—in his endeavors in behalf of the Teiseitō. The previous year he had vowed that "if my enemies make a speech, I shall make a speech; if my enemies form a political party, I must form a political party."[67] And they had done just that. Following the intense political enthusiasm of September 1881 and the subsequent announcement of plans for a constitution, many groups had become engaged in movements and campaigns (occasionally violent in nature) to influence political developments and the eventual form of the constitution. As the agitation and turmoil grew, some decided that mere spontaneity was insufficient to accomplish what they desired. Thus, late in 1881 the government's more liberal opponents, following the lead of Itagaki, joined together to form the Jiyūtō (Liberal Party), a party dedicated to French-style popular sovereignty and parliamentary government. Soon a number of newspapers announced that they would lend their columns to the Jiyūtō cause.[68] (*Nichi Nichi*, it should be noted, was thus not the only party-line paper in 1881.) On March 14, 1882, as the Jiyūtō movement seemed to be gathering force, the Kaishintō (Progressive Party) was formed by the somewhat more British-oriented followers of Ōkuma in order (like the Jiyūtō) to urge greater recognition of popular rights—and to fight both the government and the Jiyūtō.[69] It too was supported widely in the press, by such papers as *Tokyo-Yokohama Mainichi, Hōchi,* and *Yomiuri.* Fukuchi, recalling his views of a few months before, reacted predictably:

> I shuddered at the radical democracy being advocated by the newspapers and society at large. I felt that if the mood were not checked or changed, public opinion would become democratized to the extreme by 1890. The parties seemed on a collision course with the constitutional monarchy. . . . So I decided, rashly perhaps, to shoulder the task, without regard for my own capabilities.[70]

Lofty motives aside, Fukuchi was supported in this decision to start a party by a number of friends in the government who were sympathetic with the idea of a progovernment party as an effective means of checking the liberal movement. Having failed in efforts to suppress Tokyo's antigovernment papers by buying them off,[71] men like Itō, Inoue, and Yamada Akiyoshi, with Yamagata's encouragement, had begun secret consultations early in 1882 about forming a party to "organize *nonofficial* support for the government and thwart the development of other parties."[72] It was a controversial idea, however, and officials soon found themselves entangled in debate over whether such a party would accomplish enough to warrant the expense—or whether it was philosophically consistent with the kind of government they envisioned.

Fukuchi was among those consulted, and when he became fearful that the vacillation was hurting the gradualist cause, he decided to act privately. Joining fellow journalists Maruyama Sakura of *Meiji Nippō* and Mizuno Torajirō of *Tōyō Shimpō,* he announced independently on March 18 the formation of Japan's first progovernment political party, the Rikken Teiseitō.[73]

The new party's platform, published the same day in *Nichi Nichi,*[74] pledged the Teiseitō to imperial rule and gradualism, "neither adhering to conservatism nor disputing with radicalism, but constantly seeking the parallels of order and progress." It proclaimed eleven basic principles:

1. It has been made clear by imperial order that a national assembly will be convened in 1890. Our party will observe that intention; we absolutely will not discuss its alteration.

2. It has been made clear by imperial order that a constitution will be granted by the emperor. Our party will observe that intention; we absolutely will not violate the rule of the authorized constitution.

3. Sovereign power in the empire resides, indisputably, within the sole control of the emperor. The application of his will shall be regulated by the constitution.

4. We seek the establishment of two branches in the national assembly.

5. We seek to restrict the parliamentary electorate by requirements related to social standing or some such standard.

6. We believe that the national assembly should be granted authority to enact laws for promulgation throughout the land.

7. The emperor should have the authority to approve or disapprove of the national assembly's decisions.

8. We maintain that naval and army men should not take part in government or in politics.

9. We seek the independence of judicial officials, in order to maintain the purity of our legal system.

10. We support freedom of speech and assembly so long as it does not interfere with national peace and order; we also seek freedom of public lectures, newspapers and publication within the limits of law.

11. We maintain that today's inconvertible paper money should be changed gradually into convertible paper money by a reform of the monetary system.

Along with this platform, Fukuchi also published a commentary *(engi)* on the new party. The platform, he said, had been shown to several ministers and councillors who said it coincided perfectly with the aims of the cabinet. Nevertheless, he felt it necessary to place conditions on the government-party alliance: "If the cabinet members always adhere to this philosophy without betraying us, our party surely will support the government. . . . But if the cabinet members should shift or turn away from our position, we, being ruled by party philosophy, would no longer be able to assist the government even if we should want to. The debates and positions of our party serve only the interests of party philosophy, not of the government or cabinet."[75] The aim, said Fukuchi, was to serve Japan, not merely to engage in mutual recriminations, as had the Jiyūtō and the Kaishintō. "We seek internally to insure the rights, the peace and the well being of our people according to Japan's eternal *kokutai,* and externally to enhance national sovereignty by defending her glory against all countries. Moving forward within the bounds of gradualism, . . . we seek the parallels of progress and order. . . . Thus we organize this Rikken Teiseitō, desiring to move ahead with the support of all like-minded men."[76]

The party formed on this "progress and order" platform was the smallest of the period's three political organizations, claiming the allegiance of some thirty local groups compared with about forty for the Kaishintō and more than sixty for the Jiyūtō.[77] Its membership consisted mainly of rising bureaucrats, Shinto and Buddhist priests, prefectural officials, public school

teachers and a number of businessmen with government connections—mostly men without major national political influence, though its supporters did include a few prominent leaders
like Sasa Tomofusa in the Kyushu Shimeikai and, initially,
some important behind-the-scenes bureaucrats.[78]

The Teiseitō commenced its stormy public history on March
21 with a lecture meeting at Tokyo's Shintomiza, the same theater, ironically, where Fukuchi had drawn an overflow crowd for
his denunciation of *hambatsu* politics seven months earlier. All
the organizers of the new party spoke, outlining the nature and
aims of the Teiseitō, as well as their view of imperial primacy
and of the current government. The audience, though neither
so numerous nor so boisterous as it had been the previous
autumn, filled the available seats.[79] Party leaders followed this
up by organizing a supporters' club in Tokyo, called the Tokyo
Kōdōkai, and arranging lecture tours throughout western and
central Japan. In October, a three-day conclave was held in
Kyoto for several hundred of the party's supporters. Fukuchi,
who lectured at various posts along the Tōkaidō en route, served
as chairman of the gathering and issued a rather platitudinous
synopsis of the "convention," praising the "intimate friendship of like-minded men" and calling for another meeting a
year later.[80]

As one might have expected, however, the Teiseitō was too
closely tied to government positions to become truly popular.
And the indirect linkage of *Nichi Nichi* to the April stabbing of
Itagaki further diminished the party's public image. On the
evening of April 6, after one of the Jiyūtō leader's typical two-
hour speeches at Gifu,[81] a young schoolteacher charged at Itagaki with a sword, attempting unsuccessfully to kill him.
Reports of the incident—embellished with descriptions of the
falling leader gasping histrionically, "Itagaki may die but liberty never!"[82]—spread quickly through Japan, and Jiyūtō followers reacted with predictable fury, demanding recourse and hail-
ing their cause with new fervor. It was Fukuchi, however, who
proved the chief victim of the stabbing. The story spread that
the young teacher's act had been incited by *Nichi Nichi*

criticisms of Itagaki. Fukuchi made matters worse a month later
with an inflammatory editorial claiming, incorrectly, that
Itagaki had slandered the emperor.[83] The Teiseitō leader
apologized after the accusation had caused a fresh uproar,
claiming that he had received mistaken information.[84] But the
cumulative result was public sympathy for Itagaki and indignation toward the Teiseitō and its leader.

The party was even more severely damaged by the government's cool treatment and eventual withdrawal of support, as
well as by the oligarchs' determined efforts after the summer of
1882 to weaken the entire political party movement. In June,
they announced a revised law of assembly, providing that all
public meetings be approved and monitored by local authori-
ties and adding severe penalties for defying the law or disturb-
ing the peace.[85] The leading oligarchs also succeeded in getting
Itagaki and Gotō Shōjirō, the Jiyūtō's other chief luminary, to
make a trip to Europe, thus dividing and severely damaging
that party.[86] Moreover, they initiated attempts to curtail the influence of Mitsubishi, a pro-Kaishintō shipping company that
had received considerable government patronage over the past
decade,[87] and made efforts, though unsuccessful, to entice
Ōkuma to go abroad too.[88] Then in April 1883 the press laws
were revised to further curtail debate. The net effect was that
the Kaishintō and the Jiyūtō began fighting more within and
among themselves, and though they continued to exist their
vitality diminished.[89]

The impact was even greater on the Teiseitō. As the government's overt opposition to the other parties increased, its covert
support of the Constitutional Imperial Party decreased. More
and more, members of the oligarchy began espousing "trans-
cendentalism," a view that called for cabinets to stand aloof
from all political activities. Fukuchi's old friend, Itō, became
particularly cold toward the party after his return from Europe
on August 3, 1883, having become enamored with the German
idea of the supraparty cabinet.[90] As the trend became more and
more obvious, even Fukuchi's own Teiseitō colleagues began arguing for the disbanding of the party. Fukuchi continued to

hold out for a time, contending that someone must oppose the other parties. But by late September the means for supporting the party—both financial and human—had eroded drastically. So he consented and on September 24 the Teiseitō's termination was announced. The government's role, said Miyake, was that of "leading a disciple to the roof top, then pushing him off."[91]

It was a disillusioning end—particularly so for Fukuchi, the Teiseitō's head and heart. The party had not really gotten off the ground. Its popular image as an "official" organization, as well as its final failure, greatly damaged (and eventually wrecked) Fukuchi's newspaper career,[92] while the sum he spent promoting it drove him toward bankruptcy. The Teiseitō, moderate though its platform may have been in most areas, never escaped the "conservative" label, partly because Fukuchi's tendency to overreact in the heat of battle highlighted his conservative demeanor more than his popular tenets. Even the political or philosophical contributions of the party have been questioned by some, as they were by Fukuchi himself.[93] It was, said one critic, "a worthless, dream-like thing."[94] It spent too much time, said another, attacking the other parties and too little espousing positive views.[95]

Yet, to flippantly write off either the Teiseitō or Fukuchi's political contributions in this period would be a mistake. "We may have erred in raising issues without checking on the cabinet's intentions concerning the organization of a political party," wrote Fukuchi, "but one cannot say our support of imperial government in the midst of all the storms . . . did not have a certain effect."[96] One effect was just that: bringing the "other side" into the political debate of the period and thus articulating for the public certain principles that otherwise might have been forgotten by most outside the bureaucracy. Fukuchi and the Teiseitō alone among the disputants vigorously and constantly advocated such concepts as *kokutai* and loyalty to the emperor, though the underlying Teiseitō demands for "progress and order" were theoretically not far removed from the Kaishintō's own ostensible motto of supporting policies that were "slow and steady, moderate but sound."[97] While the other parties were stirring up passions in support of parliamentary government, Fukuchi was stressing traditional values. The journalist and critic Kuga Katsunan declared: "The party's role in countering popular trends and cooling down the popular rights fervor and radicalism was a necessary one."[98]

To Fukuchi also goes some credit for helping to stimulate public interest in political issues. He and his colleagues provided a target for the sharp thrusts of the liberal movement. They called public attention to the issues by their own heated volleys. If these were indeed years of preparation for constitutional, participatory government, that contribution was not insignificant. It should be noted too that the policies and concepts Fukuchi supported during this period generally were enacted or realized as Meiji Japan ran its course. His forceful articulation of *kokutai* foreshadowed the total permeation of that concept in the following decades. His absolutist view of imperial sovereignty showed up clearly in the Meiji constitution, as did his proposals for a bicameral legislature, an imperially appointed cabinet, and separation of civil and military bureaucracies.

It would be folly to credit his advocacy with primary responsibility for the adoption of such policies. But as one of the earliest Meiji advocates of *kokutai* and one of the most consistent private spokesmen for imperial sovereignty, his role cannot be dismissed. While theorists in the other two parties equivocated on the role of the emperor, claiming devoted allegiance yet often so clouding the meaning of his authority as to rob that allegiance of much of its significance,[99] Fukuchi almost alone spelled out a consistent view of imperial sovereignty. His ideas were admittedly somewhat absolutistic and thus unacceptable to twentieth-century liberals; yet as the first major Meiji journalist to consistently espouse complete fealty to the ruler from the head as well as the heart, he brought new meaning to the concept of imperial rule, at the same time offering a foretaste of late Meiji, imperialistic nationalism. The ultimate collapse of the Teiseitō robbed him of much personal influence and eventually contributed to his disillusionment with public life. But by the time of the party's collapse in September 1883, he had made a genuine mark on Meiji politics.

### The Embattled Editor

Late in December 1881, shortly after the reorganization of Nippōsha, an anonymous caller brought a small package to the *Nichi Nichi* offices and requested that it be given to Fukuchi. Removing the wrappings, the forty-year-old editor found a box inscribed "ten thousand yen gold," with a baked sweet potato *(satsumaimo)* and rice cakes *(omochi)* inside. Immediately, he said, "I recalled the riddle: 'Sweet potatoes and the rice cakes of Hagi' " *(satsumaimo to ohagi)*[100]—a reference to the leading *han* in the *hambatsu* government, Satsuma and Chōshū (Hagi was the castle town of Chōshū), and to *Nichi Nichi*'s rumored new financial ties to the government.[101] It was an amusing slander, hardly enough to give Fukuchi pause. Yet it was, in many ways, an omen. For though 1882 would prove frenetic enough to be mildly satisfying, the two years after that would involve him in life's most difficult series of events—events that would leave him alienated from older government allies, ostracized by rising younger bureaucrats, and, in the end, disillusioned with public life altogether.

One blow fell in the summer of 1883, shortly before the forced disbanding of the Teiseitō, when the government announced that it would at last begin publishing its own official "Gazette" *(Kampō)*.[102] Though *Nichi Nichi* was promised distribution rights (a promise never kept), the government made it clear that it would no longer need Fukuchi's paper to publish official notices. The financially pressed Fukuchi fought the move, just as he was fighting at the same time against the demise of the Teiseitō, maintaining that it would be more economical to make *Nichi Nichi* a *Kampō*.[103] But the fight failed, and by early fall *Nichi Nichi* had been forced to revert to a broader style of journalism than it had practiced over the last year and a half as a "true" *goyō shimbun*. Ties to the government, its editor had learned for the last time, would not work, especially when the government was itself a changeable, faction-ridden institution.

Unfortunately for *Nichi Nichi,* one result of this severing of relationships was that many junior bureaucrats now began to give voice to their own latent hostility toward Fukuchi and his paper. A new breed of young officials was beginning to exert its influence in the various ministries, men who had reached maturity after the Restoration, who had joined the government after Fukuchi's resignation from the Ōkurashō and thus did not know the *Nichi Nichi* editor personally. When senior officials read Fukuchi's defenses of political gradualism, they envisioned an iconoclastic friend, an "idea man" who had made his presence vividly felt in the government until 1874. The younger officials, however, saw only the gray conservatism of a middle-aged establishment figure, a "haughty power seeker" who might write ringing editorials but would never bother to make their personal friendship. As long as the official détente between *Nichi Nichi* and the government existed, most of them had felt obliged to conceal their personal feelings toward Fukuchi. Once the official break came, however, that obligation evaporated, and the result gave the already frustrated editor more than ample trouble.

Particularly distressing were the new difficulties it created in the gathering of news. Prior to the decision to publish an offical organ, Fukuchi had enjoyed an advantage over other papers in acquiring official documents and reports, an advantage he found justifiable in light of his special support of official policy. After that summer, the favors ended. When he called at various bureaus, petty officials would either avoid him or deliver a lecture about the vice of "leaking secrets." Some even refused him general, nonsecret information. Their attitudes "shocked" a man who had always preached and practiced personal loyalty. Had he not stood by the government at the expense of personal popularity; and did he not, as a result, deserve special treatment? As he complained in his memoirs: "It is hardly appropriate to regard foes and friends alike. How, in heaven's name, can that be called true equality?"[104]

As a result, at least partly, of the withdrawal of official support, *Nichi Nichi*'s circulation also began to decline. Actually all of the *daishimbun* suffered a drop in circulation after the political wars of 1882 and early 1883, but none was hurt more than *Nichi Nichi*. From an average daily circulation of 8,547 in 1882, the paper dropped to 5,349 in 1883, a reduction of 37 percent. In the same period, *Hōchi* dropped by 30 percent, *Chōya* by 24, while Fukuzawa's independent and less political *Jiji* tripled its subscription list. By 1885, *Nichi Nichi* had declined even further, to 4,312 subscribers a day.[105] The circulation loss came in large measure from the failure of officials and government institutions throughout the country to continue subscribing to *Nichi Nichi*. By Fukuchi's reckoning, the number of officials taking *Nichi Nichi* declined by some 40 percent between 1883 and early 1885, even while Fukuchi's competitors were enjoying a 30 percent rise in that category. This development, he said, was a "great perplexity."[106]

It should not be inferred from these troubles, however, that Fukuchi descended into oblivion.[107] For even though the retrospective view shows 1883 to be the year his fortunes started irreversibly downward, his power and influence appeared very much intact to contemporaries in the middle 1880s. That he remained one of Tokyo's most influential journalists, one of Japan's foremost citizens, shows up quite clearly both in the paper itself and in the responsibilities he shouldered in public life.

To look at the pages of *Nichi Nichi* during these years is, in fact, to see a paper deeply involved in the normal operations of a leading national publication. Writers often dramatize transition to the point of obscuring reality; nearly all have done so with Fukuchi.[108] But in truth the public image of Fukuchi shifted only slightly after mid-1883. The circulation decline would have been noticed by a few; certainly the loss of the *goyō* columns and the demise of the Teiseitō were obvious. Yet *Nichi Nichi*'s editorials continued, as they had before 1881, to support an independent gradualist course and to serve as a hub of Tokyo's political debate—at least into 1887 when Fukuchi's slipping grip at the paper become more obvious. And the paper's editor himself continued to exert an exceedingly strong influence in public circles.

Ironically, one of the positive results of Fukuchi's political failures was the resumption at *Nichi Nichi* of efforts to publish a truly journalistic newspaper concerned not just with politics but with the broad spectrum of issues that had characterized its coverage during the 1870s. Editorials on domestic politics decreased from 40 percent of the paper's total in 1882 to a more balanced 15 percent in 1885, while those in other areas increased proportionately. Economics again came to rival politics for newspaper space, with key topics including everything from public bonds and railway development to the need for speed in issuing inconvertible currency. Coverage of such heretofore minor topics as military affairs and cultural developments increased markedly. And international matters, particularly those of East Asia, became a *Nichi Nichi* forte, averaging some 32 percent of all editorials published from 1884 to 1886.[109]

In 1884, for example, Fukuchi gave over forty editorials to a discussion of China's war with France, advocating above all that Japan remain neutral, not allowing friendship with China to draw it into the conflict.[110] The China-Japan-Korea triangle dominated foreign affairs in 1885 and 1886, and again Fukuchi's writings rather accurately reflected major national concerns, consistently advocating both military preparedness and realistic restraint in handling those Korean problems that threatened so often to spark war between Japan and China. By 1887, tensions in East Asia had relaxed slightly and *Nichi Nichi*'s emphasis shifted to Europe, with some forty-four editorials on such matters as Franco-Prussian hostility and Occidental policies toward the East. Early in 1888, Fukuchi ran an incisive series on treaty reform in reaction to a much-discussed article by Edward H. House criticizing the Western powers for treating Japan unfairly.[111] He thanked the U.S. journalist for his defense of Japan but maintained in typically pragmatic fashion that House was by now "out-of-date" and too moralistic, that Japan must win treaty revision on its own by convincing foreign powers that she was genuinely ready for it.[112]

Moreover, the tone of those political editorials that Fukuchi did publish called to mind the more independent spirit of the late 1870s. Though the demise of the Teiseitō had combined with the decline of popular interest in politics to take some of the old impact out of his political writing, his articles on the developing bureaucracy frequently sparked at least hints of the old combativeness. They were, as formerly, relatively conservative in tone, yet purposefully independent. He continued to insist on imperial sovereignty, allowing that insistence to color all his other positions. He praised the institution of a cabinet system late in 1885 as a "major step on the road to constitutional government."[113] Yet he defined the ambiguous phrase "responsible cabinet" conservatively as the responsibility cabinet ministers owe to an emperor, who in turn "bears a great responsibility to his own good intentions, a great responsibility to history and a great responsibility to the gods."[114] He maintained that although "special circumstances" might sometimes call for party cabinets, such cabinets should be regarded as "makeshift" or temporary.[115]

The most spirited and fully independent of Fukuchi's latter-year political editorials came in an impressive attack early in 1886 on the ever increasing oligarchic tendencies of the government. Called simply "Satchō ron" ("On Satsuma and Chōshū"), it ran for five consecutive days and stirred enough controversy to merit reprinting in booklet form.[116] As Fukuchi's last major political blast at *Nichi Nichi* and as one of the period's more incisive critiques of clique government, it has drawn comparison to his "Kyōjaku ron" ("On strength and weakness") at *Kōko Shimbun* nearly twenty years earlier.[117] Accordingly, it deserves consideration in some detail.

To understand the import and meaning of "Satchō ron," a brief description of national political developments after the demise of Fukuchi's Teiseitō is needed. With the decline of the parties and of popular political fervor, the center of political activity had shifted to the government itself where a number of bureaucrats, under the lead of Itō, had begun intensive preparation for the drafting of a constitution. Following his study of European constitutions, the once "liberal" Itō (a man de-

scribed by one contemporary as a "smooth sailor" who "knows
how to go with the crowd"[118]) had become an advocate of non-
party government and of a Prussian-style constitution where
most power resided in the executive.

By way of preparation for the constitution, he and other oligarchs began in 1884 to set up a number of specific institutions
that would insure a smooth transition to the kind of government they envisioned. First they set up a peerage of more than
five hundred persons divided into five ranks. Then, in 1885,
they devised a modern cabinet system, headed by a prime minister, to replace the old Dajōkan, or Council of State, structure.
Both moves served to strengthen the oligarchs' own positions,
the former by constructing a conservative basis for the House of
Peers that would be set up under the constitution, the latter by
solidifying and more clearly rationalizing the executive base of
power. Other moves included adopting the German general
staff system in the army, making the military directly answer-
able to the emperor and creating a national police force under
central government control. By 1886, work was ready to begin
on the actual drafting of the constitution.

At least as significant as the nature of these creations was the
fact of who created them. By the middle 1880s a small, select
group of men including Itō, Yamagata, Inoue, Matsukata Masayoshi, and Kuroda Kiyotaka had come to completely dominate national policy. Nearly all of them hailed from the Restoration *han* of Satsuma and Chōshū. Seven of the eight men in
the first cabinet were Satchō men, and all but two of the Meiji
era prime ministers came from there. In other words, it had become clear by the middle 1880s that without the right geographical origins one's hope of attaining power in the government was slight. Though opinion leaders expressed occasional
resentment against this tendency, the options for checking it
seemed to be diminishing.

It was with this realization—as well as his own disillusionment over the Teiseitō debacle—in mind that Fukuchi thus set
out on January 19, 1886, to discuss the reasons the Meiji government had come to be called a "Satchō administration." The

Restoration, he noted, was carried out almost exclusively by Satchō forces. The consolidation of the government was planned and executed by men from those two *han*, with only a few exceptions. The newly established cabinet excluded nearly anyone who was not from those regions. There was no question, he said, about the fact that these men had served their country courageously, leading in the Restoration battles, encouraging the development of solid foreign relations, abolishing the decentralized *han*, and "destroying hundreds of years of feudalism at a single leap." The problem was that they had consolidated personal power to a point where "no man could occupy a strategic post or attain a position of genuine influence without the power of this very Satchō clique behind him. . . . Military and civil power is now controlled completely by Satsuma and Chōshū."

The following day, he discussed the conditions that had allowed this situation to develop. He saw the problem as an outgrowth of the fact that the Meiji government took root in a "feudal" period during which each *han* had distrusted all other *han*. In consolidating power, the Satchō men created widespread distrust among the leaders of other domains and, as a result, were forced by both custom and prevailing conditions to man the bureaucracy from among their own associates. This did not mean that they had desired at the time to establish permanent Satchō rule; it merely indicated that, bred in feudal practice, they had been unable to escape old ways and ideas. The men from Satsuma and Chōshū were, he suggested, like those of Sparta in ancient Greece—men of special "ability and merit." And "it is quite natural that great merit begets great strength. Even in nations like the United States, with pure democratic systems, the Republican party ruled the country for twenty years on the basis of having triumphed in the Civil War." So it was understandable, in light of both feudal custom and superior merit, that Satchō should have established a long rule.

But the time had come to end that special privilege. Even Kido had said that the "work of the Meiji government would not be fully consolidated until favoritism toward Satsuma and Chōshū had come to a halt." And had not Itō, the ruling prime minister, once called "the evil of favoritism unbearable"? The Satchō dominance was, indeed, a challenge to true imperial sovereignty, a point with which Fukuchi dealt at some length the following day.[119] Then, in a burst of sarcasm,[120] he suggested that having "restrained their personal affection for the Tokugawa . . . and their *han* lords, having suppressed their affection for their native areas, they had carried out their meritorious Restoration deeds in behalf of the court"—climbing of course to their current stations in the process. Now, to prove that they still were motivated by concern for the imperial welfare, the oligarchs should once again "bear the unbearable and suppress their affection for their own disciples" in order to abolish the despicable practice of geographical favoritism within the bureaucracy.

After a reiteration of the many areas of society dominated by Satchō men, areas ranging from banking to railway construction and shipping, Fukuchi proceeded in the final installment of the series to suggest means whereby the Satchō oligarchs could "regulate their preponderant strength."[121] "I know that power does not plan its own decline," he admitted. But he did think the ruling men had a duty at least to restrain that power. To do that he recommended that the government immediately and fully carry out a "General plan for reorganization" that had been submitted to the cabinet by Itō on December 26, whereby upper-level offices were henceforth "to be conferred only on those that successfully pass a Higher Examination."[122] "I agree with this plan," he said. "If we strictly carry it out, disciples will no longer be tools. Superiors will not be able to assist them in their climb. We will no longer follow the patronage road. Men will be promoted simply as a result of their own superior merit. . . . They will not need to depend on Satchō strength." The result, he concluded, would be a gradual decline in Satchō influence and a more impartial government.

For a man who had so often been called a *goyō*, or "kept" editor, it was a remarkable series, reminiscent of his editorials in

1880 and 1881, when his gradualism had frequently called specific government practices into question. In no way could one say that it departed from his gradualist convictions. What it did instead was to highlight, in a last grand series, the essentials of Fukuchi's mature approach to gradualism. Nation-centered "order" remained basic; the perspective of the articles was a belief in the use of talent so as to make national structures strong: indeed, the very stimulus of the series was an officially published reorganization plan. So he obviously was not opposing the established "order" per se. At the same time, "Satchō ron" asserted that still more "progress" was needed to assure the perpetuation of order and strength. The government had grown unduly despotic and inflexible. It had an insufficient number of valves through which talented men could vent their frustrations, too few ways to use such persons' talents. The situation was, in a real sense, unstable.

One suspects that personal bitterness played a certain role in inspiring the outburst against favoritism. Certainly Fukuchi's experiences with the Teiseitō and the *Kampō* had given him personal insights into the darker side of patronage politics. Talent, he had found, had never been quite adequate to compensate for his own Nagasaki origins. But the mere accusation of personal pique hardly explains away the very real nature of the problems raised in "Satchō ron." No less a figure than Ōkuma had been squeezed excruciatingly in the vise of faction politics.[123] So had Itagaki and Gotō Shōjirō. That these abuses should have been treated so forcefully by a paper still widely regarded as conservative and progovernment, however, gave the movement for their elimination greater impetus. It may have been Fukuchi's "final explosion" as a journalist. But it was a powerful one, indicating the influence the name Fukuchi still exerted in Tokyo's public circles.

Equally illustrative of his continued influence were the number and nature of his nonjournalistic activities. He continued to live a life of luxury at Ike no Hata. The home, with its massive gates overlooking the blue-green waters and yellow-pink lotus blossoms of Ueno's Shinobazu Pond, had long since become one of Tokyo's more famous abodes.[124] It was built in purely Japanese style, with a mother-of-pearl phoenix crest on each of the horizontal pillars, specially ordered *tatami* from Bingo for flooring, and a perfectly designed tea house in the courtyard. As the lord of the home, Fukuchi was known for the scores of servants he commandeered "like an army general organizing his platoons."[125] And until late in the 1880s he continued to socialize with officials and businessmen of the stature of Itō, Inoue, and Shibusawa, entertaining them lavishly at his annual cherry-blossom-viewing parties and attending their gaudy masquerade balls in return.[126] As Suezo, a hero in Mori Ōgai's *Gan* ("Wild geese") and one of Fukuchi's jealous neighbors, sneered: "How stupid to squander money like some men, like Fukuchi for example . . . strutting openly on the streets and followed by . . . expensive geisha."[127]

Fukuchi was also much in demand during these years as a lecturer and a sponsor of philanthropic organizations—teaching recent history at a widely acclaimed "scholarly research association" *(gakujutsu kōkyū kai)* launched in February 1884,[128] serving as a founding director of Japan's Red Cross in 1887, continuing on the Tokyo city council into the 1890s. When *Konnichi Shimbun* conducted a poll in the spring of 1885 to find "today's ten most outstanding men," some 1,406 persons named Fukuchi first in the field of journalism and second in overall balloting. His 1,089 votes followed only those of Fukuzawa (1,124 votes) and led such men as Itō (leading politician: 927 votes) and Shibusawa (businessman: 596 votes).[129] It was hardly a scientific poll, yet its testimonial to Fukuchi's continuing prominence was undeniable.

Prominence was not enough to satiate Fukuchi, however. He had tasted not just prominence but dominance, and as the second decade of Meiji neared a close the old combatant began showing signs of growing weary of public life. His efforts to revive *Nichi Nichi* did yield mild success, as the paper's circulation increased by about 15 percent between 1886 and 1888.[130] But it was too slight a change for a man whose paper had ruled society. Moreover, the press itself had begun changing significantly in these years, and Fukuchi seemed to lack the inclination to keep abreast.

By the latter half of the 1880s, a new generation was spearheading the drive for journalistic modernization—young intellectuals such as Tokutomi Sohō and Kuga Katsunan, business entrepreneurs such as Murayama Ryūhei—men who saw journalism not merely as a step to political prominence but as a fulfilling profession in and of itself. They, along with the established independent journalists at *Yomiuri* and *Jiji,* introduced numerous new elements into the respectable press: cartoons, novels, serials, interviews, unabashed commercialism. Indeed, by 1890 nearly all of the old distinctions between the *daishimbun* and *shōshimbun* would have been obliterated by the spread of this true commercial journalism. But Fukuchi was not psychologically prepared to keep pace. He could not really bring himself to publish novels or to edit for the sake of entertaining.[131] Progressive though he was in the field of economics, he could not escape the Confucian-based view that commercialism debased a paper. He had been the servant of political interests too long to be capable of genuine editorial objectivity. Even news he still regarded as secondary to political comment. In 1888, when asked to speak into Japan's first phonograph machine, he took the microphone and said: "This sort of invention will make things hard for a newspaperman."[132] A decade earlier he might have hailed its possibilities. But now the innovator had become a conservator. It was almost as though he had formed his ideas about the press by age thirty-five, then refused to change.

To make matters worse, Fukuchi grew poor. He had gone into heavy debt in promoting the Teiseitō, only to see the party fail.[133] *Nichi Nichi*'s declining revenues had forced him to take a salary cut, and by the end of the 1880s he was approaching bankruptcy.[134] "I was being pressed in every direction by force of circumstances," he wrote. "I no longer loved reading as in the past. . . . It was not too late to change my line of debate and join the liberal forces, but it seemed wasteful to turn on friends of past years and return to old pet theories just to gain personal fame. So I saw no choice now but to retire from debating circles."[135] It was the complaint of a mentally exhausted man.

Yamagata, among others, urged Fukuchi to take a temporary leave from the paper and travel abroad, a course of action that might have refurbished both his enthusiasm and his viewpoint just as it had in 1865 and 1871.[136] But even that failed now to interest him. Instead, early in 1887, he began relinquishing control at *Nichi Nichi*. On January 4, he turned the proprietorship *(mochinushi)* of the paper over to Ishikawa Shukō, though maintaining personal direction of the editorial writing. The company's announcement of the transfer, published in Fukuchi's name, indicated that an internal power struggle had perhaps already begun. It cited the paper's "difficult straits" as the reason for the shift and added, somewhat defensively: "I am still managing Nippōsha, and I am still carrying on as usual in matters pertaining to the writing of *Nichi Nichi Shimbun*."[137] Just what control Fukuchi actually maintained is unclear, as no one chose to record the details of internal struggles.

In the middle of the next year, however, Fukuchi, clearly under pressure, severed all formal connections with *Nichi Nichi*. On July 10, 1888, a company advertisement stated: "Nippōsha president Fukuchi Gen'ichirō, being unable to continue exhausting work due to a nervous disorder, has been discharged. Seki Naohiko has been selected to be in charge." Fukuchi would remain as an informal consultant *(kyakuin)*, willing to give "friendly service," but his formal ties to *Nichi Nichi* were severed.[138] Suematsu Kenchō, a former *Nichi Nichi* writer and now an official in the Home Ministry, was at first invited to assume the editorial reins, and when he declined Seki was called home from a *Nichi Nichi* assignment in Europe to take over.[139] It was a whimpering end to a dynamite career— surprising in its final suddenness, yet somehow fitting in the life of a mercurial man.

### The Gradualist Journalist: An Evaluation

The discouragement Fukuchi carried with him from *Nichi Nichi* was, in many ways, unnecessary. Events of recent years had, admittedly, been disappointing. Yet the overall effect of his life since the Restoration had been one of remarkable contribution and influence, shown as much by the controversies that plagued him as by the achievements that followed him. Competitors frequently had damned him as a "kept editor," an "old-fashioned conservative" or a powermonger, but friends had described him as independent, truly civilized, a "man of the century." Which, one finds oneself asking, were correct? In what ways did both groups approximate the truth? More important, what were the dominant or consistent strands of his thought, the actual contributions he made to the politics and journalism of his day?

Looking first at the specific, evolving meaning of Fukuchi's political thought, one finds not only a distinct delineation of the issues that dominated early Meiji society but also a general statement of most of the basic principles that underlay those issues. His view was, with some exceptions, purposefully similar to that of the government's leading oligarchs; so his articulation and defense of gradualism tells much about the general course the government itself pursued.

First of all, Fukuchi never failed to demand the *drafting and promulgation of a constitution*—as soon as Japan was ready for it. Within a month after initiating editorial columns at *Nichi Nichi,* he had begun discussing the need for constitutional government.[140] In 1880 he called for a national assembly to draw up a constitution under imperial direction.[141] His 1881 outline of a constitution was one of the first private drafts to appear in the press. He claimed late that year that it was the emperor's concrete promise of constitutional government that made it imperative to renew his support of the government. As he wrote in September 1881: "When we can establish joint rule of the people and the sovereign, opening an assembly and establishing a constitution, then we will have been able to carry out our desires."[142] That, to him, was the bedrock foundation of gradualism.

Second, Fukuchi's gradualism never ceased to call for steady movement toward *establishment of a "popular assembly."* The

Fukuchi Gen'ichirō in 1903, at age 62. *(Photo courtesy of Mainichi Shimbunsha Shi Henshūshitsu)*

idea of some kind of cooperation between the rulers and the people appealed to him from the first, though he felt that *heimin* were not yet ready to assume major political responsibilities in 1874. They had been nurtured in subservience, he said, hence should be tutored in self-government by the creation of local cooperatives and assemblies before a national legislative body was established. In 1879 he illustrated what he meant by accepting the presidency of Tokyo's first drastically limited city council; his constitutional draft called for a relatively strong assembly; and while his views on the nature of the assembly narrowed after 1882, bringing him to warn more and more forcefully against allowing an assembly to curtail imperial power,[143] never did his support of an assembly system per se waver. "The two most important tenets of gradualism," he wrote, "are the promulgation of a constitution and the convening of an assembly."[144] His view of representative government may not have been thoroughgoing or Western; neither could it be shaken.

Third, Fukuchi never abandoned his contention that one of the prime purposes of the constitution was to insure *the public's right to "enjoy freedom,"*[145] though once again his was a peculiarly Japanese, "order"-oriented definition of freedom. In his initial argument on a popular assembly, he maintained that the entire point of gradually developing representative government was to train people to grasp and maintain their own rights. His constitutional draft assured the right of people to own property, to enjoy freedom of speech and religion within legal limits, and to receive equal treatment before the law. Even the Teiseitō platform called for "freedom of speech and assembly, as long as it does not interfere with national peace and order."[146] Unfortunately, the legal limitations Fukuchi would have placed on such freedoms indicated a significant inconsistency, a flaw born of traditional Confucian training, in his stated concern for civil rights. That he genuinely believed that a government must serve the populace seems unassailable. But he was not a populist, not a true democrat. He never moved beyond the parallel belief that the people must also serve the government. Reforms in the direction of rational, orderly government were essential to the movement toward a strong nation. But always the emphasis was on *tenka kokka*, the nation above, rather than on *shimin kokka*, a nation in which government belonged to the people. Popular freedom was more a component of modernization than an end in itself. But, as a component, he desired it.

The reason for this likely lies in the fourth aspect of Fukuchi's gradualism: his emotional and undying *support of Japan's tra-*

*dition and historical polity*, or *kokutai*, as an absolute essential
if progress were to be genuine. Perhaps the most forceful aspect
of many of his debates was his assertion that liberal opponents
used "desk top" arguments that ignored Japan's distinctive tradition.[147] With the passing of years, few positions became so
fraught with emotion to most Japanese as the uniqueness of
their land, its traditions and history. One of the Meiji press' earliest articulators of this emotional attachment to the national
spirit, to "all that could not be touched,"[148] was Fukuchi.
From the early Nagasaki days, Fukuchi regarded himself as a
historian. "My impression," said one student of the press, "is
that his historical view shines through all of his articles. . . . I
think one root of his gradualism lies there."[149] For that reason,
it was quite natural that he, more than most (and earlier than
most), would view progress in the light of what he saw as
*kokutai*, or the historical Japanese way. To be a good dramatist,
he admonished a student, one must: "Know Japan! Know
Japan!"[150] He felt the same way about the man who would
write a constitution.

Closely related was Fukuchi's *forceful defense of imperial
sovereignty* as the heart of *kokutai*. More than his contemporaries, he espoused both of what Robert N. Bellah has referred to
as the "father figure" and the "mother figure" images of the
emperor. The emperor was, to him, both the essential samurai
—the remote, elevated, demanding hero—and the "warm, accepting *Gemeinschaft*," the "shield from anxiety."[151] Already
at *Kōko Shimbun*, his attacks on the Meiji government went to
some lengths to point out that he firmly supported the principle of imperial sovereignty. In his first year at *Nichi Nichi* he
declared the primary purpose of a constitution to be "service to
the will of the emperor."[152] Some fifteen editorials were given
to an impressive, almost reverent consideration of the imperial
line in early 1879.[153] Both his constitutional draft and his contribution to the "Imperial precepts to soldiers and sailors"
highlighted a fervent loyalty to the "divine emperor." While
the platform and party prospectus of the Jiyūtō contained
"scarcely a reference to the Emperor,"[154] Fukuchi's Teiseitō

made loyalty to the ruler basic in its party statements. And his attachment to that view grew more intense as time passed. "I thought that public opinion could not disagree with my position" that "sovereignty always resides in the king," he wrote of the 1882 sovereignty war.[155] In 1886, he described those who would support popular sovereignty as violators of Japan's history.[156]

The sixth and final pervasive tenet of Fukuchi's philosophy, a tenet that summarized all the rest, was a profound belief in *the orderliness of progress*. Undue haste in fostering new ways, he said so often, would bring chaos and disorder. He found the middle road "indispensable to the spirit of a nation," to making it possible to support "good and beautiful governmental reforms" without introducing unnecessary disruption.[157] That, to him, meant that Japan must progress into the contemporary world by drawing up a constitution, opening a popular national assembly, and assuring certain human rights, but that it must at the same time safeguard tranquility and all that was good about Japanese tradition by basing progress on *kokutai* and imperial sovereignty—a philosophy, in other words, of specific progressive tenets circumscribed by generalized conservative traditions. As he said in the Teiseitō platform: "We seek the parallels of progress and order."[158]

Gradualism, to Fukuchi, was thus a blend—sometimes inspirational and sometimes oppressive, often inconsistent yet always pragmatic—a philosophy fitted uniquely to the rapidly changing country and government he served. His early advocacy of *kokutai* and absolute imperial sovereignty made him a forerunner of nationalistic movements that would eventually sweep Japan and propel it toward a cataclysmic clash with the Western world. His attacks on *hambatsu* factionalism prefigured the well-known "conservative opposition" of the late 1880s and 1890s.[159] His limited definitions of popular rights and representative government found general embodiment in the Meiji constitution itself. If one were to choose a phrase descriptive of the essence of Fukuchi's (and, one might say, the government's) gradualism, it would be: "orderly Japanese progress." Certainly, he felt, Japan must evidence progress if she were to enter international society. Certainly that progress must be orderly. And order could be assured only if progress were consistent with Japanese tradition. With the realization of these three points Fukuchi would be satisfied.

Turning from the abstract world of political thought to the more concrete sphere of journalistic practice, one sees at least as many different evaluations, as curious a blend of the weak and the strong, the conservative and the progressive, as one does in the "political" Fukuchi.

One is struck first with the weaknesses that prevented him from realizing his full potential. Nearly all observers have commented, for example, on his personal eccentricities: the arrogance that offended acquaintances and often robbed his writings of their logical impact; the self-confidence that led him to spread his talents over too many areas; the tendency to prodigality that made him vulnerable to attack, to charges of corruption. Yet at least two other, more basic, weaknesses appear to have detracted even more significantly from his journalistic contributions.

The first of these lies in Fukuchi's failure to develop a clear philosophy regarding *the nature and role of news reporting*. He had, admittedly, studied the Western press more diligently than had most of his contemporaries; and we have seen that his view of reporting was well in advance of that of other journalists in the 1870s. Yet, as in so many of the early Japanese contacts with the West, Fukuchi seems to have grasped (often intentionally, one suspects) only selective aspects of the institution. He failed, in the final analysis, to carry even those aspects that impressed him to logical conclusions. The political influence of European papers impressed him deeply, the informational role much less. Consequently, as one reads the pages of Fukuchi's *Nichi Nichi*, one is struck with the constant subordination of news to opinion. Even if he developed the art of reporting more fully than did his early contemporaries—and even if the subordination of news might be said to have represented a natural response to a period of national turbulence and awakened political consciousness—still, the marked tendency to slight news coverage cannot be ignored.

The result was a lack (though not an absence) of objectivity and breadth, as well as an overemphasis on those items that best coincided with Fukuchi's gradualist point of view. When he went to Kyushu in 1877, for example, his reports stressed government triumphs to the point of inaccurately downplaying rebel strength. And though he wrote on many topics, his focus continued always to be those matters most related to politics and economics. The obscene scandalmongering of the *shōshimbun* was, of course, taboo to Fukuchi; but so was the less political news orientation of *Yomiuri* and *Osaka Asahi Shimbun*, which emerged as Japan's first genuinely commercial newspaper during the 1880s. Because of this heavy political orientation, Fukuchi was never able to offer his readers a full complement of news and features, not even a genuine balance of opinion. A full century later, press critics were complaining that Japan's newspapers often denied their readers a broad spectrum of political viewpoints.[160] Even in that respect, Fukuchi may have been a forerunner, though one could hardly call it a salutary distinction.

Second, Fukuchi never seems to have developed a definite policy regarding *the proper relationship between the government and the press*. The early years at *Nichi Nichi* found him speaking out for the Kido faction. After Kido's death he became increasingly independent, even while identifying generally with the policies of such Chōshū oligarchs as Yamagata and Itō. In August and September 1881, he broke completely with the oligarchy, only to become its devoted servant during 1882 and 1883. It would appear, in other words, that two forces vied constantly for Fukuchi's loyalty, creating a struggle that would finally destroy him as a journalist. On the one hand, there was his bright vision of the press as a political instrument, his desire that *Nichi Nichi* become the people's window to the government and that its editor become the popular articulator of official positions. On the other hand, Fukuchi ever remained too proud and self-confident to suppress his own points of view.

Hence, he generally demanded the right to independence even when supporting the government line, and he always insisted that the press be accorded the basic legal freedoms then enjoyed by Western newspapers. It was an anomalous position, born more of emotional reaction than of philosophical commitment. And it was a personally ruinous position; for even as it kept him from establishing the principle of genuine press freedom, it also prevented him from realizing his own dream of establishing a government newspaper. "Being a non-*hambatsu* official," he wrote in his first novel, "is like walking a tight rope. You never know on what day or at what time you will fall."[161] The same might have been said of a government-oriented journalist who, one suspects, helped stretch his own rope.

Unfortunately, many press historians become so impressed by Fukuchi's final tragedy that they fail, except in the use of a few sweeping platitudes, to evaluate his positive contributions. Yet, for all his failings, he was a leader of his times, one whose contributions dramatically outweighed his failures.

In the first place, Fukuchi, by the very act of becoming a journalist, had much to do with raising the press from a position of social contempt to one of respect. At the time he joined *Nichi Nichi,* reporters generally were scorned as mediocrities; news was unreliable, opinion pieces limited largely to essays contributed by outside experts. Fukuchi's courage (and it was that) in making the leap from the bureaucracy to journalism, however, influenced others, and within the next few years the press became a haven for ambitious youths and bright but bitter bureaucrats—men like Tokutomi Soho (whose first journalistic impulse came from a dream of being "like Fukuchi"[162]), Yano Fumio, Saionji Kimmochi, Taguchi Ukichi, Inukai Tsuyoshi, and Hara Satoshi. In the exaggeration of Inukai, by the late 1870s newsmen had become "the most learned people of the age, . . . greatly respected by the public."[163] In that transition, Fukuchi must be granted a measure of credit.

He also deserves credit for introducing the daily editorial into Japanese journalism, and with it the idea of maintaining a fixed company philosophy. The climate was ripe for the publication of daily editorials when Fukuchi changed *Nichi Nichi*'s format in late 1874. He had been invited to the paper largely because of the increasing politicization of the press. So once *Nichi Nichi* instituted its page one editorials, such columns were rapidly copied by other papers. By the spring of 1875, the editorial, or *ronsetsu*, had become a focal point of Tokyo's political discussions. One might indeed say that Fukuchi's editorials were too successful. Not only did they draw heated responses; their influence undoubtedly contributed to the overpoliticization of the press during the first two decades of Meiji, a politicization that caused the press' temporary decline when political fires dampened, and contributed to the relatively slow growth of other features of modern journalism.

Fukuchi, in the third place, deserves credit for introducing—at least encouraging—a miscellany of other Western concepts to Japanese journalism, concepts that he never fully developed but that came to fruition in the writings and management of others. "He knew China, the West and Japan like no other person of his day," said Nishida Taketoshi of the Meiji Shimbun Zasshi Bunko, Japan's leading repository of nineteenth-century press archives; "so he was the only one, except perhaps Fukuzawa, capable of showing newspapers the way of modernization."[164] Though his concept of the press' informational role never matured, he did advance the art of reporting to new levels, encouraging highly paid reporters *(kisha)* not to consider themselves above digging out facts, and winning imperial recognition for his own reportorial efforts in the Satsuma Rebellion. He taught, likewise, the need for versatility in the press, lambasting those editors who wrote only about politics, introducing every topic from economics and culture to journalism and religion into *Nichi Nichi*'s editorial columns. As Inukai put it: "When I think about it, no one else was as well qualified as a newspaper reporter. He excelled in *kambun*, yet was well-versed in Japan's own literature and language. Being versatile, . . . he was also intimate with entertainers. The breadth of his knowledge was frightful."[165]

In many respects, Fukuchi also showed the way in newspaper

management and technology. He pioneered in company management practices by reorganizing *Nichi Nichi* as a joint-stock company in 1877 and by introducing unified control over the business and editorial sides of his paper. He was the first editor of a *daishimbun* to purchase steam-run presses, which meant that although *Nichi Nichi*'s circulation in 1881 was similar to that of its major competitors, *Chōya* and *Hōchi*, its work force was only two-thirds as large.[166] He introduced color advertising to Japan. And the result of this willingness to innovate technically was that *Nichi Nichi* became, until 1881, the most profitable *daishimbun* in the nation.[167] The advantage evaporated when men like Murayama at *Osaka Asahi* began running papers as truly commercial ventures in the 1880s; but, once again, Fukuchi had at least pointed the way.

"As long as there are newspapers in Japan," said Tsukahara Jūshien, "Koji will be our honored teacher."[168] *The* modernizer of the press? *A* modernizer of the press? The leading voice of his time? The father of true journalism in Japan? Fukuchi has been called all of these. Without deciding which label is most accurate, the best summary of all is perhaps the retrospective evaluation of one of his fiercest competitors, *Hōchi*'s Yano Fumio:

> Fukuchi's *Nichi Nichi Shimbun* editorials led and dominated society. . . . They exerted an authority unseen among newspaper editorials elsewhere. The reason was that Fukuchi, having early traveled to the West and investigated new matters in various societies and systems, possessed the greatest learning of the time. Both government and people were overwhelmed by the feeling that in order to understand the strengths of Europe and America, it was necessary to look at Fukuchi's *Nichi Nichi* editorials. . . . I have not in all my life seen a time that a newspaper's editorials have so guided society.[169]

Fukuchi was thus a complex man, driven as a youth by ambition and visionary ideas, hindered in his late forties by a seeming ossification of those ideas. It was almost as though "progress and order" had become as much the symbols of his personal life as they were the standards of his public postures. At an early age he had set goals: he wanted to influence his country, from as high a position as possible, toward the creation of a stable, modern state worthy of international respect; he wanted to edit a newspaper for the sake of shaping political opinion. When those goals were achieved, he rested. Times and trends, of course, kept evolving, but his journalistic and political goals really did not. So, disillusioned by personal loss of influence, he left those two worlds. There was, however, still another segment of society—the world of literature and drama—that had not yet come abreast of all his youthful ideas. So rather than hewing new courses or dreaming new ideas as a politician or journalist, he simply switched. He would, he decided, see what could be done with his ideas in the arts.

# CHAPTER V

# The After Years:
# 1888–1906

> *People long on talent and rich in knowledge
> are likely to be dissatisfied with conditions in
> today's society. Becoming strangely cynical
> about the world . . . they may well find plea-
> sure in making fun of society . . . through
> the medium of humorous novels.* [1]

The late nineteenth century in Japan was an era of mind-shattering transformation, a period so dramatic in its introduction of change that Basil Hall Chamberlain found it no hyperbole in 1904 to comment that "having arrived in Japan in 1873, we ourselves feel well-nigh four hundred years old."[2] Yet, by the late 1880s, the middle years of Meiji, one also could find a full complement of feudal remnants, one of the chief of which was the pervasive tendency to regard men of literature merely as idle practitioners of a "useless pursuit."[3] Even the eclectic Fukuzawa Yukichi said of Japan's first "modern" novelist, Tsubouchi Shōyō: "It is quite beneath the dignity of a person holding a Bachelor of Arts degree to engage in such a vulgar occupation as the writing of novels."[4]

Social ostracism was not, however, sufficient cause to keep Fukuchi out of a profession. At least twice in his first forty years he had defied friends' advice, to enter forbidden worlds, first in 1859, when he forsook the "safe" field of Chinese studies to become a student of the West and, second, when he left the Finance Ministry in 1874 to become a journalist. Both times he had proved his friends wrong and his own instincts right, using despised talents to win personal success and power. So it was not out of character that he should hesitate but briefly after leaving *Nichi Nichi* in 1888 before plunging into a third forbidden world, that of literature. Disillusioned with politics and journalism, his personal fortune largely dissipated, he saw in literary

writing the promise of financial (if not social) success. He harbored, moreover, numerous ideas about the reform of drama
and literature and possessed full confidence in his own ability as
a writer. So he made another dramatic plunge, severing many of
the old ties and creating a new world of friends and acquaintances. Though the years that followed this plunge lie largely
outside the scope of our study of Fukuchi's public life, they did
bring him sufficient success of a new kind to demand a summary.

### A Man of the Arts

The development of Fukuchi's interest in literature and drama
was, as we have noted, not an overnight thing. Like many other
samurai of his own generation, he had approached manhood
under the onus of a paternal admonition "never to set foot in a
theater";[5] but the trips to the West had robbed the warning of
its impact. In Europe, he was frequently escorted to the theater
by Western officials, and though English or French dramas initially put him to sleep, in time they came to stimulate his curiosity nearly as much as the newspaper once had in Nagasaki.
Soon, he was reading the plots of plays before going to the
theater, and by 1865 he had begun reading such authors as William Shakespeare, Edward Gibbon, and Montesquieu for pleasure.[6] He even made some crude efforts at writing fiction in the
years just before the Restoration.[7]

Nor did the interest wane once Fukuchi became editor of
*Nichi Nichi.* He took part throughout the newspaper years in
gatherings of *rakugo* (comic tale) storytellers,[8] encouraged the
development of several drama reform groups,[9] and published
numerous editorials on both literature and drama.[10] He also
formed the friendship of Ichikawa Danjūrō IX, a famous
kabuki actor whose temperament and artistic outlook closely
paralleled Fukuchi's. And from 1874 onward he collected over
six hundred old theater texts *(marubon),* which contained the
kinds of historical stories that he hoped would someday become
a source for the reform of Japanese drama.[11]

It thus came as no particular shock when Fukuchi's name surfaced in the fall of 1888 as the instigator of one of Tokyo's most ambitious kabuki enterprises. Specifically, it was announced that he would team up with Chiba Katsugorō, a relative of one of his former *Nichi Nichi* partners, to construct the largest kabuki theater yet built in Japan, a theater to be named simply the Kabukiza. Construction was begun with considerable fanfare early in 1889,[12] and by the time the doors opened that fall, the new building was being hailed as an important tribute to an upsurge of interest in the theater.[13] It was, said an observer, "an epoch-making theater,"[14] larger by far than any previous kabuki hall, made elegant by the winglike shape of its front exterior, built over a period of eight months at a cost of more than 35,000 yen.[15] Its name also standardized for the first time the *kanji*, or characters, used in the word "kabuki."[16]

Though the financially pressed Fukuchi eventually was forced to sell his share in the company to Chiba,[17] he became the theater's chief playwright, and between 1890 and 1903 turned out no fewer than forty-four kabuki plays (see Table 2).[18] The plays were written specifically to exhibit the talents of his friend, the famed Ichikawa, and drew largely on Fukuchi's knowledge of history and the tales he had collected from *marubon*. Among the better known were *Kasuga no Tsubone* ("Lady Kasuga"), first performed in 1891; *Gogiwashi* ("Mutual suspicions"),[19] produced in 1894; and *Kyōkaku harusame no kasa* ("Gallant in the spring rain") and *Ōmori Hikoshichi*, both produced in 1897. The last and probably most famous of these detailed the attempt of a princess to avenge the slaying of her warrior-father by killing Ōmori, the general responsible for his death.[20] She failed but came back after her own death to bewitch the offending general in a climactic demon dance that sufficiently pleased audiences that the play was still being performed decades later. So successful, in fact, were many of Fukuchi's plays that a European visitor to Japan in the 1890s described him as "Japan's most eminent dramatist and the greatest of living writers."[21]

Fukuchi was regarded in his day as a dramatic innovator. While still at *Nichi Nichi* he had called for Japan's dramatists to "free our art" from the current tendency "to revel in the im-

TABLE 2
*Fukuchi's literary works, 1888–1905, by year and type* *

| Year | Plays | Novels: Political Satire | Novels: Romance | Novels: History | History | Total |
|---|---|---|---|---|---|---|
| 1888 | 0 | 3 | 0 | 0 | 0 | 3 |
| 1889 | 0 | 1 | 0 | 0 | 0 | 1 |
| 1890 | 2 | 5 | 2 | 0 | 0 | 9 |
| 1891 | 7 | 0 | 4 | 0 | 0 | 11 |
| 1892 | 4 | 6 | 0 | 2 | 1 | 13 |
| 1893 | 5 | 1 | 7 | 1 | 0 | 14 |
| 1894 | 3 | 2 | 4 | 1 | 1 | 11 |
| 1895 | 2 | 4 | 2 | 1 | 1 | 10 |
| 1896 | 2 | 0 | 2 | 0 | 0 | 4 |
| 1897 | 7 | 2 | 2 | 1 | 1 | 13 |
| 1898 | 0 | 0 | 1 | 0 | 2 | 3 |
| 1899 | 4 | 0 | 0 | 1 | 0 | 5 |
| 1900 | 1 | 1 | 1 | 0 | 0 | 3 |
| 1901 | 2 | 0 | 2 | 1 | 0 | 5 |
| 1902 | 2 | 0 | 2 | 3 | 2 | 9 |
| 1903 | 3 | 0 | 1 | 0 | 1 | 5 |
| 1904 | 0 | 0 | 0 | 2 | 0 | 2 |
| 1905 | 0 | 0 | 1 | 0 | 0 | 1 |
| TOTAL | 44 | 25 | 31 | 13 | 9 | 122 |

*Adapted from Yanagida Izumi, *Fukuchi Ōchi*, pp. 294–316.

purities of the world and to take pleasure in the rank odor of ig-
nobility.''[22] He had taken part in most of Japan's mid-Meiji
drama reform movements. At the Kabukiza he offered better
lighting and new-style programs.[23] And, more important, the
study of the old *marubon* and Western theater had convinced
him that the secret to appealing drama lay in "natural" plots
where characters did what one might expect them to do in real
life rather than what stylized art forms dictated. Thus, his plays
became somewhat more realistic and episodic.[24] His goal, according to his foremost critic, was to use traditional Japanese
material and impose upon it the naturalness and plot of the
Western theater,[25] with a result generally known as "Ōchi
Kabuki.''[26]

No scholar claimed, however, that the old *Nichi Nichi* mentor really took Japanese drama far down the road of reform. He
was much too deeply rooted in traditional Japan, too conservative in nature to introduce far-reaching changes. In a series of

interviews with British traveler Mortimer Menpes he showed just how traditional his thinking was. Japanese theater was superior to that of Europe, he told Menpes, because of its revolving stage and its *hanamichi,* the flower path that was of such "tremendous advantage" dramatically.

He defended the role of the female impersonator and charmed Menpes with a quaint (though itself rather innovative) description of his vision of the ideal playwright, whose duty it was to "arrange everything," including stage settings, plot, and costuming. "If an actor or an actress were permitted a choice as to the color or form of costumes," he said, "the work would of necessity be ruined"; artistic balance would be lost. "The dramatist must be supreme."[27] He demonstrated to Menpes, in great detail, how he even insisted on sketching out the stage settings for the carpenter. To write a play, he said, one needed to envision a "series of pictures," then describe those pictures in writing.[28] Such a view was hardly typical in a land where kabuki actors had been central. Nevertheless, most of his ideas were those of a traditionalist, an artist bred in the Tokugawa era who depended primarily on the acting of one man, Danjūrō, for his own artistic expression and who actually withdrew from the world of kabuki when the great actor died late in 1903. Fukuchi's playwriting was more like that of the historian or journalist than of the gifted dramatist, more, in fact, like the "old-fashioned *kyōgen* writer."[29] He was a leader in an important transitional period of the theater, a prime mover in raising the prestige of kabuki. But true reform would have to await his successors.[30]

Fukuchi also left a mark on the world of literature, writing no fewer than sixty-nine novels in just eighteen years after leaving *Nichi Nichi*![31] Having lost much of his fortune before retiring from the newspaper world, he badly needed funds to continue the life-style he had come to enjoy, and the writing of novels seemed one of the most promising sources of income. Asahina Chisen, a later editor of *Nichi Nichi*, recalled that one day early in the 1890s Fukuchi brought a political novel to the Nippōsha office, to the same room where "he used to consult in his golden years," and asked the paper to serialize it for two yen a day ("a relatively large sum then") simply "because I need money." Asahina agreed quickly, later claiming himself moved nearly to tears by the sight of his former hero trying to sell a manuscript.[32] Fukuchi himself wrote in 1902 that he was forced to "make up some novels to get enough money to pay for rice and medicine."[33] While both statements must be regarded as exaggerations, reflections both of the period's patronizing or derisive view of the literary profession and of an artistic propensity to self-denigration, they illustrate a financial condition greatly deteriorated from the blossom-viewing days at Ike no Hata. Hence, his prodigious average of six novels a year from 1890 to 1897.

Published initially in such newspapers as *Jiji, Nichi Nichi, Yamato Shimbun,* and *Kokumin Shimbun,* most of the works fell into three classes: romantic novels,[34] which simply related old, often moralistic, tales; historical novels,[35] which faithfully treated such famous events or lives in Japanese history as the Mongol invasion and Minamoto Yoshitsune; and satirical *(fūshi)* or political novels *(seiji shosetsu),*[36] drawn largely from Fukuchi's own experiences.

Of the three groups, the political satires have drawn the largest share of attention—hardly a surprising situation, since few men ever stepped onto the literary stage with a richer store of insights into the operations of all levels of public life. Of two dozen such political novels, few attracted more comment or shed more light on its author than the first one, *Moshiya sōshi* ("What if . . . "), a work that sold an extraordinary three thousand copies after publication late in 1888.[37] Described by one critic as "a direct expression of the shadows of his heart,"[38] it probed into an imaginary future to describe the vicissitudes of one Shimizu Kiyoshi, who supposedly went abroad as a student in 1888 and returned to Japan in 1903, aiming to become a scholar. Soon after returning, however, he gravitated to the political world; then, being too astute and honest a man to settle amicably into the politicized society of his day, he made a series of shifts from the Foreign Ministry to the Finance Ministry to banking to party politics, and thence into commerce, then the Diet, journalism—and finally back to scholarship. One of his friends and advisers also followed a similar, though somewhat less complicated route, eventually becoming a member of the House of Representatives and, later yet, a social critic, while Shimizu's wife became an actress to help lift her husband out of severe financial straits.

In each of these occupations (and one could hardly expect a greater or more varied offering in a single novel!), Fukuchi explained the foibles and iniquities that trapped men of genuine talent or integrity. He told of candidates for official posts being asked to write "joke books" on their civil service examinations. Nobles were seen as "mere puppets" of crude "mushroom millionaires." Diet members were self-seeking manipulators who staged their legislative debates and hired audiences to listen. Even newspapers, though claiming to be organs of principle, switched sides at will for the sake of financial gain. "With this book at one's side," quipped one critic, "even the inexperienced or unimaginative should be able to become a novelist or a playwright."[39]

Fukuchi denied in the introduction that *Moshiya sōshi* was meant to "ridicule or insult" society or that it was written to vent personal frustrations. "I implore my readers," he said, "to read it at will and evaluate it freely; but it bears no relation to Koji."[40] It was not a convincing disclaimer, however, coming from a man who had himself worked in most of the professions described in the book. Much to the contrary, one of the chief characteristics of his satirical novels was their realistic, autobiographical nature. They were not, said Yanagida Izumi, noted student of Meiji literature, truly literary, nor were they truly philosophical; they merely showed a worldly-wise man "turning the world inside out."[41]

Fukuchi's satire frequently was too coarse or too bitter. But few men in the period knew Japanese society quite so completely and at the same time possessed a basic literary competence. Hence, his political novels, even if not masterpieces, have been described as possessing a depth of social understanding reminis-

cent of the works of Charles Dickens. They presented a
"panorama of society," as useful in explaining the real world of
Meiji as any formal social history of the period.[42] And "considering the times in which they were written," adds Yanagida,
"they were among the best of all political novels"—works de-
serving of further study.[43]

A third literary area in which Fukuchi involved himself after
1888 was the writing of history. His interest in that field actually never subsided after those early days when his father had introduced him to Confucian classics and sent him off to study
under Nagasaki's most prominent historians. During the *Nichi
Nichi* years, the historian's method showed up in his annual
"Kiji hommatsu," a series of perhaps half a dozen early January
editorials in which he would summarize the developments of
the preceding year. His forceful advocacy of adherence to
*kokutai*, or the national essence, also reflected the historian's
view. "My proper role," he wrote in 1889, "is that of the historian. You ask about drama? It is just my sideline."[44]

That may have been an exaggeration. But there is no gainsay-
ing the fact that the most lasting of his latter-day works were his
historical writings. He produced nearly a dozen such works in
this period. Among them: *Bakufu suibō ron* ("On the decline
and fall of the bakufu");[45] *Bakumatsu seijika* ("Political
leaders of the Bakumatsu");[46] *Takashima Shūhan*, an 1898 biography of a famous Nagasaki and Edo military strategist and
artillery maker; and *Nagasaki sanbyakunenkan gaikō hensen jijō* ("The vicissitudes of 300 years of foreign exchange in Nagasaki"). One of his last political novels, *Gengō monogatari*,
treated the Mongols' thirteenth-century invasion and has, accordingly, been classified by some as a historical work, "one of
the masterpieces of his life."[47] In addition, he began but died
before finishing monumental histories of the life of Tokugawa
Keiki[48] and of the Tokugawa era, the latter projected to reach
ten thousand pages.[49]

Most influential of these volumes was his *Bakufu suibō ron*, a
work Tokutomi Sohō felt would bring him "immortality."[50]
Until its publication, Meiji historians had, quite understand-

ably, viewed the Tokugawa era and especially the shogunal family in an unfavorable light. Fukuchi, deciding it was time to balance the picture, agreed when Tokutomi asked him in 1891 to prepare a late bakufu history for *Kokumin no Tomo* magazine.[51] His aim, he said, was to show both the outlines and the causes of the Tokugawa fall, as seen from the viewpoint of the bakufu itself. Earlier works "might be labeled histories of the Meiji Restoration," he said, "but they could not be described as records of the Tokugawa demise."[52] He would correct that.

Accordingly, the book asserted that while it was feudalism and the seclusion of the country that had maintained the Tokugawa bakufu for 280 years, it was also feudalism and isolation that destroyed it during the reign of the fifteenth generation of the Tokugawa family. For thirty-three chapters, he attempted to support that point, discussing first the general nature of shogunal administration—the foreign policy, reforms, diplomacy and domestic policy—then outlining each of the significant events leading up to the pivotal battle of Toba-Fushimi. The Tokugawa were not opposed to the throne, he wrote; they were not usurpers or insurgents as recent scholars had maintained. Indeed, he argued that the Tokugawa had itself fostered devotion to the emperor, requiring faithful retainers to invoke the emperor's name in giving advice to a shogun, requiring imperial sanction of official appointments. And it was the growth of this very loyalty to the emperor, tied to the intervention of foreign elements into domestic Japanese affairs, that eventually led to the Restoration. "Without those two factors," he said, "ten Satchō cliques or a hundred Saigōs and Kidos could not have moved the Tokugawa bakufu."[53]

It had, in other words, been absolutely essential at first to institute a feudal system and to exclude foreign intercourse in order to stabilize seventeenth-century Japan. Later, in the days of Yoshimune, the eighth shogun, it had been further necessary to encourage the acquisition of Western knowledge so as to preserve order and growth. But this encouragement, along with growing foreign pressure, eventually led to a fierce debate over the opening of the country. Once the bakufu decided it was necessary to permit the entry of foreigners, the nonbakufu forces began increasingly to oppose it; and the bakufu, unable to act resolutely because of immobilizing feudal attitudes, finally collapsed. To really understand this, he said, one had to look at the entire 280-year history of the Tokugawa. Only then could one see that the Tokugawa were not usurpers, that decline came as much from within a legitimate (even though increasingly inept) system as from without.[54]

*Bakufu suibō ron* was not the most balanced piece of historical scholarship, lacking objectivity and careful reliance on sources. Nor did it have the depth or prose quality of Gibbon's *Decline and Fall of the Roman Empire* or Thomas Babington Macaulay's *History of England,* the works Fukuchi sought to imitate.[55] It was, rather, as a memoir, written to a large extent "on the basis of my memory,"[56] that it became one of the "more . . . influential . . . productions" of the period.[57] More than most early and mid-Meiji historical works, it attempted to be fair and honest; more than most, it included frank analysis. It opposed the current view, which aimed primarily at legitimating Satchō involvement in the Restoration, and it refused to dismiss the Tokugawa as usurpers. It also offered a wealth of source material for students of the period. It must be read, said Tokutomi, by anyone who wants to understand the Bakumatsu period.[58]

Clearly, Fukuchi's post–*Nichi Nichi* days were not spent in idleness. In the fifteen years from 1889 to 1903, he published no fewer than 116 literary works, including more than 40 plays, 9 historical volumes, and more than 60 novels, an average of nearly 8 works a year. It should not seem surprising that his literary output never showed the elegance born of painstaking care. Indeed, one can but shake his head in amazement that a single man could write so prolifically and at the same time turn out as many solid works as he did. Nor were the novels, dramas, and historical volumes all that he wrote. He also translated several Western works into Japanese,[59] lectured frequently on the arts, and contributed numerous articles to leading newspapers and journals.[60] And he wrote regular, often daily, articles for

*Yamato Shimbun* during 1901 and the first half of 1902.[61] During the 1890s, Fukuchi's lifelong friend, Jōno Dempei, had solicited occasional articles as that paper's chief writer on the arts and society, and when he died in November 1900, the *Yamato* president asked Fukuchi to enter the company in something resembling a supervisor-teacher post. Fukuchi declined formal appointment, having no desire to become involved again in the battles he had once fought at *Nichi Nichi,* but he did consent to becoming a consultant and regular contributor. As at *Nichi Nichi,* his articles covered the gamut from politics and economics to international affairs, though now the emphasis was more on literature and culture.

Late in December 1903, the *Tokyo Asahi Shimbun* ran an item to the effect that Fukuchi, "who had been hidden in the world of drama for some time," was thinking about "blossoming again in his old age." He had decided to run for the Diet.[62] The item was correct, and when the voters went to the polls several months later, they selected him as one of Tokyo's fifteen members of the lower house.[63] Unfortunately, however, the election held more sentimental than real significance for the much-scarred warrior. Though his political and legislative aspirations were genuine, the prevailing international situation and increasing health problems prevented him from making an impact. Both of the 1904 Diet sessions[64] were held during the Russo-Japanese War, a period that provided little chance for political initiative; and by the time the twenty-second Diet convened on December 28, 1905, Fukuchi had been prostrated by kidney trouble, tuberculosis, and pneumonia. A week later, at 2:00 A.M. on Thursday morning, January 4, 1906, "Japan's premier journalist"[65] died at the age of sixty-four. "Death," said one paper, "overtook him just as a new career of distinction seemed to be dawning."[66]

Elaborate funeral services were held at Tokyo's Zōjōji temple two days later. The papers eulogized him as one of "Japan's greatest celebrities in the literary world."[67] Famous friends mourned his passing. Yamagata Aritomo eventually had the fifteen-foot-high marker referred to on the first page of this study erected in his memory at Tokyo's largest temple, the Asakusa Kannon. Yet there was no denying the irony, even the bitterness, of his passing. Life, which seemed promising but uncertain the day he first sailed out of Nagasaki harbor half a century earlier, had given him more of travel, of success, of fame than he might have hoped. Yet when his star had begun rising fastest at *Nichi Nichi,* it had fallen, tossing him eventually into the world of drama and fiction. Now, as he once again had begun to experience a measure of public confidence and a new shimmer of expectation, sickness had felled him; health had slipped away. Life, for Fukuchi, had never been predictable, never tranquil. The circumstances of his death were not either.

### The Years in Review

Few people have contributed more to their society than did Fukuchi. Nor have many contributed in more varied ways. Yet, in the final accounting, how should one evaluate those contributions? How, indeed, can one individual *ever* accurately evaluate another? Perhaps a man of history can best be measured by the people he knew, or by those he influenced. Perhaps one should look at the popularity he gained, the positions he articulated, the offices he held. Sometimes the influence he exerted on specific developments is most important. Certainly, all such factors must be studied in most lives, and even then one must remain humble about the ability to evaluate. For there is no tangible accounting, no ''correct'' way to determine an individual's value. Yet evaluate one must. History is affected by individuals. The more one knows about those who influence or represent their times, the better one can understand the times themselves and the historical context into which they fall.

It would be reason enough in Fukuchi's case to have studied him merely for the inescapable fascination inherent in a highly unusual life. From the quarrels that drove him from the Namura home in Nagasaki to the sympathetic efforts of fellow townsmen electing an old man to the Diet half a century later, from the lonely entry into the swirl of Edo society in 1859 to positions of power at *Nichi Nichi,* his was a life of more intriguing twists than most novelists would dare to sketch in their more fanciful works. Even more significant were the specific contributions Fukuchi made: his authorship of Meiji's first sympathetic history of the Tokugawa house, his role in constructing the Kabukiza and writing two score plays that helped rejuvenate the popularity of kabuki theater, his pragmatic leadership in the fields of economics[68] and diplomacy,[69] and, of course, his numberless contributions as the "father" of modern journalism and the "great gradualist" in politics.

Interesting and significant as these events and contributions were, however, there remains one more important strand for the evaluating student to draw from Fukuchi's life: namely, the greater understanding his variegated experiences provide regarding the nature of human existence itself during the first half of the Meiji era. More than most men, his activities and interests spread across a wide range of activity, typifying in so many ways the spirit of his age—the exuberant quest for knowledge, the zest for sampling new world pleasures, the embarrassment at Japanese "backwardness," the desire to maintain what seemed best in national tradition, the constant searching for safe ways to foster enlightenment. In other words, though Fukuchi's life is extremely important for its obvious and direct contributions, it is perhaps almost as much so simply for its illumination of an age. Through that life we can see in a clearer, new way several of the most salient characteristics of the late-nineteenth-century environment. A look at those features of civilization that he illuminated seems a fitting way to conclude the study of his life.

The first such characteristic one notices is *the way in which vestiges of the Tokugawa era continued to pervade Meiji society*. Meiji was an age of enlightenment. Fukuchi himself frequently spoke with amazement of the rapidity with which change occurred. Yet, as Fukuchi would learn again and again, surface changes frequently masked the subsurface persistence of old norms.

Throughout life he was affected, for one thing, by the patterns of personal patronage politics that had long characterized bakufu administration. In his own bakufu years, he had decried those aspects of the system that allowed incompetents to head bureaus, lead missions, even command armies. He despaired when foreign office officials vacillated for weeks during the sensitive negotiations over the Richardson affair, and he called many of his superiors "wooden monkeys."[70] All too often clique politics affected him personally, cutting him out of one foreign mission, dictating the closing of his first language school because the "other side" regarded his views and manners as dangerous. And he found that aspect of administration nearly as pervasive after the Restoration. His entry into the government resulted from friendships with the "proper" persons, as did his selection as a member of the Iwakura mission in 1871. After the mission's return, the loss of power by his own patrons in the Ōkurashō led to his resignation from the government. At the same time, he was able to assert *Nichi Nichi*'s influence at least partly because the Chōshū faction to which he maintained close ties wielded such influence. Unfortunately, when the faction chose to withdraw its support from his Teiseitō in 1883, Fukuchi found that the resources for keeping it alive also dried up, as did much of his influence. Talent, he found, was not sufficient in early Meiji; one's factions or friendships had to be kept in order too. Hence, his assertion in 1886 that "no man can occupy a strategic post or exert actual influence without the power of the Satchō clique behind him."[71] All governments experience a measure of this phenomenon. Fukuchi's life illustrates what an acute, lingering problem it was in Meiji Japan.

Closely tied to personal patronage politics among the bakufu remnants was the continuing influence of the old Confucian emphasis on loyalty to one's lord or superior. Chu Hsi teachings on proper relations between people, as well as popular feudal beliefs in the essential nature of loyalty to both superiors and personal friends had permeated Tokugawa society, and though he seldom delved into theoretical treatises about the nature and logic of such tenets, the emotional attachment to concepts of human trust and imperial loyalty remained fundamental in Fukuchi's approach to life. It was, as we have seen, a traditional view of loyalty to one's lord that made it psychologically impossible for him to join the Meiji government until nearly two and a half years after the Restoration. A similar view of loyalty to the nation undergirded his emotional defense of imperial sovereignty. And a firm belief in loyalty to friends made him bitter over the government's treatment of the Teiseitō. When he attacked the attorneys for abusing the legal system, his main charge was that they were subverting the time-honored concepts of personal "humility and subservience."[72] "Loyalty," said the "Imperial precepts to soldiers and sailors," is the "essential duty."[73] It was a concept that his Nagasaki father taught him, a concept he and most contemporaries hated to see die.

Another carryover from the hierarchical Tokugawa days was the elitist tendency to despise certain vocations as base or unworthy. For centuries men had been taught that society was divided into four levels: warrior-officials, farmers, artisans, and merchants, in that order,[74] while writers, actors, and the like had not even made the list, at least as a class. Samurai were not to visit theaters, and those who did went disguised. Such stratification supposedly ended in Meiji, the age when the emperor himself attended a kabuki play,[75] when leading officials staged elaborate masquerade parties and merchants assumed positions of respect. But as Fukuchi found more than once, some taboos die only with a struggle. Hence, when he left the Ōkurashō to become a journalist, most friends remonstrated that he was throwing away his future by entering such a lowly profession. But times changed and journalists soon came to be respected nearly as much as officials. Then, in 1888 he shifted again, this time to the world of drama and literature; and again he felt the scorn of his friends. Literature was still being "pushed aside into a corner by society . . . a sort of outcast kept deliberately in obscurity."[76] This time he entered the field from a position of weakness, however, and though gaining a certain eminence among his colleagues, he never fully escaped society's pity or contempt. This kind of narrow-mindedness was not exactly what he had in mind in his calls for maintaining national tradition. But he found that centuries-old ideas are not easily shaken.

Looking at Fukuchi's contemporaries, one scholar has noted

that the "Japanese coming to manhood at Perry's arrival . . .
had not felt in their upbringing the full force of cultural
change; they had grown up in a rapidly changing but not yet
'broken' world."[77] It must be seen as quite natural that such
people would retain many of their pre-Restoration attitudes and
practices. They might borrow from the West, but the eyes
through which they perceived Western culture would be traditional Japanese eyes; the hands that borrowed would be culturally conditioned Japanese hands. Hence, "Western journalism" to Fukuchi and his contemporaries would emphasize press
freedom and political power but would fail for years to include
such basic pillars as journalistic independence or the press' informational role. Democracy and politics would be an elitist
phenomenon in which "heirs of the Bakumatsu *shishi*" engaged each other in battle with a "spirit of military adventure,"
rather than out of civic-mindedness.[78] Fukuchi's idea of Western drama would include only "natural plots," leaving out
such basic concepts as realistic characterization and natural stag-
ing. The transformation of early Meiji society was, in other
words, a spotty thing, colored always by the persistence of
Tokugawa legacies.

A second general societal characteristic illustrated by
Fukuchi's life was *the importance of Western knowledge in establishing many men as national leaders.* Despite the subsurface
reservoir of entrenched ideas, the conscious goal of most early
Meiji leaders was to stimulate national enlightenment, a goal
usually identified with grand-scale importation of ideas, techniques, and gadgets from Europe and the United States. A man
of Fukuchi's nature and background probably never could have
entered the world of public prominence without his study of the
West. It was, in fact, the Western orientation that led to Edo in
the first place, the knowledge of Dutch and English that won
him a bakufu post, the same language ability that secured a
spot for him on two early missions to Europe. And it was the experience gained on those foreign trips that earned him a place
in a Meiji bureaucracy heavy with Satsuma and Chōshū retainers
and that gave such force to his editorials at *Nichi Nichi.*

It has been noted that most early Meiji intellectuals "received Westernization from books and not from direct contact with the West."[79] The fact that Fukuchi's comments on the West were, by contrast, squarely based on a total of nearly four years' travel abroad gave his voice a particular power. "His detailed knowledge of the West surpassed that of most others," remarked Nishida Taketoshi, student of that period's press; "the result was that he had a marked influence on modernization."[80] Added one of Fukuchi's contemporaries: his editorials "had an authority unseen elsewhere. . . . The reason was that Fukuchi had early traveled in the West, investigated new matters in various societies and systems, and come to possess the greatest learning of the time."[81] It was not an understated evaluation of Fukuchi; nor was it faint praise for the influence of the West.

At the same time, it was this very Western experience that also made Fukuchi more skeptical than some about the wholesale importation of Western culture and philosophy. As a Nagasaki youth, he wrote an early poem referring to foreign shippers as "jackals and wolves" who "plunder our blessed provisions,"[82] and in his "internationalist" days as a translator in the Yokohama foreign office he often became irate over Western merchants' lack of culture or courtesy. Even the trips abroad convinced him of Western weaknesses as well as strengths. As a consequence, he refused to accept the more extreme, superficial imitations of Western culture and, at times, shunned even some of the more logical Western offerings. He criticized, for example, attempts at democratization that would merely copy English or French systems; and he despised the uncritical aping of Western fashions. The whole point of westernization, Fukuchi maintained, was not merely to force wholesale a new way of life on Japan but to introduce culture to a broad segment of society and to gain the Western respect that would enable Japan to assume its deserved place in the family of nations. Like so many leaders of his day, he saw westernization not as an end in itself but as one essential ingredient in the "orderly and systematic cultural development" of a nation seeking worldwide influence.[83]

A third societal characteristic pointed out rather dramatically by Fukuchi's experiences was *the difficulty of balancing the two worlds*. Japanese of his day craved something they called "modernity," yet frequently shuddered in apprehension over the danger inherent in wholesale rejection of their own culture. The result was a tension, sometimes dynamic and sometimes paralyzing, between West and East. During Fukuchi's Edo years, for example, he was ignored by some and threatened by others, merely because he chose to study the West. His loquacity, born of a fascination with Western ideas, frequently robbed his talents of their usefulness in the bakufu foreign office. And though the overt opposition to internationalism largely subsided after the Restoration, the inner struggles between the two strains continued through life.

Fukuchi suffered, quite obviously, from what he described as that "ebb and flow . . . within my breast" of both liberal and conservative, Western and Eastern thought,[84] an ebb and flow that kept him within the gradualist stream, yet made his defense of government causes difficult, if not a bit tortured, on occasion. His contributions to the "Imperial precepts to soldiers and sailors" serve as a case in point. Written at a time when Fukuchi had become a sincere advocate of greater "civil liberties," of a strong legislature and the early drafting of a constitution, it nevertheless evidenced numerous traditional, conservative tendencies: a belief that the emperor was sovereign and divine, that soldiers had no duty greater than loyalty, that hierarchical patterns were still best in society. It may, of course, be argued that these conservative tenets were not fully traditional, that they had been fabricated by the architects of the Meiji state to consolidate their own control; yet their roots, at least in the mind of Fukuchi, lay in traditional Japan. Thus, it would seem that Fukuchi's elitist, hierarchical, Neo-Confucian upbringing made the easy or wholesale adoption of Western political theory impossible. Yet total rejection of Western political modes was rendered equally impossible by his dedication to national transformation. The balance was found in a somewhat contorted effort to clothe late Tokugawa emphases on *kokutai*, imperial divinity, and loyalty in the garb of the Western phrases constitutionalism, imperial sovereignty, and soldierly duty.

In other words, Fukuchi had come to espouse such Western terms as "civil rights" and "popular suffrage"; yet he defined those terms in a peculiarly Japanese way and limited their meaning by tying them to traditional concepts of *kokutai* and loyalty to the emperor. The tensions and contradictions thus created plagued his writing through life. It was not an unusual problem. Times of drastic transition can be expected to create tensions. And certainly individuals in every area of Japanese life experienced similar problems. One of Fukuchi's contemporaries commented in 1888 that of all Japan's recent controversies, "the one that has attracted the widest attention . . . is . . . the debate over Westernism and Japanism."[85] It was certainly that debate and its ramifications that most often dominated Fukuchi's own life.

One sees in Fukuchi's career, fourthly, a vivid portrayal of the *renaissancelike breadth and turbulence of the Meiji era.* Nearly all periods offer their own attractions to innovative minds, but rarely has any land experienced such a bombardment of new ideas and experiences, such encouragement to expanding mental and cultural horizons, so many fresh new avenues to success for so many people in such a brief span of years. Nor have many men delved seriously into as many of those areas as did Fukuchi. He was, at least in his breadth of experience, a renaissance man.

Almost from the day of birth he encountered experiences that had been closed to his fellow countrymen for centuries—the chance to meet Western merchants, to study English, to travel abroad, to ride in a train, to dance, to visit with foreign statesmen, to attend the theater, to read Western history and literature. The French historian Jules Michelet has described the European Renaissance as a "discovery of the world and of man," as the birth of the modern spirit. Such certainly was the impact and thrust of Fukuchi's own lifelong encounters and studies.

Inherent in each of his Bakumatsu experiences was a universe of new ideas. Early on in Nagasaki, he became fascinated by the possibility of communicating events through a newspaper. At the customshouse in Yokohama, he began to question the idea that merchants should be the lowest social class. On his first trip to Europe, he saw a "parliament," a governing body elected by the people themselves. The second trip to the West introduced him to Western literature and law. Later on, with the coming of Meiji, he encountered new ideas about banking, currency, technology, education, music, and a host of other matters. He reached manhood in a new age when old concepts were being questioned, when new knowledge was valued as supreme. To the end of life, his relatives recalled him regularly "sitting inside a mosquito net, reading by candle light until late at night."[86] Experience breeds ideas—and Fukuchi loved ideas.

Another mark of this renaissancelike breadth was the diversified nature of Fukuchi's occupations and interests. The preceding pages already have detailed many of the areas in which he made major contributions. Equally impressive is a list of the matters, both major and minor, in which he pioneered. He traveled, for example, on the second modern mission ever to leave Japan for the West, became the first Japanese to visit Jerusalem (en route home from the Iwakura mission), was the first person in his land to make a recording.[87] In the field of economics, he introduced the idea of Western banking, helped found the Tokyo Trade Association and the city's first stock exchange, and in 1876 published the country's first economic newspaper, the *Chūgai Bukka Shimpō*. His "firsts" in the field of journalism were innumerable: he was the first important journalist jailed for his writing, the first editor to attempt to cover *all* types of news in his paper, the first writer of daily editorials, a member of the first journalism "guild," the first publisher to run color ads, the first journalist granted an imperial interview. As a politician, he was secretary of the first Conference of Local Officials, first president of a Tokyo city Council, head of the first progovernment political party. As a writer and dramatist, he built the largest kabuki theater of his era and wrote the first Bakumatsu history favorable to the Tokugawa. One could add a host of similar pathbreaking efforts at the expense of boredom. The point of such a list, however, should already be clear: Fukuchi lived in a transitional period, and by taking the broadest possible advantage of myriad opportunities he won the right to be called a "renaissance man"—if by that phrase one intends the "break in historical continuity," the birth of modernity and eclecticism described by scholars such as Jakob Burckhardt, rather than the mere revival of ancient culture once seen as necessary to a renaissance.[88]

Unfortunately, such a period also has drawbacks. For even while stimulating consciousness and encouraging breadth, a renaissance period such as Meiji frequently introduces stormy elements into personal lives, a fact to which Fukuchi's career bears equally dramatic testimony. Even near the end of the Edo period, one sees a young man already frustrated by the very knowledge that has brought him fame, sometimes by the unwanted idleness, once by the forced closing of his language school, frequently by a mediocre superior's refusal to listen to his overly innovative proposal. From the beginning of the Meiji period, these clashes of new and old created even more serious troubles for Fukuchi. There was, for example, the problem of what to do with Western individualism, a concept basic to European definitions of the word "renaissance." In one sense, Fukuchi's fascination with new world ideas led him, as we have seen, to insist that commoners (not just former samurai) be given political rights. Yet his upbringing was too rigid, too hierarchical to allow real liberation of the common man or to enable him to oppose the elitist style of government that prompted Fukuzawa's comment that "we have no citizens, . . . only a government."[89] Moreover, even his eventual decline in influence at *Nichi Nichi* appears to have been related to the knowledge explosion of the period. For when, in mature years, he became more rigid personally, he found his own influence diminishing. Most unfortunate of all, in a personal sense, was the fact that in his fascination with myriad, diverse fields of knowledge he failed to reach his full potential in any one of them. While contemporaries felt he might have become an Itō had he concentrated on politics or a Shibusawa had he limited himself to business,[90] he reacted to his era like the glutton at a smorgasbord, and in the end, having been temperamentally unable to place a limit on his "specialties," to concentrate to the point of fulfillment, he died a disappointed man. It was, in part, the potential fate of any life in renaissance times.

It should be noted, in the fifth place, that Fukuchi's life and writings dramatically illustrated the *important role played by intellectuals in the early Meiji era*. Political sociologist S. N. Eisenstadt has noted the danger inherent in considering only liberals or social critics in studies of intellectual history. Intellectuals, he says, are both "creators and carriers of tradition,"[91] not merely critics of the past; hence "conservative" intellectuals frequently become as important as liberals in the transmission of culture. To understand their role, he says, one must recognize that most of the world's effective intellectuals—whether conservative or liberal—are rather constantly involved in a two-sided struggle, seeking to maintain autonomy even while attempting to gain the official recognition that will assure influence and guarantee safety for the free expression of their views. And in most cases "thinkers" become vastly important to the government itself as "legitimators" of official policy.[92]

Few lives or periods more precisely illustrate these points than that of Fukuchi in his years at *Nichi Nichi*. Though regarded by contemporaries as a conservative, he was, without question, both a creator and a carrier of tradition, bombarding society with new ideas about popular suffrage, economics, diplomacy, drama, and journalism even while constantly attempting to fit progress into the framework of national tradition. He vividly displayed the dichotomous struggle between personal autonomy and public power, thus illustrating the tensions experienced by an effective intellectual in a dynamic society. The press, he maintained, must be free: a man must always be true to his creed; yet, as we have seen, no man in the period attempted so constantly to use official connections to buttress his own editorial authority and influence. And throughout much of his time at *Nichi Nichi* government leaders relied on his editorials as their chief popular source of legitimacy and defense.

To specifically quantify the degree of influence exerted by those editorials, or by any of his fellow intellectuals in the press, would, of course, be impossible. But the very public passions aroused by their writings, as well as the close relations most of them maintained with officials or out-of-power politicians, testify to the fact that the Meiji government, operating in a new era and a new world, was both deeply interested in, and often dependent upon, the thought, the suggestions, and the rationales of the world of the intellectual. Eisenstadt credits the mass-communications leader (probably the leading type of intellectual in early Meiji Japan[93]) with "a central role in the broad process of construction and transmission of tradition."[94] Certainly, it would seem, that was true of Fukuchi's Japan.

Finally, Fukuchi's life and thought foreshadowed the *national particularism that would become so important in the later Meiji years* and on into the middle of the twentieth century.[95] Beginning in the 1880s, Japanese speakers and writers constantly emphasized *kokutai,* the national heritage and tradition that made Japan unique among nations. "The Crown," said Itō in later years, "was, with us, an institution far more deeply rooted in the national sentiment and in our history than in other countries. It was indeed the very essence of a once theocratic State. . . . It was not the people who forcibly wrested constitutional privilege from the Crown *as in other countries,* but the new regime was to be conferred upon them as a voluntary gift."[96] Japan was, in other words, unique.

Fukuchi was one of the earliest Meiji writers to emphasize that point. One wonders if early embarrassment at his nation's seeming "backwardness" did not make it psychologically necessary for him to compensate by insisting that there were areas in which Japan always had been—and always would be—superior. His emphasis would no longer be as abstract as the "Western science–Eastern ethics" rationale of the Tokugawa period. Instead he would point to those specific areas that made Japan so unusual—to that "general uniqueness" embodied in historic emphases on filial piety, on harmony between citizens, on the mystical unity that bound Japanese together, and, above all, on loyalty to one's ruler. It was an emphasis that led him in an increasingly conservative direction during his latter years at *Nichi Nichi*. But perhaps that fact too was reflective of the times. For it was most certainly just such a growing belief in Japan's unique qualities and her resultant national destiny that led many an otherwise progressive thinker of late Meiji into the trap of imperialism, expansionism, and uncritical allegiance to the government. It was just such a belief that helped propel Japan down the tragic road toward twentieth-century militarism.

Fukuchi was, then, in so many ways, a reflection of his own country in one of its more exciting eras. Never, to the end of life, did he (or his fellow countrymen) really reject such traditional concepts as Confucian-style loyalty or social elitism. Yet, like others of his age, he saw in Western knowledge a chance for both personal and national success; and like most Meiji leaders he found the balancing of the old and new difficult but exhilarating at times, necessary yet debilitating at others. The eclectic nature of his interests and vocations, moreover, bespoke an impressive national transformation in knowledge and culture. And his rather determined effort to give a confusing period meaning and stability by enunciating a belief in Japanese particularism reflected a general, growing mid-Meiji nationalism shared by most of his contemporaries. It would seem safe to say, in short, that nearly every aspect of Fukuchi's personal career mirrored, in an unusual way, the broader nature of his nation as a whole. He was a shaper of his times, a reflection of his times, even a victim of his times. He was, one might conclude, an embodiment of the "spirit of Meiji."

Chronology
Notes
Bibliography
Glossary
Index

# Fukuchi's Life:
# A Brief Chronology

| | | |
|---|---|---|
| 1841 | | Birth in Nagasaki (May 13). |
| 1848 | Age 7 | Commenced study of history under Osagawa family. |
| 1855 | 14 | Began studying Dutch at Namura home. |
| 1857 | 16 | Interpreting at Deshima and teaching Dutch at Aku-no-Ura. |
| 1858 | 17 | In charge of Nagasaki interpreters connected to foreign shipping (September). |
| 1859 | 18 | Arrived in Edo. Entered Moriyama home to study English (May). Went to work in bakufu foreign office on June 26. |
| 1861 | 20 | Married Kaneda Satoko. Present when *rōnin* attacked British legation on July 5. Chosen for Japan's second embassy to the West (November). |
| 1862 | 21 | Traveled in Egypt, France, England, Holland, Russia, Germany, and Portugal as interpreter on bakufu mission. |
| 1863 | 22 | Back in Japan. Not used much by bakufu, due to propensity to talk too freely. Took part in *rōjū* Ogasawara's abortive plan to attack Kyoto (July). |
| 1864 | 23 | Ill and idle during first half of the year. Helped with talks on Shimonoseki indemnity. |
| 1865 | 24 | Second trip to Europe, to study the construction of naval works. Also studied literature and drama. |
| 1866 | 25 | Back in Tokyo (March 5). Opened a language school during leisure time. |
| 1867 | 26 | Closed language school on bakufu orders. Went to Osaka in December to assist in the opening of a port there. |

| | | |
|---|---|---|
| 1868 | 27 | Fled Osaka after Meiji Restoration. Published anti-Meiji *Kōko Shimbun* (May 24 to July 9); first major journalist jailed for his writings (July 12). Dropped out of public life. |
| 1870 | 29 | Prepared *Kaisha ben* at government request. Entered Finance Ministry in December. |
| 1871 | 30 | Went to the United States with Itō to study financial systems. Returned to Japan in June. Worked for Ōkurasho before being chosen a first secretary on Iwakura embassy to the West. |
| 1872 | 31 | Traveled with Iwakura embassy in the United States and Europe. |
| 1873 | 32 | Studied "mixed courts" in Egypt, returning to Japan in July. Employed again by Ōkurasho, but increasingly dissatisfied with bureaucratic life. |
| 1874 | 33 | Left the government in midsummer. Joined *Nichi Nichi*. Instituted editorial columns. |
| 1875 | 34 | Participated in editorial war over the opening of a national assembly. Served as secretary in first Conference of Local Officials (June and July). Opposed new government press laws. |
| 1876 | 35 | Led journalistic profession, as editor of *Nichi Nichi*. Began *Chūgai Bukka Shimpō*. |
| 1877 | 36 | Covered the civil rebellion in Kyushu; drafted letter to Saigō for Yamagata, urging a surrender. |
| 1878 | 37 | Especially active in economic circles. Elected to Tokyo-*fu* council in November. Wrote important editorials on economics. |
| 1879 | 38 | Elected president of the Tokyo-*fu* council. Entertained Ulysses S. Grant during his Tokyo sojourn. Published key editorials on treaty revision and imperialism. |
| 1880 | 39 | *Nichi Nichi* editorials becoming increasingly independent of government. Several series on treaty reform. |
| 1881 | 40 | Published a controversial draft constitution. Engaged in acrimonious dispute with Tokyo attorneys' association. Broke dramatically with the government over Hokkaido land sales, then returned to government camp after an imperial promise of a constitution and an assembly. |

| 1882 | 41 | "Imperial precepts to soldiers and sailors" (which he helped draft) published in January. Engaged in editorial war on the locus of sovereignty. Founded Rikken Teiseitō on March 18. |
| 1883 | 42 | Disbanded Teiseitō in September under government pressure. Hurt by government creation of *Kampō* in July. |
| 1884 | 43 | Resigned as president of Tokyo-*fu* council. |
| 1885 | 44 | Greater emphasis on economics and culture in *Nichi Nichi* editorials. Went to China to cover the Li-Itō negotiations following violence in Korea. |
| 1886 | 45 | Criticized oligarchy in controversial series "Satchō ron." Made vigorous efforts to revive *Nichi Nichi*'s sagging circulation. |
| 1887 | 46 | Relinquished proprietorship of Nippōsha, but remained as *Nichi Nichi* editor. |
| 1888 | 47 | Resigned from *Nichi Nichi* (July 10). Made plans to construct the Kabukiza. Published three novels. |
| 1889 | 48 | Opened the Kabukiza amid great fanfare; became the theater's chief playwright. |
| 1890 | 49 | Published five political novels and two kabuki plays. |
| 1892 | 51 | Published *Bakufu suibō ron.* |
| 1893 | 52 | Produced five plays and nine novels; his most prolific literary year. |
| 1894– | 53– | |
| 1899 | 58 | Turned out an average of eight literary works a year. |
| 1900– | 59– | |
| 1902 | 61 | Consultant and regular writer for *Yamato Shimbun.* |
| 1903 | 62 | Stopped writing drama after Ichikawa Danjūrō died late in the year. |
| 1904 | 63 | Elected to the Diet in March. |
| 1905 | 64 | Ill most of the year; wrote one novel. |
| 1906 | 65 | Died January 4 of kidney ailment, pneumonia, tuberculosis. |
| 1919 | | Widow, Satoko, died on April 15. |

# Notes

*Introduction*

1. Yano Fumio, writing in Kubota Tatsuhiko, ed., *Nijūichi daisenkaku kisha den* (Osaka, 1930), pp. 65–66.

2. He is nearly as well known by the pen name, Ōchi, which he used as an author during his latter years. Koji was another of his pseudonyms.

3. Fukuchi Gen'ichirō, *Shimbunshi jitsureki*, in *Fukuchi Ōchi shū*, ed. Yanagida Izumi, vol. 11 of *Meiji bungaku zenshū* (Tokyo, 1966), p. 328.

4. Georg W. F. Hegel, *Philosophy of Right* (London, 1942), p. 295.

5. Robert N. Bellah, "Intellectual and Society in Japan," *Daedalus* (Spring 1972):103.

6. These phrases are from Kenneth B. Pyle, *The New Generation in Meiji Japan: Problems of Cultural Identity, 1885–1895* (Stanford, 1969), chaps. 6 and 7.

*Chapter One: The Clash of Two Worlds*

1. Fukuchi Gen'ichirō, *Kaiō jidan*, in *Fukuchi Ōchi shū*, ed. Yanagida Izumi, vol. 11 of *Meiji bungaku zenshū* (Tokyo, 1966), p. 278.

2. Dates have been converted to the Western calendar, using Paul Y. Tsuchihashi, *Japanese Chronological Tables* (Tokyo, 1952).

3. Descriptions of the interpreters' lives and work are few. See, however, Donald Keene, *The Japanese Discovery of Europe, 1720–1830*, rev. ed. (Stanford, 1969), pp. 11, 17–20, 75–76, 123, Itazawa Takeo, "Rangaku no igi to Rangaku sōshi ni kansuru ni-san no mondai," *Rekishi Chiri* 59 (1932): 460–461. See also James Murdoch, *A History of Japan* 3, pt. 2 (New York, 1964):537–550.

4. Junesay Idditti, *The Life of Marquis Shigenobu Ōkuma* (Tokyo, 1956), p. 11.

5. An additional annual "diversion" was the forced visit of the Dutch captain to Edo to offer presents to the shogun.

6. C. P. Thunberg, *Travels* (London, 1795), 3:64, quoted in Keene, *Japanese Discovery*, p. 9.

7. An excellent description of Nagasaki's development in the Tokugawa

period is Fukuchi's own *Nagasaki sanbyakunenkan gaikō hensen jijō* (Tokyo, 1902).

8. Rutherford B. Alcock, *The Capital of the Tycoon: A Narrative of a Three Years' Residence in Japan* (London, 1863), 1:98.

9. Fukuchi, *Nagasaki sanbyakunenkan*, pp. 152–155. The entire text of the "expulsion decree" is included.

10. Years later Fukuchi credited the Dutch king's letter with exerting an influence on the bakufu's conciliatory response when Perry arrived in Uraga with his Black Ships in 1853. See ibid, p. 164.

11. Ibid., p. 175.

12. Cited in Yanagida Izumi, *Fukuchi Ōchi* (Tokyo, 1965), pp. 19–20.

13. Facts on Fukuchi's ancestors are scarce. His claim to samurai status has never been disputed, but the lack of family records has left even that dependent primarily on the fact that the family had a surname. The best single account of the family's history is in ibid., pp. 1–17.

14. Ibid., p. 6. Actually, Fukuchi's father, Kōan, was adopted into the Fukuchi household after leaving the Rai San'yō school and traveling to Nagasaki in search of employment. At one point he left Nagasaki for Edo, hoping to become a Confucian scholar. But when that venture failed, he returned to the Fukuchi household and settled down to the practice of medicine.

15. Translation from Tamura Hisashi, *Fukuchi Ōchi,* in vol. 3 of *Sandai genronjin shū*, ed. Jiji Tsūshinsha (Tokyo, 1962), p. 16.

16. The name Gen'ichirō was assumed when Fukuchi reached the age of sixteen. Fukuchi also bore the alias *(azama)* Shōho and used Seiō as his first pen name. He took the pseudonym of Ōchi at the age of twenty-one, reportedly after he became enchanted with a geisha named Ōji in Edo's Yoshiwara section. See Tamura, *Fukuchi Ōchi,* pp. 107–108. He also became well known in later years by the pseudonym Koji.

17. Shōwa Joshi Daigaku Kindai Bungaku Kenkyūshitsu, "Fukuchi Ōchi," in *Kindai bungaku kenkyū sōsho* (Tokyo, 1958), 8:358.

18. Quoted in Yanagida, *Fukuchi Ōchi,* p. 29.

19. Fukuchi Gen'ichirō, "Ōchi Koji jihitsu jiden," in Nozaki Sukefumi, *Watakushi no mita Meiji bundan* (Tokyo, 1927), p. 101.

20. Among other possible explanations for Kōan's consent: (1) There already was an adopted son in the Fukuchi family, adopted prior to Gen'ichirō's birth; (2) coercion could have been a factor, though no existing records hint at it; (3) Gen'ichirō and his adopted elder brother may not have gotten along well, a possibility for which there does seem to be some evidence. See Yanagida, *Fukuchi Ōchi,* p. 35.

21. Ibid., p. 36.

22. Fukuchi, *Shimbunshi jitsureki,* in *Fukuchi Ōchi shū,* ed. Yanagida Izumi (Tokyo, 1966), p. 325.

23. Ibid.

24. Yanagida, *Fukuchi Ōchi,* pp. 39–41.

25. Fukuchi, *Kaiō jidan*, p. 264.

26. Tamura, *Fukuchi Ōchi*, p. 19. This same ship was to take Japan's first mission to America little more than a year later.

27. Scholars disagree on the date of Fukuchi's transfer to Edo, some placing it in 1858, most citing January 1859. The bulk of the evidence seems to support 1859, as the earlier date leaves too little time to crowd in the events that occurred before his departure from Nagasaki. See Yanagida, *Fukuchi Ōchi*, pp. 43–44.

28. George B. Sansom, *Japan: A Short Cultural History* (New York, 1962), p. 524.

29. See Naitō Akira, *Edo no toshi to kenchiku* (Tokyo: Mainichi Shimbunsha, 1972), pp. 23–25; cited in Gilbert Rozman, "Edo's Importance in the Changing Tokugawa Society," *Journal of Japanese Studies* 1, no. 1 (Autumn 1974):93.

30. Rozman notes that Edo was largely a "male city," with entertainment that catered to male tastes. Houses of prostitution, he says, ran on a system of reservations—"the counterpart of modern corporation-owned season tickets parcelled among employees"; "Edo's Importance," pp. 103–104.

31. Shibusawa Eiichi Denki Shiryō Kankōkai, ed., *Shibusawa Eiichi denki shiryō* (Tokyo, 1955), 1:170.

32. For a complete list, see Fukuchi, *Kaiō jidan*, p. 278.

33. Fukuchi Gen'ichirō, *Bakumatsu seijika*, in *Bakumatsu ishin shiryō sōsho* (Tokyo, 1968), 8:381–382. *Bakumatsu seijika*, a historical work in which Fukuchi reviews the lives of leading late Tokugawa statesmen, includes much material of an autobiographical nature.

34. Fukuchi, *Kaiō jidan*, p. 278.

35. Yanagida, *Fukuchi Ōchi*, p. 66.

36. Ibid., p. 49.

37. Ibid., p. 66.

38. Fukuchi Gen'ichirō, "Seiō shisō," in Fukuchi Nobuyo, ed., *Kankon shiryō* (private collection, 1918), notes that Fukuchi quickly used up all his money in the early days of Edo pleasures and for a few weeks was driven to the life of a vagabond in the regions north of the Tokugawa capital. The "pains" of those wanderings, he later claimed, prompted him to limit his excesses and pursue more serious scholarship (p. 8).

39. Fukuchi, *Kaiō jidan*, p. 278. The *kurokuwa* were very low-ranking vassals, often of poor farm families, hired by the Tokugawa family to work as palace guards or in various types of construction. Hayashi's idea was that by becoming a *kurokuwa* Fukuchi could gain easy access to the Tokugawa house; then, as a member of the house, he could request an exam and be assured of rapid promotion as a Confucian scholar. An exam system provided one means for promotion in rank.

40. Maruyama Masao, *Studies in the Intellectual History of Tokugawa Japan*, trans. Mikiso Hane (Tokyo, 1974).

41. See, in English, H. D. Harootunian, *Toward Restoration, the Growth of Political Consciousness in Tokugawa Japan* (Berkeley, 1970), pp. 47–128; Tetsuo Najita, *Japan* (Englewood Cliffs, N.J., 1974), pp. 45–51.

42. See Harootunian, *Toward Restoration,* pp. 184–245. For biographical detail, see David M. Earl, *Emperor and Nation in Japan* (Seattle, 1964), pp. 109–160.

43. Fukuchi, *Kaiō jidan,* p. 278.

44. See Fukuzawa Yukichi, *The Autobiography of Yukichi Fukuzawa,* trans. Kiyooka Eiichi (New York, 1966), pp. 98–99, for a fascinating account of this episode.

45. Fukuchi, *Kaiō jidan,* p. 267.

46. Maruyama, *Intellectual History,* p. 307, quoting Ōhachi Totsuan.

47. This is especially well discussed in W. G. Beasley, *The Meiji Restoration* (Stanford, 1972), pp. 117–139.

48. Yamaguchi-ken Kyōikukai, ed., *Yoshida Shōin zenshū* (Tokyo, 1938), 6:122; cited in Maruyama, *Intellectual History,* p. 362.

49. For Alcock's account of this event, see Alcock, *Capital of the Tycoon,* pp. 93–102.

50. See Roger F. Hackett, *Yamagata Aritomo in the Rise of Modern Japan, 1838–1922* (Cambridge, Mass., 1971), p. 11.

51. Fukuchi, *Kaiō jidan,* p. 264.

52. Ibid., p. 265.

53. For a text of that treaty, see, among other references, "Treaty of Amity and Commerce between the United States of America and Japan, Edo, July 17, 1858," *The Meiji Japan through Contemporary Sources* (Tokyo, 1969), 1:27–36.

54. Payson J. Treat, *Diplomatic Relations between the United States and Japan, 1853–1895* (Stanford, 1932), 1:87.

55. Alcock, *Capital of the Tycoon,* p. 138.

56. Treat, *Diplomatic Relations,* 1:86.

57. Fukuchi, *Bakumatsu seijika,* p. 383.

58. Ibid. Mizuno admitted privately to Fukuchi that Yokohama had been selected "by accident" (lending support to the "second Deshima" theory), but maintained that it had already turned out to be "the most propitious place, commercially."

59. Fukuchi, *Kaiō jidan,* pp. 267–268.

60. Ibid., p. 269.

61. See ibid. for an explication of this feeling.

62. "Treaty of Amity," *Contemporary Sources,* 1:31–32.

63. For a vivid description of the effect of this maneuver, see Samuel Mossman, *New Japan, the Land of the Rising Sun* (London, 1873), p. 105.

64. See Fukuchi, *Kaiō jidan,* p. 269; Alcock, *Capital of the Tycoon,* pp. 145–149.

65. Treat, *Diplomatic Relations,* 1:89.

66. "Treaty of Amity," *Contemporary Sources*, 1:32.

67. Fukuchi, *Kaiō jidan*, pp. 268–273, 293–296. For a full treatment of currency issues, see Peter Frost, *The Bakumatsu Currency Crisis* (Cambridge, Mass., 1970).

68. Fukuchi, *Kaiō jidan*, p. 273.

69. Yanagida, *Fukuchi Ōchi*, p. 62.

70. Fukuchi, *Kaiō jidan*, p. 277.

71. Ibid., p. 278.

72. Ibid., pp. 284–285.

73. See Alcock, *Capital of the Tycoon*, pp. 151–170, for a detailed, if rather biased, account of the attack.

74. This summer also saw his marriage to Kaneda Satoko, whom he apparently met at a brothel. Unfortunately, little information about her appears in any of Fukuchi's writings. See Yanagida, *Fukuchi Ōchi*, p. 65; see also Kawabe Shinzō, *Fukuchi Ōchi* (Tokyo, 1942), p. 327. Facts about Fukuchi's family also are scarce. Five boys were born to him (mostly by mistresses), but only Nobuyo, the fifth, lived beyond childhood. Fukuchi also adopted one of the daughters of his patron, Moriyama. See also Yanagida, *Fukuchi Ōchi*, pp. 12–13.

75. Fukuchi, *Shimbunshi jitsureki*, p. 325.

76. See Hanazono Kanesada, *Journalism in Japan and Its Early Pioneers* (Osaka, 1926), p. 24.

77. See Fukuchi's comments in *Kaiō jidan*, p. 287.

78. Ibid.

79. Nozaki Sukefumi, "Ōchi Koji jihitsu jiden," in *Watakushi no mita Meiji bundan* (Tokyo, 1927), p. 103, says he returned in the spring of 1863. This must be an error in memory. The embassy returned in December 1862, and no records show Fukuchi returning separately. See also *Kaiō jidan*, p. 293.

80. "Great Britain. London Protocol. June 6, 1862," *Contemporary Sources*, 1:49–51.

81. Yanagida, *Fukuchi Ōchi*, p. 72.

82. See Fukuchi, *Kaiō jidan*, pp. 273–274, for Fukuchi's role in that dispute during his first two years in the foreign office.

83. Ibid., p. 291.

84. Ibid., p. 293.

85. Ibid., pp. 273, 293.

86. Wataru Ichikawa, "A Confused Account of a Trip to Europe, Like a Fly on a Horse's Tail," trans. Henry Satow, in *Chinese and Japanese Repository of Facts and Events: Science, History and Art, Relating to Eastern Asia* (July 1865), p. 367.

87. Letter from Fukuchi to his father, July 14, 1862; Kawabe, *Fukuchi Ōchi*, p. 53. Unfortunately, Kōan had died on June 14, before the letter was sent.

88. For a vivid account of the embassy's consternation over British politics, see Fukuzawa, *Autobiography*, p. 134.
89. Kawabe, *Fukuchi Ōchi*, pp. 54–55.
90. Wataru, *Confused Account*, p. 374.
91. Fukuchi, *Shimbunshi jitsureki*, p. 325.
92. Fukuchi, *Kaiō jidan*, p. 293.
93. Ibid.
94. Hackett, *Yamagata Aritomo*, p. 21.
95. Yanagida, *Fukuchi Ōchi*, p. 81.
96. See Beasley, *Meiji Restoration*, pp. 189–190.
97. Fukuzawa, *Autobiography*, p. 143.
98. Fukuchi, *Kaiō jidan*, p. 310.
99. All three incidents are vividly recounted in ibid., pp. 310–311.
100. Ibid., pp. 293, 302–303.
101. Fukuchi's role in this episode was minor—and Mizuno saw to it that he was sent to Osaka "on official business" when it was clear that the expedition was about to abort; thus his name remained clear. The undertaking is described in *Kaiō jidan*, p. 301.
102. Ibid., p. 310.
103. Ibid., p. 303. He also wrote during this period a five-volume report on the mission for presentation to the *rōjū*. Once delivered to the proper officials, however, it "disappeared"—being either lost or destroyed due to its sensitive nature. Fukuchi described it as being "as incisive as Fukuzawa's *Seiyō jijō*." See *Kaiō jidan*, p. 292.
104. The entire trip is discussed in Fukuchi, *Kaiō jidan*, pp. 304–309.
105. Hanazono, *Early Pioneers*, p. 37. See also Tamura, *Fukuchi Ōchi*, pp. 24–25.
106. Fukuchi, *Shimbunshi jitsureki*, p. 326. Fukuchi's emphasis.
107. These conversations are discussed in Fukuchi, *Bakumatsu seijika*, p. 382, and in *Kaiō jidan*, pp. 294–296.
108. See Fukuchi, *Kaiō jidan*, pp. 298–299.

*Chapter Two: The Search for a Vocation*

1. Fukuchi, speaking to Ōkubo Toshimichi, in Fukuchi Gen'ichirō, "Ishin no genkun," *Taiyō* 1 (April 1895):34.
2. Fukuchi Gen'ichirō, *Kaiō jidan*, in *Fukuchi Ōchi shū*, ed. Yanagida Izumi, vol. 11 of *Meiji bungaku zenshū* (Tokyo, 1966), p. 314.
3. Ibid., p. 317. Fukuchi drew up three alternative strategies for Tokugawa resistance. By the first plan the shogun would stay in Osaka, placing a naval blockade around Osaka and Hyogo, erecting parapets along the road from Nishinomiya to Osaka and fortifying the Yodo River. By defending Osaka, he felt, the Tokugawa could in time defeat any opponents. A second plan called for the shogun to go to Edo, while Aizu and Kuwana troops defended Osaka castle, gradually extending control to a wider area. By his third plan, if Toku-

gawa troops decided to attack Kyoto, they were to use the Yamazaki route, by all means avoiding the direct routes through either Toba or Fushimi. He advocated, above all, caution and movement only from the Tokugawa's strongest positions. Yanagida, *Fukuchi Ōchi,* pp. 107–108, sees in this strategy the influence of Napoleon's military strategems—not an unlikely analysis, since Fukuchi was at this time finishing a translation of the memoirs of Napoleon I. See also Tamura Hisashi, *Fukuchi Ōchi,* in vol. 3 of *Sandai genronjin shū,* ed. Jiji Tsushinsha (Tokyo, 1962), pp. 28–29.

4. Fukuchi, *Kaiō jidan,* p. 321. The entire story of Fukuchi's month and a half at Osaka, described in detail in pp. 314–321, is fascinating, full of the poignant emotions that engulfed many Tokugawa retainers then.

5. Ibid., p. 321.

6. See Shimane Kiyoshi, *Tenkō, Meiji ishin to bakushin* (Tokyo, 1969), pp. 165–168.

7. Fukuchi Gen'ichirō, *Shimbunshi jitsureki,* in *Fukuchi Ōchi shū,* ed. Yanagida Izumi (Tokyo, 1966), p. 326. For a discussion of *why* Fukuchi remained loyal to the Tokugawa, see Yanagida Izumi, *Fukuchi Ōchi* (Tokyo, 1965), pp 100–101. Among other things, he cites emotional ties, hatred of Satsuma, and personal ambition.

8. Yanagida, *Fukuchi Ōchi,* p. 122.

9. Fukuchi Gen'ichirō, *Kōko Shimbun,* no. 1 (May 25, 1868), in Osatake Takeki, ed., *Bakumatsu Meiji shimbun zenshū* (Tokyo, 1934–1935), 4:3. This series contains the entire twenty-two issues of *Kōko Shimbun,* published from May 24 to July 9, 1868. Hereafter cited as *BMSZ.*

10. Ono Hideo, *Shimbun no rekishi* (Tokyo, 1961), p. 18. The best study of the development of this premodern form of journalism is Ono Hideo, *Kawaraban monogatari. Edo jidai masu komi no rekishi* (Tokyo, 1960).

11. From 1856 to 1861, this office was known as the Bansho Torishirabedokoro. After 1863, the name was again changed, this time to Kaiseijo. This office was the forerunner of Tokyo University.

12. Actually, the *Batabia Shimbun* was preceded by *The Japan Herald* in 1861 as Japan's "first newspaper." Western-language newspapers have not been included in this study, however, since they were published by foreigners for foreigners and exerted a marginal impact on the Japanese. An excellent list of Western newspapers is the unpublished manuscript of Robert M. Spaulding, Jr., "Bibliography of Western-language Dailies and Weeklies in Japan, 1861–1961" (University of Michigan). See also Endō Motō and Shimomura Fujio, *Kokushi bunken kaisetsu* (Tokyo, 1956), 2:429–444.

13. The *Shimbunshi*'s publisher, Kishida Ginkō, later became famous as a reporter on Fukuchi's own *Tokyo Nichi Nichi Shimbun.*

14. Harry Emerson Wildes, *The Press and Social Currents in Japan* (Chicago, 1927), p. 17.

15. Kawabe Kisaburō, *The Press and Politics in Japan* (Chicago, 1921), p. 43.

16. Hanazono Kanesada, *The Development of Japanese Journalism* (Osaka, 1924), pp. 11–12.

17. Nishida Taketoshi, *Meiji jidai no shimbun to zasshi* (Tokyo, 1966), pp. 16–17.

18. Albert Altman, "Shimbunshi: The Early Meiji Adaption of the Western-style Newspaper," in W. G. Beasley, ed., *Modern Japan: Aspects of History, Literature and Society* (California, 1975), p. 55. For a list of these papers, see Altman's "The Emergence of the Press in Meiji Japan" (Ph.D. diss., Princeton University, 1965), p. 58. See also Meiji Bunka Kenkyūkai, ed., *Shimbun hen*, in *Meiji bunka zenshū* (Tokyo, 1968), 4:605–606.

19. Altman, "Shimbunshi," pp. 55–57.

20. Scholars once attributed the papers' demise solely to government suppression. Altman argues effectively, however, that they would have died anyway with the defeat of the pro-Tokugawa troops whose cause they espoused. Most really were not so much newspapers as polemical sheets. See Altman, "Emergence," pp. 81–82. Altman also includes an insightful discussion of these early papers' social and political roles in "Shimbunshi," pp. 57–59.

21. Fukuchi, *Shimbunshi jitsureki*, p. 326. These men would remain closely tied to Fukuchi's journalistic efforts throughout the next decade.

22. *Kōko Shimbun*, no. 20 (July 7, 1868), *BMSZ*, p. 75.

23. Yanagida, *Fukuchi Ōchi*, pp. 114–115. See also Ono Hideo, " 'Moshiogusa' oyobi 'Kōko Shimbun' no kaisetsu," *BMSZ*, pp. 12–13.

24. *Kōko Shimbun*, no. 1 (May 24, 1868), *BMSZ*, p. 3.

25. Phonetic Japanese symbols appended to the side of Chinese characters to facilitate understanding. Overuse was considered unscholarly.

26. See Sugiura Tadashi, *Shimbun koto hajime* (Tokyo, 1971), p. 105.

27. Evaluation of Ono, "Kaisetsu," pp. 12–13.

28. "Satchō" is the term commonly used to refer to Satsuma and Chōshū, the two *han* whose men led in the Restoration and in consolidating the Meiji government.

29. Fukuchi, *Shimbunshi jitsureki*, p. 326.

30. See Yanagida, *Fukuchi Ōchi*, p. 117.

31. Figures based on a study by Sugiura, *Hajime*, p. 110.

32. *Kōko Shimbun*, no. 21 (July 9, 1868), *BMSZ*, pp. 76–77.

33. Ibid., no. 16 (June 24, 1868), *BMSZ*, pp. 61–64.

34. The agreement of scholars that Fukuchi wrote the "Kyōjaku ron" is unanimous. Fukuchi himself said he wrote everything in *Kōko Shimbun* (*Shimbunshi jitsureki*, p. 326). See also Midoro Shōichi, *Genron hen*, in *Meiji Taishō shi* (Tokyo, 1930), 1:7; Ono, "Kaisetsu," p. 12; Sugiura, *Hajime*, p. 112.

35. The "Genki-Tensho" period, generally said to have run from 1570 to 1586; *Kōko Shimbun*, no. 16 (June 24, 1868), *BMSZ*, p. 62.

36. The decisive battle of 1600 in which the Tokugawa established suprem-

acy over Japan. Fukuchi here seems to refer not so much to the Tokugawa victory as to the seriousness of the division.

37. Letter to Kitayama Ansei, quoted in Maruyama Masao, *Studies in the Intellectual History of Tokugawa Japan* (Tokyo, 1974), p. 311.

38. See, for example, Robert N. Bellah, *Tokugawa Religion* (Glencoe, Ill., 1957), pp. 188–192.

39. Fukuchi, *Shimbunshi jitsureki,* p. 326.

40. Yanagida, *Fukuchi Ōchi,* p. 118.

41. Ono, "Kaisetsu," p. 2.

42. See Sugiura, *Hajime,* pp. 106–110.

43. Ibid., pp. 113–114.

44. Mori Shina, "Meiji gannen Fukuchi Ōchi gokuchū bemmeisho," *Bungaku* (November 1968):1342.

45. Sugiura, *Hajime,* p. 115

46. Fukuchi, *Kaiō jidan,* p. 323.

47. Ibid.

48. Fukuchi himself recalled the arrest as coming on July 7; *Shimbunshi jitsureki,* p. 327. He apparently erred in memory, however. All records set the date at July 12. See Sugiura, *Hajime,* p. 117; Yanagida, *Fukuchi Ōchi,* p. 123; and others. The fact that issues of *Kōko Shimbun* appeared on July 9 and 11 also refutes Fukuchi's recollection.

49. Here again Fukuchi's memory appears mistaken. He claimed to have been taken to the *chinjōfu,* an impossibility since the new government office by that name was not established until August. According to documents uncovered recently in the Imperial Household Agency archives, his arraignment was at the Wadakura Mon *kyūmonjo.* See Mori, "Bemmeisho," p. 1341.

50. Fukuchi, *Shimbunshi jitsureki,* p. 327.

51. Ibid.

52. Tsukahara Jūshien, a reporter for Fukuchi several years later at *Tokyo Nichi Nichi Shimbun,* quoted by Sugiura, *Hajime,* p. 120.

53. Sugiura, *Hajime,* p. 121; Yanagida, *Fukuchi Ōchi,* p. 123. Many scholars credit Kido with the prime responsibility for Fukuchi's release—owing to the intimacy of Kido and Sugiura, and to Fukuchi's own, later friendship with the oligarch. There is little possibility, however, that Kido actually played a role. Throughout July, he was in Nagasaki, handling the "dispersion of 3,000 Christians" there, and he did not enter Edo once after the Restoration until August of that year. There is no mention of Fukuchi in Kido's diary during the period in question. See Kido Kōin, *Kido Kōin nikki,* 1 (Tokyo, 1932), May–June 1868. See also Thomas W. Burkman, "The Urakami Incident and the Struggle for Religious Toleration in Early Meiji Japan," *Japanese Journal of Religious Studies* 1, nos. 2–3 (June–September 1974): 184–185.

54. June 20, 1868. Here again, the facts differ somewhat from traditional

accounts. Fukuchi (*Shimbunshi jitsureki*, p. 327) said he was confined for "more than twenty days," a statement repeated by most scholars. Sugiura has, however, found Tokyo city records ("Tokyo shi shikō") from the period stating that on "July 20 the matter was settled and he returned home"; *Hajime*, p. 121. The records appear more reliable than Fukuchi's memory, which already has been found faulty on dates and statistics.

55. The full text of his "petition" and "defense" is reprinted in Mori, "Bemmeisho," pp. 1341–1344. It also is evaluated, from a psychological standpoint, in Shimane, *Tenkō*, pp. 132–139. Shimane finds the "servile" tone of Fukuchi's confessions a "blot" on his character and the first step in his conversion to the Meiji regime.

56. Mori, "Bemmeisho," p. 1343.

57. Ibid., p. 1342; Sugiura, *Hajime*, pp. 122–123.

58. W. W. McLaren, ed. and trans., "Japanese Government Documents," *Transactions of the Asiatic Society of Japan* 62, pt. 1 (Tokyo, 1914):530. Earlier laws regulating publication had been issued in the spring and summer of 1868. They were, however, more like "policy statements," not fully developed press codes. See Peter Figdor, "Newspapers and Their Regulation in Early Meiji Japan, 1868–1883," *Papers on Japan* (Harvard University, 1972), 6:3–6. See also Altman, "Shimbunshi," pp. 59–60.

59. *Moshiogusa* and *Naigai Shimbun*; Ono, *Shimbun no rekishi*, p. 23.

60. Fukuchi, *Shimbunshi jitsureki*, p. 327.

61. Kido, *Nikki* 1 (August 17, 1868):64; quoted in Sidney D. Brown, "Kido Takayoshi and the Meiji Restoration: A Political Biography, 1833–1877" (Ph.D. diss., University of Wisconsin, 1952), p. 126.

62. Kenneth Pyle, *The New Generation in Meiji Japan: Problems of Cultural Identity 1888–1895* (Stanford, 1969), p. 3.

63. Fukuchi, *Kaiō jidan*, p. 324; Yanagida, *Fukuchi Ōchi*, p. 125. The nature of the government summons has not been recorded, though it seems likely that it came from the foreign affairs bureau.

64. Letter from Fukuchi to his wife early in November 1868, quoted in Yanagida, *Fukuchi Ōchi*, p. 126.

65. Fukuchi, *Kaiō jidan*, p. 324. Edo's name was changed to Tokyo on September 3, 1868.

66. Yanagida, *Fukuchi Ōchi*, p. 129.

67. See, for example, H. D. Harootunian, *Toward Restoration, the Growth of Political Consciousness in Tokugawa Japan* (Berkeley, 1970), pp. 403–410; W. G. Beasley, *The Meiji Restoration* (Stanford, 1972), pp. 423–424.

68. The titles, however, were not preserved for posterity; Yanagida, *Fukuchi Ōchi*, pp. 128–130. His translations included *Gaikoku kōsai kōhō* ("The law of nations"), adapted apparently from an English translation of

Georg Friedrich von Marten's *Compendium of the Law of Nations*. See Kawabe Shinzō, *Fukuchi Ōchi* (Tokyo, 1942), p. 89; see also Yanagida, *Fukuchi Ōchi*, p. 131.

69. See Kawabe, *Fukuchi Ōchi*, p. 88; Yanagida, *Fukuchi Ōchi*, p. 134. One of the school's students was Nakae Chōmin.

70. Fukuchi Gen'ichirō, *Kaisha ben*, in Meiji Bunka Kenkyūkai, ed., *Keizai hen*, vol. 12 of *Meiji bunka zenshū* (Tokyo, 1968), pp. 93–110. The work, a translation and abridgment of books by J. S. Mill and Francis Wayland, both of them entitled *Elements of Political Economy*, explained the role of "exchange" in an economy; the functions, operation, and regulation of a banking system. It has been called a "pioneer work." Fukuchi himself indicated that *kaisha* should be translated "bank," p. 96.

71. Fukuchi, "Ishin no genkun," p. 31.

72. See Shimane, *Tenkō*, pp. 141–142, 159–176.

73. Translation in Ryusaku Tsunoda, William Theodore de Bary, and Donald Keene, eds., *Sources of Japanese Tradition* (New York, 1964), 2:136–137.

74. Brown, "Kido Takayoshi," p. 120.

75. From an analysis of statistics compiled by Kee Il Choi, "Shibusawa Eiichi and His Contemporaries" (Ph.D. diss., Harvard University, 1958), pp. 43–49.

76. Fukuchi, *Kaiō jidan*, p. 304.

77. *Hoshi beikoku nikki*. The original manuscript has been lost, but major portions are, fortunately, included in Kawabe, *Fukuchi Ōchi*, pp. 92–109.

78. Letter, Itō Hirobumi to Hamilton Fish, March 31, 1871, U.S. Department of State, *General Records*, "Notes from the Japanese Legation to the Department of State," vol. 1, 1858–1875.

79. Kawabe, *Fukuchi Ōchi*, pp. 101–102.

80. Ibid., p. 96.

81. Yanagida, *Fukuchi Ōchi*, pp. 141–142.

82. Fukuchi, "Ishin no genkun," p. 32.

83. See Choi, "Shibusawa Eiichi," pp. 224–227.

84. Itō became official head of the Kōbushō on November 2, 1871.

85. Choi, "Shibusawa Eiichi," p. 226.

86. Yanagida, *Fukuchi Ōchi*, p. 142.

87. Fukuchi, "Ishin no genkun," p. 32, describes infighting between Inoue Kaoru, Saigō Takamori, and Kido over whether Fukuchi should be sent along.

88. Marlene Mayo, "The Iwakura Mission to the United States and Europe, 1871–1873," *Researches in the Social Sciences on Japan* (Columbia University: East Asian Institute Studies No. 6 [June 1959]), 2:28.

89. Chitoshi Yanaga, *Japan since Perry* (New York, 1949), p. 179.

90. Translation adapted from Charles Lanman, *Leaders of the Meiji Restoration in America* (Tokyo, 1939), pp. ix–x. See, for an account of the meeting at which Fukuchi made these remarks, *Yomiuri Shimbun,* March 22, 1902, in Nakayama Yasuaki, *Shimbun shūsei Meiji hennenshi* (Tokyo, 1934–1936), 11:191–192. A useful analysis of the mission's official journal is Eugene Soviak, "On the Nature of Western Progress: The Journal of the Iwakura Embassy," in *Tradition and Modernization in Japanese Culture,* ed. Donald Shively (Princeton, 1971), pp. 7–34.

91. Cited by Shimane, *Tenkō,* p. 169; Fukuchi, "Ishin no genkun," p. 31.

92. Fukuchi, "Ishin no genkun," p. 34.

93. Hanazono Kanesada, *Journalism in Japan and Its Early Pioneers* (Osaka, 1926), p. 26. Hanazono says that Fukuchi was the first Japanese to visit the Holy Land.

94. Fukuchi Gen'ichirō, "Gaikoku tachiai saiban hōkoku" (unpublished manuscript in Naikaku Bunko, no. 271–22–19653 [July 1873]).

95. The salient features of the system were also outlined in a *Tokyo Nichi Nichi Shimbun* editorial, February 7, 1876, and reprinted in *Japan Weekly Mail,* February 12, 1876, p. 1478. For a history of the Egyptian system, see John Marlowe, *A History of Modern Egypt* (Hamden, Conn., 1965), pp. 85–90.

96. See Inō Tentarō, *Nihon gaibun shisō shi ronkō* (Tokyo, 1966), 1: 233–234, for a discussion of Fukuchi's report on the "mixed courts."

97. Choi, "Shibusawa Eiichi," pp. 235–236.

98. Fukuchi, "Ishin no genkun," p. 35.

99. Fukuchi, *Shimbunshi jitsureki,* p. 327.

100. Nishida, *Shimbun to zasshi,* p. 48. The Hōritsu Kogikai was later reorganized as the Ōmeisha, a political organization that early in the 1880s aligned with the Kaishintō (Progressive Party) of Ōkuma Shigenobu.

101. Fukuchi, "Ishin no genkun," p. 32.

102. For a detailed, colorful, progovernment account of this expedition, see Edward H. House, *The Japanese Expedition to Formosa* (Tokyo, 1875).

103. Fukuchi, *Shimbunshi jitsureki,* p. 328.

104. See Tamura, *Fukuchi Ōchi,* p. 27.

105. *Kōko Shimbun,* no. 16 (June 24, 1868), *BMSZ,* p. 64.

106. Fukuchi Gen'ichirō, *Bakumatsu seijika,* in *Bakumatsu ishin shiryō sōsho* (Tokyo, 1968), 8:382.

107. The defense *(engi)* of Fukuchi's political party, the Rikken Teiseitō, in 1882, quoted in Yanagida, *Fukuchi Ōchi,* p. 246.

### Chapter Three: Years of Power at Nichi Nichi

1. Fukuchi Gen'ichirō, *Shimbunshi jitsureki,* in *Fukuchi Ōchi shū,* ed. Yanagida Izumi, vol. 11 of *Meiji bungaku zenshū* (Tokyo, 1966), p. 341.

2. Yanagida Izumi, "Fukuchi Ōchi," in *Fukuchi Ōchi shū,* p. 409.

3. Miyake Setsurei, *Dōjidaishi* (Tokyo, 1954), 3:484.

4. Miyake Setsurei, "Ijin no ato," quoted by Yanagida Izumi, *Fukuchi Ōchi* (Tokyo, 1965), p. 341.

5. Zushikawa Chōko, "Ōchi Koji no tsuioku," *Denki* 2 (February 1935):23.

6. Ozawa Ryōzō, "Fukuchi no shōgai," in *Onnagata konseki dan* (Tokyo, 1941), p. 50. The writings of the psychiatrist L. Takeo Doi on *amaeru*, the dependency on another's love or indulgence, also seem pertinent to Fukuchi. His loyalty had an idealistic, Confucian tinge, but strictly emotional aspects also were present. See Doi, "Amae: A Key Concept for Understanding Personality Structure," in R. J. Smith and R. K. Beardsley, eds., *Japanese Culture: Its Development and Characteristics* (Chicago, 1962); reprinted in T. S. Lebra and W. P. Lebra, eds., *Japanese Culture and Behavior* (Honolulu, 1974), pp. 145-154.

7. Kawabe Shinzō, quoting Tsukahara Jūshien, in *Fukuchi Ōchi* (Tokyo, 1942), p. 331.

8. Yanagida, "Fukuchi Ōchi," p. 416.

9. Zushikawa, "Tsuioku," p. 19.

10. Ibid., p. 23.

11. Fukuchi, *Shimbunshi jitsureki*, p. 328. See also Nishida Taketoshi, *Meiji jidai no shimbun to zasshi* (Tokyo, 1956), p. 44.

12. The *Shimbunshi*, founded in 1864, has been called Japan's first daily newspaper. It only lived two months, however; most historians cite *Yokohama Mainichi* as the first true daily paper.

13. Fukuchi, *Shimbunshi jitsureki*, p. 328.

14. John R. Black, *Young Japan* (London, 1881), 2:371.

15. Albert A. Altman, "Shimbunshi: The Early Meiji Adaptation of the Western-style Newspaper," in W. G. Beasley, ed., *Modern Japan: Aspects of History, Literature and Society* (California, 1975), p. 61, contains a chart showing the geographical diffusion of the early Meiji press by year.

16. Ibid. A helpful account of government aid to the press during these years is Peter Figdor, "Newspapers and Their Regulation in Early Meiji Japan, 1868-1883," *Papers on Japan* (Cambridge, Mass., 1972), 6:8-9.

17. Principal authors of the memorial were Itagaki Taisuke and Gotō Shōjiro. The full text is translated in W. W. McLaren, ed., "Japanese Government Documents," *Transactions of the Asiatic Society of Japan* 42, pt. 1 (1914), pp. 426-432.

18. Nishida, *Shimbun to zasshi*, p. 28.

19. See Nihon Shimbun Remmei, ed., *Nihon shimbun hyakunen shi* (Tokyo, 1962), p. 825. See also Tamura Hisashi, *Fukuchi Ōchi*, in vol. 3 of *Sandai genronjin shū*, ed. Jiji Tsūshinsha (Tokyo, 1962), p. 46.

20. All of the initial editors had helped Fukuchi at *Kōko Shimbun;* most prominent was the writer, Jōno Dempei.

21. See Itō Seitoku, "Sosei kara Meiji ki," in Nihon Shimbun Remmei, *Hyakunen shi*, p. 219.

22. See Fukuchi, *Shimbunshi jitsureki*, p. 328. Fukuchi later claimed to have entered the company as *shusai*, or chairman (*Tokyo Nichi Nichi Shimbun*, January 17, 1879). *Shuhitsu* is the title most often assumed correct, however.

23. Records on the actual date of Fukuchi's assumption of the *Nichi Nichi* editorship are nonexistent. Scholars have traditionally held that he took over on December 2, 1874, the date on which the paper made major format changes. It appears, however, that he took control somewhat earlier. It would have taken time to have planned the editorial changes, making it unlikely that he would have entered on the day of their execution. Moreover, the editorial of December 3 is the sixth in a series on his specialty, foreign relations, which commenced on October 4. And the secural of *Nichi Nichi*'s right to publish Dajōkan materials came on October 27 (*Nichi Nichi*, October 27, 1874). Fukuchi said he began writing for *Nichi Nichi* "from time to time" until "before long it became, as it were, a public secret" (*Nichi Nichi*, no. 8000, quoted in Sugiura, *Hajime*, p. 270). The fact that the last of his "contributed articles" *(tōsho)* at *Hōchi* ran on October 28, 1874, also coincides with the late October date for his assumption of duties at *Nichi Nichi*.

24. *Tōnichi nanajūnen shi* (Tokyo: Tokyo Nichi Nichi Shimbunsha, 1942), p. 25.

25. Fukuchi, *Shimbunshi jitsureki*, p. 328.

26. Sugiura, *Hajime*, p. 278; Fukuchi, *Shimbunshi jitsureki*, p. 334; Kawabe, *Fukuchi Ōchi*, p. 156.

27. Nihon Shimbun Kyōkai, *Nihon shimbun shi chihō betsu* (Tokyo, 1956), p. 175. See also narrative by Inukai Tsuyoshi in *Daigaku Hyōron* (August 1917), quoted by Kawabe Kisaburo, *The Press and Politics in Japan* (Chicago, 1921), p. 86.

28. Nishida, *Shimbun to zasshi*, pp. 44–45; Yanagida, "Fukuchi Ōchi," p. 411.

29. Sugiura, *Hajime*, p. 272.

30. Translated by Ryusaku Tsunoda, William Theodore deBary, and Donald Keene, *Sources of Japanese Tradition*, paperback (New York, 1958), 2:145.

31. Nishida Taketoshi, "Ōchi no shimbun kiji ni tsuite," in Yanagida, *Fukuchi Ōchi shū*, p. 456.

32. *Nichi Nichi*, July 28, 1875.

33. Fukuchi, *Shimbunshi jitsureki*, p. 334.

34. Ibid., pp. 331–334.

35. Ibid., p. 334.

36. See Yanagida, "Fukuchi Ōchi," p. 413.

37. The price was doubled to three sen per issue; Nihon Shimbun Kyōkai, *Shimbun shi chihō betsu*, p. 118.

38. See evaluation of Kawabe, *Fukuchi Ōchi*, p. 5; Tokutomi Sohō, in Kubota Tatsuhiko, ed., *Nijūichi daisenkaku kisha den* (Osaka, 1930), p. 66. *Chōya Shimbun* began such a column slightly earlier, but not as a *daily* column adhering to a consistent point of view.

39. Yone Noguchi, "Journalism in Japan," *The Bookman* 19 (April 1904):50.

40. *Nichi Nichi*, February 12, 1875.

41. Statistics are based on a list of *Nichi Nichi* editorials from 1874 to 1887, compiled by the author on the basis of several other compilations: Nishida Taketoshi, "Meiji shoki shimbun ronsetsu sakuin," *Meiji Bunka Kenkyū*, no. 3, pp. 182–190; no. 5, pp. 250–260; no. 6, pp. 180–189 (October 1934–November 1935), for editorials from 1874 to 1877; Nishida, "*Tokyo Nichi Nichi Shimbun* shasetsu sakuin" (unpublished manuscript from Nishida's personal collection), for editorials from 1878 to 1882; Nishida, "*Tokyo Nichi Nichi Shimbun* shasetsu mokuroku" (mimeographed), for 1883–1887. Also, Showa Joshi Daigaku Kindai Bungaku Kenkyūshitsu, "Fukuchi Ōchi," in *Kindai bungaku kenkyū sōsho* (Tokyo, 1958), 8:274–326.

42. Japan's newspapers then were generally called either *daishimbun* or *shōshimbun* (minor papers), depending on their content. The *daishimbun* focused on political opinion and eschewed fiction, scandal, crime news, and the like. The *shōshimbun*, which ran more salacious stories and took more extreme positions, often had larger circulations. Scholars of the press differ on the pronunciation of the characters, with some rendering them *ōshimbun*, others *daishimbun*. I have opted for the latter on the basis of Nishida Taketoshi's support for that pronunciation. See Nishida, *Shimbun to zasshi*, p. 289. See glossary.

43. At first, Fukuchi also used such other terms as *Ga* and *Wagasō* to refer to himself, but in time Gosō became standard.

44. Tsukahara Jūshien, quoted by Kawabe, *Fukuchi Ōchi*, p. 6.

45. Fukuchi Gen'ichirō, "Bunsho no hiketsu," *Seinen Bungaku* 4 (July 1891), in Yanagida, *Fukuchi Ōchi*, p. 334.

46. Debate with Narushima Ryūhoku of *Chōya Shimbun* in summer of 1875, quoted by Tamura, *Fukuchi Ōchi*, p. 75.

47. *Nichi Nichi*, March 17, 1880.

48. *Yubin Hōchi Shimbun*, *Nichi Nichi*'s chief competitor, began running daily editorials on March 16, 1875. Others, like *Chōya* and *Akebono*, began about the same time.

49. Shimada Saburō, *Taikan* (October 1918), p. 202, quoted by Kawabe Kisaburo, *Press and Politics*, p. 82.

50. *Nichi Nichi*, December 2, 1874.

51. Fukuchi Gen'ichirō, *Shimbunshi jitsureki*, p. 331.

52. See, for example, "Nippōsha ni okeru gosō sensei," *Nichi Nichi*, January 5, 1906.

53. Kawabe, *Fukuchi Ōchi*, pp. 324–326.

54. *Yūbin Hōchi* ran the story on November 24 in its correspondence column, claiming without factual foundation that Mitsui, Ono's partner in Dai-ichi and a financial power with close ties to the Ōkurasho, had also folded. *Nisshin Shinjishi* failed to mention the bankruptcy until November 27, and then treated it only in briefest detail.

55. "Dajōkan kiji inkō goyō." This was first run on October 27, 1874, and appeared daily thereafter.

56. *Nichi Nichi,* December 2, 1874.

57. Itō, "Sōsei kara Meiji ki," p. 236.

58. Fukuchi, *Shimbunshi jitsureki,* p. 330.

59. Ibid., p. 335.

60. *Nichi Nichi,* December 27, 1874.

61. He severely criticized the "self-serving" Religion Ministry (Kyōbusho) on May 24, 1875.

62. Nishida, *Shimbun to zasshi,* p. 92. In the same year, *Chōya Shimbun* and *Hōchi,* Fukuchi's antigovernment competitors, each had five men jailed.

63. See *Nichi Nichi,* December 27, 1874. It should be noted that the government had stopped purchasing all papers except *Nichi Nichi* during November 1874. In May 1875 it stopped the purchase of newspapers altogether. See Okudaira Yasuhiro, "Nihon shuppan keisatsu hōsei no rekishiteki kenkyū josetsu," *Hōritsu jihō,* vol. 34, no. 7, p. 41.

64. Sugiura, *Hajime,* p. 274.

65. Fukuchi's friendship with Yamagata is less often cited but seems to have been as intimate. In early 1874, for example, they both belonged to the Yūhōsha (Like-minded Club), which met often to discuss religion, the arts, and so on, and which opposed the Taiwan expedition. See Kawabe, *Fukuchi Ōchi,* p. 193; see also Roger Hackett, *Yamagata Aritomo in the Rise of Modern Japan, 1838-1922* (Cambridge, Mass., 1971), p. 74. The two worked together during the Satsuma Rebellion and on drafting the "Imperial precepts to soldiers and sailors" in 1882.

66. Fukuchi, *Shimbunshi jitsureki,* p. 335.

67. Fukuchi, "Ishin no genkun," *Taiyō* 2, no. 4 (April 1895):36.

68. Fukuchi, *Shimbunshi jitsureki,* p. 329.

69. It should be made clear that these were not the first Meiji discussions of assembly or constitutional government. As George Akita points out, such discussions went back to the beginning of the period. The Saigō crisis merely served to push such matters to the front of public debate. See George Akita, *Foundations of Constitutional Government in Modern Japan, 1868-1900* (Cambridge, Mass., 1967), pp. 6–14. See also Ike Nobutaka, *The Beginnings of Political Democracy in Japan* (Baltimore, 1950), pp. 60–77; Robert Scalapino, *Democracy and the Party Movement in Prewar Japan* (Berkeley, 1953); Ōtsu Jun'ichirō, *Dai Nihon kensei shi* (Tokyo, 1927–1928), 1:783–842.

70. For a helpful summary of the positions taken, see William R. Braisted, trans., *Meiroku Zasshi: Journal of Japanese Enlightenment* (Tokyo, 1976), pp. xxxiii–xl. See also Joseph Pittau, *Political Thought in Early Meiji Japan, 1868–1889* (Cambridge, Mass., 1967), pp. 37–71; Kosaka Masaaki, *Japanese Thought in the Meiji Era*, trans. David Abosch (Tokyo, 1958), pp. 137–146.

71. Quoted by Sugiura, *Hajime*, p. 281.

72. Ono Hideo, *Shimbun no rekishi* (Tokyo, 1961), p. 31, quoting Narushima Ryūhoku of *Chōya Shimbun*.

73. *Hyōron Shimbun* in March 1875, quoted by Ono, *Shimbun no rekishi*, p. 27; see also *Sōmō Zasshi*, June 1, 1876.

74. *Hōchi Shimbun*, January 29, 1875; Sugiura, *Hajime*, p. 282.

75. *Yūbin Hōchi*, April 4, 1875; Sugiura, *Hajime*, p. 286.

76. *Nichi Nichi*, December 6, 1874.

77. Fukuchi, *Shimbunshi jitsureki*, p. 329.

78. *Nichi Nichi*, November 19, 1874; see similar arguments in editorials of December 5, 1874, and December 28, 1875.

79. *Nichi Nichi*, December 5, 1874.

80. Ibid., April 14, 1875.

81. Ibid., December 28, 1875.

82. Maruyama Masao, "Meiji kokka no shisō," in *Nihon shakai no shiteki kyūmei*, comp. Rekishigaku Kenkyūkai (Tokyo, 1949), p. 200; trans. Akita, *Constitutional Government*, p. 23.

83. *Nichi Nichi*, March 12, 1875.

84. Ibid., March 23, 1875.

85. *Hōchi*, March 24, 1875.

86. *Nichi Nichi*, March 25, 1875.

87. Ibid., March 27, 1875.

88. The April 14 decree grew from the Osaka Conference in which Kido and Itagaki agreed to return to the government in return for promises of more participatory government. Translation by Scalapino, *Democracy and the Party Movement*, p. 60. For a perceptive, interpretive discussion of the conference, see Akita, *Constitutional Government*, pp. 21–24.

89. See *Yūbin Hōchi*, April 16, 1875.

90. *Nichi Nichi*, April 14, 1875.

91. Nozaku Sukefumi, "Ōchi Koji jihitsu jiden," in *Watakushi no mita Meiji bundan* (Tokyo, 1906), p. 112.

92. See, for example, Tamura, *Fukuchi Ōchi*, p. 113; Itō, "Sosei kara Meiji ki," p. 226.

93. See Maruyama Masao, *Studies in the Intellectual History of Tokugawa Japan* (Tokyo, 1974), p. 354.

94. Ibid., pp. 309–310.

95. Earl Kinmonth, "Fukuzawa Reconsidered: *Gakumon no susume* and Its Audience," *Journal of Asian Studies* 37, no. 4 (August 1978):696. Kin-

month argues, on the basis of a careful analysis of *Gakumon no susume,* that Fukuzawa has been misinterpreted by modern scholars due to "a preconception derived in part from an uncritical acceptance of the role and importance Fukuzawa ascribed to himself, and in part from the desire of scholars to find a figure such as Fukuzawa alleged himself to have been" (p. 695).

96. *Nichi Nichi,* April 14, 1875.

97. Kido wrote a friend during the conference: "I feel as if I have fallen into hell. . . . But I am holding on for the sake of the people." Quoted in Albert Craig and Donald Shively, eds., *Personality in Japanese History* (Berkeley, 1970), p. 293.

98. Yanagida, *Fukuchi Ōchi,* pp. 166–167.

99. Kawabe, *Fukuchi Ōchi,* p. 194.

100. Sugiura, *Hajime,* p. 276.

101. Evaluation of Sidney Brown, "Kido Takayoshi and the Meiji Restoration" (Ph.D. diss., University of Wisconsin, 1952), p. 346. See also Walter McLaren, *A Political History of Japan during the Meiji Era, 1867-1912* (New York, 1965), pp. 134–135. For the conference's constitution, see McLaren, "Documents," pp. 502–512. See also Ōtsu, *Kensei shi,* pp. 863–865.

102. Cited by Brown, "Kido Takayoshi," p. 349.

103. *Nichi Nichi,* June 25, 1875. *Nichi Nichi* also ran evaluations of the conference on July 7, 9, 10, 14, 15, 1875.

104. Ibid., June 22, 1875, cited in McLaren, "Documents," p. lxxvii. See also Sugiura, *Hajime,* p. 176.

105. Fukuchi served as secretary of this conference too, this time under Itō. *Nichi Nichi* editorials evidencing impatience over government postponement of the conference appeared on July 10, 1876; August 31, 1877; and March 7, 1878. See also Fukuchi, *Shimbunshi jitsureki,* p. 331.

106. The law is translated in McLaren, "Documents," pp. 539–543, and discussed in Figdor, "Newspapers and Their Regulation," pp. 15–16.

107. Sugiura, *Hajime,* p. 289. See also Braisted, *Meiroku Zasshi,* pp. xli–xlii.

108. Ono, *Shimbun no rekishi,* p. 28. A helpful account of the reaction of other papers to the press laws is found in Shimane Kiyoshi, *Tenkō: Meiji ishin to bakushin* (Tokyo, 1969), pp. 150–151.

109. Ono, *Shimbun no rekishi,* p. 28.

110. Quoted by Sugiura, *Hajime,* p. 291. The manuscript of this article is preserved in the Mainichi Shimbunsha archives. It fits Fukuchi's prose style and philosophy and, according to Sugiura, appears to have been written in his brush style.

111. Ibid., p. 292.

112. See Nishida, *Shimbun to zasshi,* p. 92; Midoro, *Meiji Taishō shi* 1:59–60; see also Harry Emerson Wildes, "Press Freedom in Japan," *American Journal of Sociology* 32 (January 1927):605.

113. Fukuchi, *Shimbunshi jitsureki*, pp. 331–332.
114. For a translation of a number of these drafts, see George M. Beck-mann, *The Making of the Meiji Constitution: The Oligarchs and the Constitutional Development of Japan, 1868–1891* (Lawrence, Kans., 1957), pp. 120–125. See also Akita, *Constitutional Government*, pp. 15–30.
115. *Nichi Nichi*, January 17, 1879; for other editorials on the constitutional issue, see September 12, 28, October 9, 10, 1876; September 3, 1877; February 5, March 12–30, 1879.
116. Ibid., January 22, 1879. Emphasis mine.
117. See, for example, ibid., January 18, May 11, 1878; December 2–5, 1879.
118. See series in ibid., June 26–July 11, 1880; evaluation of Yanagida, *Fukuchi Ōchi*, p. 190.
119. *Nichi Nichi*, July 3, 1878.
120. Ibid., March 27, 30, 1880.
121. Ibid., March 12, 1879; a favorite expression of Fukuchi in these years was *ōdō*, the "way of righteous rule." The articles on *ōdō* firmly placed the locus of this way in the imperial institution.
122. Ibid., January 13, 1880.
123. Ibid., May 12, 1880. *Nichi Nichi*'s first call for such a convention had come on March 17, 1880.
124. Ibid., May 12, 1880. See also editorials of May 6, 12, June 11, 18, August 10, 11, October 1, 9, December 9, 10, 1880.
125. Ibid., March 17, 1880.
126. Ibid., March 27, 1880.
127. Ibid., May 12, 1880.
128. Ibid., April 4, 1881.
129. Ibid., March 30–31, April 1–16, 1881. They have been reprinted in *Seishi hen,* no. 2, vol. 10 of *Meiji bunka zenshū,* ed. Meiji Bunka Kenkyūkai (Tokyo, 1968), pp. 377–405. They are excerpted in Inada Masatsugu, *Meiji kempō seiritsu shi* (Tokyo, 1962), 1:375–382; and Kawabe, *Fukuchi Ōchi,* pp. 237–244.
130. Meiji Bunka Kenkyūkai, ed., *Seishi hen,* no. 2, pp. 382–384.
131. Ibid., pp. 384–386.
132. See Inada, *Kempō seiritsu shi,* 1:377.
133. See McLaren, "Documents," pp. 170–211, especially pp. 171-1/2; see also Meiji Bunka Kenkyūkai, ed., *Seishi hen,* no. 2, pp. 390–396.
134. See Pittau, *Political Thought,* pp. 100–101. The paper, formerly the *Yokohama Mainichi,* was renamed on November 18, 1879.
135. Inada, *Kempō seiritsu shi,* 1:380. It is worth noting that Fukuchi's efforts to inculcate imperial sovereignty and popular rights in a single system based on the unique nature of Japan's imperial institution have a ring highly similar to that of the "liberal" Yoshino Sakuzō during the Taisho era. See

Yoshino's *Mimpon shugi ron,* translated in Ryusaku Tsunoda, William deBary, and Donald Keene, eds., *Sources of Japanese Tradition* (New York, 1958), 2:218–238.

136. *Nichi Nichi,* March 17, 1880.

137. Ibid. The same statement was made in *Nichi Nichi* on September 30, 1881.

138. *Chōya Shimbun,* June 24, 1876, in Nihon Shimbun Remmei, *Hyakunenshi,* p. 793.

139. Narushima Ryūkoku, *Chōya Shimbun,* January 1877; quoted by Kawabe, *Fukuchi Ōchi,* p. 155.

140. This would have equaled more than 2 million dollars in 1980. Income figures are based on lists compiled by Itō Myoji, proprietor of *Nichi Nichi* from 1891 to 1904; Kawabe, *Fukuchi Ōchi,* p. 275. The comparison with current value relates to the fact that *Nichi Nichi*'s foremost reporter received 1,200 yen a year at this time, an amount safely assumed to have been worth at least a $24,000 salary today. Jōno, for example, received just 600 yen a year; Fukuchi, 3,000. See Hanazono, *Pioneers,* p. 28.

141. Kawabe, *Fukuchi Ōchi,* pp. 155–156; Nihon Shimbun Remmei, *Hyakunenshi,* p. 826.

142. The cartoon is reproduced in the unnumbered foreword pages of Sugiura, *Hajime.*

143. Sugiura, *Hajime,* p. 297.

144. Nishida, *Shimbun to zasshi,* p. 50.

145. One *ri* equals 2.44 miles.

146. *Nichi Nichi,* March 23, 1877. On the fighting here, see Augustus H. Mounsey, *The Satsuma Rebellion, an Episode of Modern Japanese History* (London, 1879), pp. 154–167.

147. Fukuchi in a private letter home, quoted by Kawabe, *Fukuchi Ōchi,* p. 183.

148. Itō, "Sosei kara Meiji ki," p. 242. *Hōchi*'s reporter was Inukai Tsuyoshi, a persistent young writer who would one day become prime minister.

149. Nishida, *Shimbun to zasshi,* p. 45.

150. Quoted by Hanazono, *Pioneers,* p. 28.

151. *Nichi Nichi,* April 12, 1877; Yanagida, *Fukuchi Ōchi shū,* p. 352.

152. Asahina Chisen, "Kisha no omoide," quoted by Kawabe, *Fukuchi Ōchi,* pp. 183–184. Asahina, one of Fukuchi's successors at *Nichi Nichi,* claimed that Yamagata told him "in direct conversation" that Fukuchi wrote the letter. The fact that the letter was sent on April 23 corroborates Asahina's assertion, since it coincides with Fukuchi's return to Kyushu after the imperial audience on April 6.

153. Translated by Hackett, *Yamagata Aritomo,* p. 80, from Tokutomi Iichirō, *Kōshaku Yamagata Aritomo den* (Tokyo, 1933), 2:741–742. See also *Nichi Nichi,* October 23, 1877.

154. Tsukahara Jūshien, "Nakae Chōmin," *Taiyō* 18, no. 9 (June 15, 1912), quoted in Showa Joshi Daigaku, "Fukuchi Ōchi," p. 346.
155. Tamura, *Fukuchi Ōchi*, p. 15.
156. Sugiura, *Hajime*, p. 277.
157. See Table 1, p. 89. List adapted from compilations of editorial titles and topics by Nishida Taketoshi, "Meiji shoki shimbun ronsetsu sakuin," *Meiji Bunka Kenkyū*, no. 5, pp. 251–260, no. 6, pp. 180–189; Nishida, "*Tokyo Nichi Nichi Shimbun* shasetsu sakuin," pp. 1–88, 1–39; Showa Joshi Daigaku, "Fukuchi Ōchi," pp. 175–188.
158. *Nichi Nichi*, January 24, 1876.
159. Ibid., March 3, 1876.
160. Ibid., January 24, February 16, March 3, 6, 7, 9, 12, 1876. See Hilary Conroy, *The Japanese Seizure of Korea: 1868–1910* (Philadelphia, 1960), pp. 61–69, for a discussion of these events.
161. See *Nichi Nichi*, October 24, December 9, 10, 1879, for example.
162. Ibid., February 5, 6, 7, 1876; reprinted in *Japan Weekly Mail*, February 12, 1876, pp. 146–148. He later came to oppose mixed courts as ineffective aids to the elimination of extraterritoriality.
163. *Nichi Nichi*, November 26–30, 1877; see also *Tokio Times*, December 15, 1877, for reference to the *Nichi Nichi* series. See, in addition, Payson J. Treat, *Diplomatic Relations between the United States and Japan, 1853–1895* (Stanford, 1932), 2:33.
164. *Nichi Nichi*, August 7, 1878.
165. Cf. evaluation of Tamura, *Fukuchi Ōchi*, p. 93.
166. Yanaga Chitoshi, *Japan since Perry* (New York, 1949), pp. 140–141.
167. William Lockwood, *The Economic Development of Japan: Growth and Structural Change, 1868–1938* (Princeton, 1954), pp. 15–16.
168. Quoted by Kubota Tatsuhiko, ed., *Nijūichi daisenkaku kisha den* (Osaka, 1930), p. 66.
169. See, for example, *Hōchi*, September 26–October 12, 1876; Tamura, *Fukuchi Ōchi*, p. 99.
170. *Nichi Nichi*, August 9, 1876. See also a series of *Nichi Nichi* editorials on the rice exchange, October 19–24, 1876.
171. Ibid., March 4, 1875. See also *Nichi Nichi*, November 1, 1877; July 5, 11, 13, 15, 18, 20, August 19, 1878.
172. Fukuchi, quoted by Kada Tetsuji, *Shakai shi* (Tokyo, 1940), pp. 147–148.
173. *Nichi Nichi*, August 10, 1876; November 1, 1877; September 18, 1880; April 18, 1881.
174. Ibid., July 18, 1877.
175. Ibid., June 26–July 11, 1880; these are reprinted in Watanabe Shujirō, ed., "Kokusai shihei shimatsu ni tsuite" (Tokyo, 1880).
176. Watanabe, "Kokusai shihei," p. 96.

177. Ibid., p. 70.
178. Ibid., p. 71. My italics.
179. Tamura, *Fukuchi Ōchi,* pp. 13, 75. For a brief, sympathetic description in English of Ōkuma's economic policies in this period, see Joyce C. Lebra, *Ōkuma Shigenobu, Statesman of Meiji Japan* (Canberra, 1973), pp. 15–36.
180. Ozawa, "Fukuchi no shōgai," p. 57.
181. See *Nichi Nichi,* December 23, 1878; Nakayama Yasuaki, *Shimbun shūsei Meiji hennenshi* (Tokyo, 1934–1936), 3:486.
182. *Nichi Nichi,* January 17, 1879; Nakayama, *Hennenshi,* 4:13; also Bunkaido, *Tokyo rinji fu kai bōchōroku* (January 1879), pages unnumbered. After losing the presidential election, Fukuzawa resigned from the vice-presidential post, claiming the "press of business."
183. Miyake, *Dōjidaishi,* 2:87.
184. *Nichi Nichi,* December 13, 1875. For an explanation of the *kaigisho,* see Kyugoro Obata, *An Interpretation of the Life of Viscount Shibusawa Eiichi* (Tokyo, 1938), pp. 142–143.
185. Fukuchi also took part in May 1878 in the formation of *Rizai Shimpō,* a journal that in January 1879 merged with the *Ginkō Zasshi* to form another of the Meiji era's leading economic publications, the *Keizai Zasshi.* See Nishida, *Shimbun to zasshi,* p. 81.
186. See Miyake, *Dōjidaishi,* 4:251; see also *Nichi Nichi,* March 9, 1878.
187. Yanagida, *Fukuchi Ōchi,* pp. 177, 192; *Nichi Nichi,* November 2, 1886.

*Chapter Four: Years of Struggle at* Nichi Nichi

1. *Tokyo Nichi Nichi Shimbun,* January 21, 1879.
2. Nishida Taketoshi, "Meiji jūichinen—dō jūyonnen no shimbunkai," in Osatake Takeki, ed., *Meiji bunka no shinkenkyū* (Tokyo, 1944), p. 373.
3. Yanagida Izumi, *Fukuchi Ōchi* (Tokyo, 1965), p. 184.
4. Ibid., pp. 194–197; Nishida, "Jūichinen—dō jūyonnen no shimbunkai," p. 372; Kawabe Shinzō, *Fukuchi Ōchi* (Tokyo, 1942), pp. 206–216. According to George Akita, *Foundations of Constitutional Government in Modern Japan, 1868–1900* (Cambridge, Mass., 1967), p. 222, n. 70, Inoue discussed the project with Fukuchi on January 16, 1881. A helpful discussion is also found in Joyce C. Lebra, *Ōkuma Shigenobu, Statesman of Meiji Japan* (Canberra, 1973), pp. 40–41.
5. Fukuchi Gen'ichirō, *Shimbunshi jitsureki,* in *Fukuchi Ōchi shū,* ed. Yanagida Izumi, vol. 11 of *Meiji bungaku zenshū* (Tokyo, 1966), p. 335. See also Shimane Kiyoshi, *Tenkō, Meiji ishin to bakushin* (Tokyo, 1969), p. 172.
6. *Nichi Nichi,* March 14, 1881.
7. *Chōya Shimbun,* May 20, 1881; Nakayama Yasuaki, ed., *Shimbun shūsei Meiji hennenshi* (Tokyo, 1934–1936), 4:393–394.
8. Tokyo Nichi Nichi Shimbunsha, ed., *Tōnichi nanjūnen shi* (Tokyo,

1941), p. 62. The entire court battle is reprinted verbatim in Satō Shūkichi, ed., *Meiyō kaifuku soshōroku: Tokyo daigen kumiai yori Nippōsha e kakaru* (Tokyo, 1881).

9. *Chōya*, August 18, 1881; Nakayama, *Hennenshi*, 4:429.

10. According to Nishida Taketoshi (interview, April 21, 1971), the enmity won in this struggle was a prime factor in the eventual decline of Fukuchi's public standing.

11. See Joyce C. Lebra, "Ōkuma Shigenobu and the 1881 Political Crisis," *Journal of Asian Studies* 18 (August 1959):475–487. See also Akita, *Foundations of Constitutional Government*, pp. 31–57. Akita says that Ōkuma had little to do with the Hokkaido rumors, that political rivals merely linked his name to them to discredit him. The most likely possibility is that Ono Azusa, a confidant of Ōkuma and a member of the Bureau of Audit, leaked the story to *Nichi Nichi* and to *Hōchi*. According to Sandra T. W. Davis, the credit for this, as well as "most of Ōkuma's actions" in the political sphere during 1881 and 1882 should go to Ono (personal correspondence, May 2, 1975). See Sandra T. W. Davis, "Ono Azusa and the the Political Change of 1881," *Monumenta Nipponica* 25, nos. 1–2 (1970):137–154.

12. Yanagida, *Fukuchi Ōchi*, p. 200.

13. *Nichi Nichi*, August 10, 1881.

14. Ibid., August 11, 1881; see also Inada Masatsugu, *Meiji kempō seiritsu shi* (Tokyo, 1962), 2:509.

15. Ono Hideo, *Shimbun no rekishi* (Tokyo, 1961), p. 34.

16. *Tokyo Akebono Shimbun*, August 25, 1881; Nakayama, *Hennenshi*, 4:433.

17. Kawabe, *Fukuchi Ōchi*, p. 220.

18. Fukuchi, *Shimbunshi jitsureki*, p. 336.

19. Ibid., p. 335.

20. Translation from Joseph Pittau, *Political Thought in Early Meiji Japan, 1868–1889* (Cambridge, Mass., 1967), p. 92.

21. Fukuchi, *Shimbunshi jitsureki*, p. 336.

22. Shimane, *Tenkō*, p. 173.

23. See Yanagida, *Fukuchi Ōchi*, p. 209, for a vivid account of the reaction.

24. See, for example, *Chōya*, September 24, 1881; Nakayama, *Hennenshi*, 4:458.

25. See Yanagida, *Fukuchi Ōchi*, pp. 206–208.

26. *Nichi Nichi*, November 25, 1881.

27. Fukuchi, *Shimbunshi jitsureki*, p. 337.

28. See Yanagida, *Fukuchi Ōchi*, p. 214. Among the stockholders were Shibusawa Eiichi (10,000 yen), Masuda Takashi (5,000), Jōno Dempei (2,500), Seki Naohiko (1,500). Fukuchi's stock, worth 12,500 yen, pushed total purchases to 75,000 yen.

29. *Nichi Nichi*, December 20, 1881.

30. Fukuchi, *Shimbunshi jitsureki,* p. 337.
31. For a description of this, see my "Contemporary Idioms," *The Japan Interpreter* 11, no. 4 (Spring 1975):505–515.
32. See Yanagida, *Fukuchi Ōchi,* pp. 213–218.
33. On December 20, 1881, for example, *Nichi Nichi* claimed "pure independence." The meaning seems, however, to have been that the paper had chosen its course freely, not that all positions would henceforth be decided irrespective of official policy.
34. Roger F. Hackett, *Yamagata Aritomo in the Rise of Modern Japan, 1838–1922* (Cambridge, Mass., 1971), p. 86, citing Osatake Takeki, *Meiji bunka sōsetsu* (Tokyo, 1934), p. 182.
35. Hackett, *Yamagata Aritomo,* pp. 86–87.
36. Translation from Arthur E. Tiedemann, *Modern Japan, a Brief History* (New York, 1955), pp. 107–112.
37. Hackett, *Yamagata Aritomo,* p. 86.
38. For the draft, see Umetani Noboru, *Gunjin chokuyu seiritsu shi no kenkyū,* in *Osaka Daigaku Bungakubu Kiyō,* no. 8 (1961):112–116. Nishi's role is described in Thomas Havens, *Nishi Amane and Modern Japanese Thought* (Princeton, 1970), pp. 212–215. Scholars have long debated the truth of assertions that Fukuchi drafted the rescript. Yamagata, however, reportedly stated personally to Asahina Chisen that "Fukuchi wrote it"; see Kawabe, *Fukuchi Ōchi,* pp. 188–192. Nishida Taketoshi says that "Fukuchi alone could have written such prose." Umetani has laid doubts to rest with secural of all five major drafts that went into the precepts. Fukuchi's was the fourth draft (Umetani, *Chokuyu seiritsu shi,* pp. 134–140), the fifth being but a final polishing of Fukuchi's product. Others who worked on the documents were Inoue Kowashi and Motoda Eifu.
39. Umetani, *Chokuyu seiritsu shi,* p. 180. A provocative discussion of the evolving role and status of the emperor, as evidenced in imperial decrees, is found in Marius B. Jansen, "The Monarchy and Modernization in Japan," *Journal of Asian Studies* 36, no. 4 (August 1977): 611–622.
40. *Mainichi,* November 9, 1881; Pittau, *Political Thought,* p. 107.
41. *Kōchi Shimbun,* October 7, 1881; Inada, *Kempō seiritsu shi,* 1:601.
42. *Nichi Nichi,* November 5, 6, 1881.
43. Ibid., January 14, 16, 17, 1882.
44. The *Mainichi* view, which ran from January 15 to 24, is summarized by Ono, *Shimbun no rekishi,* p. 38. See also Inada, *Kempō seiritsu shi,* 1:604–605; Pittau, *Political Thought,* pp. 108–109.
45. Fukuchi, *Shimbunshi jitsureki,* pp. 338–339.
46. *Nichi Nichi,* January 14, 1882.
47. Quoted by Pittau, *Political Thought,* pp. 110–111.
48. See David Earl, *Emperor and Nation in Japan* (Seattle, 1964), pp. 87, 236; Yamaguchi-ken Kyōikukai, comp., *Yoshida Shōin zenshū* (Tokyo: Iwa-

nami Shoten, 1938–1940), 3:606–607. For a discussion of Fukuchi's role as the only advocate of *kokutai* in this editorial war, see Pittau, *Political Thought,* p. 124.

49. *Nichi Nichi,* January 26, 1882; cited by Tamura Hisashi, *Fukuchi Ōchi,* in vol. 3 of *Sandai genronjin shū,* ed. Jiji Tsūshinsha (Tokyo, 1962), p. 88.

50. Cited by Ozawa Ryōzō, "Fukuchi Ōchi no shōgai," *Onnagata konseki dan* (Tokyo, 1941), p. 75, from "Shuken bemmō," *Nichi Nichi,* January 24–28, 1882. See also Tamura, *Fukuchi Ōchi,* pp. 150–168.

51. *Nichi Nichi,* January 28, 1882.

52. Ibid., November 8–10, 1882, cited by Kawabe, *Fukuchi Ōchi,* p. 254.

53. Tamura, *Fukuchi Ōchi,* p. 112. Seki defines the book as the university text of a "venerable Mr. Austin," likely a reference to John Austin (1790–1859), prominent English jurist. Austin's chief works were *The Province of Jurisprudence Determined* and *Lectures on Jurisprudence.*

54. Fukuchi, *Shimbunshi jitsureki,* p. 339.

55. H. D. Harootunian, *Toward Restoration* (Berkeley, 1970), p. xii.

56. *Nichi Nichi,* January 20, 1882.

57. Ibid., April 25, 26, 27, 1882.

58. Ibid., May 17, 1882.

59. Ibid., November 6, 1881.

60. Ibid., May 3, 1882.

61. A discussion of Fukuchi's initial proparty position is found in Inada, *Kempō seiritsu shi,* 1:646.

62. *Nichi Nichi,* March 25, 1882; see Ōtsu Jun'ichirō, *Dai Nihon kensei shi* (Tokyo, 1945), 2:552, for interesting comment in this area.

63. Inada, *Kempō seiritsu shi,* 1:648–649.

64. *Nichi Nichi,* May 3, 1882.

65. Ibid., May 9, 1882.

66. See a series of *Nichi Nichi* editorials, May 27–30, 1882; Inada, *Kempo seiritsu shi,* 1:652–653.

67. Fukuchi, *Shimbunshi jitsureki,* p. 338.

68. Nishida Taketoshi, *Meiji jidai no shimbun to zasshi* (Tokyo, 1956), pp. 100–108, includes a list of the papers associated with the various parties.

69. Actually, the Jiyūtō and Kaishintō consisted of a loose network of scores of small parties in harmony with Itagaki's and Ōkuma's views.

70. Fukuchi, *Shimbunshi jitsureki,* p. 337.

71. See, for example, Miyake Setsurei, *Dōjidaishi* (Tokyo, 1954), 2:165. He lists payments to such papers as *Meiji Nippō, Akebono, Yomiuri, Chōya, Hōchi, Nichi Nichi,* and *Mainichi.* See also Nishida, *Shimbun to zasshi,* p. 105. Despite payments, most papers refused to support the government's cause.

72. Hackett, *Yamagata Aritomo,* pp. 98–99. My italics.

73. Miyake, *Dōjidaishi,* 2:164, says that Itō and others planned first to

launch a party under the leadership of Yamada Akiyoshi but when that plan collapsed Fukuchi and several colleagues took their own initiative to form the party.

74. The platform also is found in Yanagida, *Fukuchi Ōchi,* pp. 240–242; Miyake, *Dōjidaishi,* 2:162–163; Ōtsu, *Kensei shi,* 2:550–551; George Uyehara, *The Political Development of Japan, 1867–1909* (New York, 1910), pp. 92–93. (Translation here is by the author.)

75. Quoted by Sashihara Yasuzō, *Meiji sei shi* (Tokyo, 1893), 2: 1293–1296. See also Yanagida, *Fukuchi Ōchi,* pp. 242–246; Ōtsu, *Kensei shi,* 2:552–553.

76. "Engi," quoted by Yanagida, *Fukuchi Ōchi,* pp. 245–246.

77. For a list of Teiseitō affiliates, see Osatake Takeki, *Nihon kensei shi taikō* (Tokyo, 1939), 2:636–637. See also Ono, *Shimbun no rekishi,* p. 35.

78. See Osatake, *Kensei shi,* 2:635. For a discussion of the Shimeikai, see Ōtsu, *Kensei shi,* 2:560–562.

79. Sashihara, *Meiji sei shi,* 2:1296.

80. The second meeting was never held, since the party folded in September 1883. Sashihara, *Meiji sei shi,* 2:1340–1342; Ōtsu, *Kensei shi,* 2:559; Fukuchi, *Shimbunshi jitsureki,* p. 335.

81. The speech is included in Itagaki Taisuke, ed., *Jiyūtō shi,* vol. 2, revised by Tōyama Shigeki and Satō Shigerō (Tokyo, 1958), pp. 120–135.

82. It probably never will be clear whether the colorful statement was actually that of Itagaki or a fabrication of an onlooker. See Sakai Kunio, *Ijin ansatsu shi* (Tokyo, 1937), p. 154. See also Ike Nobutaka, *The Beginnings of Political Democracy in Japan* (Baltimore, 1950), pp. 150–151. For a full account of the incident see Sakai, *Ijin ansatsu shi,* pp. 137–171; see also Itagaki, *Jiyūtō shi,* 2:105–154. The intensity of Itagaki's personal distaste for Fukuchi showed up that year in an interview with Tokutomi Sohō. He referred to Fukuchi as a "sour, petty man without integrity." See Irokawa Daikichi, *Shimpen Meiji seishin shi* (Tokyo, 1973), p. 381.

83. *Nichi Nichi,* May 6, 1882.

84. Ibid., May 12, 1882; Sakai, *Ijin ansatsu shi,* p. 169.

85. See Walter W. McLaren, "Japanese Government Documents," *Transactions of the Asiatic Society of Japan* 43, pt. 1 (1914), pp. 495–501.

86. The government's complicity in the effort to get Itagaki to go abroad is well illustrated in a letter from Yamagata to Itō in June 1882: "Your plan has been realized, and Itagaki has decided to go." Quoted by Hackett, *Yamagata Aritomo,* p. 101.

87. See Ono, *Shimbun no rekishi,* p. 39.

88. See Lebra, *Ōkuma Shigenobu,* pp. 77–78. She notes that government pressure even reached the extreme of sending detectives into the classrooms at Ōkuma's Tokyo Semmon Gakkō (now Waseda University) to check on what was being taught.

89. Among other causes of the parties' decline: internal factionalism, lack

of committed leadership, lack of wide support, the shifting mood of the country, and their undemocratic underpinnings. See Robert Scalapino, *Democracy and the Party Movement in Prewar Japan* (Berkeley, 1953), pp. 117–145, for an insightful analysis.

90. See Kawabe, *Fukuchi Ōchi*, p. 271.
91. Miyake, *Dōjidaishi*, 2:164.
92. See Fukuchi, *Shimbunshi jitsureki*, p. 338.
93. Ibid.
94. Yanagida, *Fukuchi Ōchi*, p. 255.
95. Kuga Katsunan, "Kinji seiron kō," in Nishida Taketoshi and Uete Michiari, eds., *Kuga Katsunan zenshū* (Tokyo, 1968), 1:56.
96. Fukuchi, *Shimbunshi jitsureki*, p. 338.
97. Lebra, *Ōkuma Shigenobu*, p. 70.
98. Kuga, "Kinji seiron kō," p. 56.
99. See Scalapino, *Democracy and the Party Movement*, pp. 75–81, for an instructive analysis of the views of the Kaishintō and the Jiyūtō regarding the emperor.
100. Yanagida, *Fukuchi Ōchi*, pp. 214–215.
101. Fukuchi, *Shimbunshi jitsureki*, p. 337.
102. July 2, 1883, was the day *Kampō* was launched.
103. Fukuchi, *Shimbunshi jitsureki*, p. 339.
104. Ibid., p. 340.
105. Statistics are based on Nishida, *Shimbun to zasshi*, p. 147. He gives only yearly circulation figures. The daily figure was derived by dividing the yearly total by 298, the number of papers published in an average year. See also Nishida, "Jūichinen—dō jūyonnen no shimbunkai," p. 407.
106. Fukuchi, *Shimbunshi jitsureki*, p. 340. Another major factor in the circulation decline was the general loss of public interest as the political climate cooled off in 1883.
107. Another "trouble" was Fukuchi's involvement in the summer of 1884 in a city council scandal regarding alleged bribery in setting rates at Yoshiwara brothels. Fukuchi was cleared in the courts, but the clouds remained. Materials on the episode are scarce, but some detail is given by Kawabe, *Fukuchi Ōchi*, pp. 313–314.
108. This is notably true in the biographies by Yanagida, Tamura, and Kawabe, as well as in Ono's writings. All largely dismiss Fukuchi as a man of influence after mid-1883. A slightly more balanced picture is found in Nishida's *Shimbun to zasshi*.
109. For statistics, see Table 1, p. 89.
110. See, for example, *Nichi Nichi*, August 29–30, September 13, 1884.
111. E. H. House, "The Thraldom of Japan," *Atlantic Monthly* (December 1887):721–734.
112. Translated in *Japan Weekly Mail*, March 24, 1888, pp. 268–269.
113. *Nichi Nichi*, December 25, 1885.

114. Ibid., May 14, 1886.

115. Ibid., May 16, 1886.

116. Fukuchi Gen'ichirō, *Satchō ron* (Tokyo, 1886). It initially ran in *Nichi Nichi*, January 19–23, 1886, and has been reprinted in Yanagida, *Fukuchi Ōchi shū,* pp. 379–386.

117. Fukuchi himself confused the two, referring to his "Kyōjaku ron" as the "Satchō ron"—hardly a surprising slip since both attacks were directed at the same Meiji oligarchs. Fukuchi, *Shimbunshi jitsureki,* p. 326.

118. See Uchimura Kanzō, *The Complete Works of Uchimura Kanzō,* in vol. 7, *Essays and Editorials—III* (Tokyo, 1973), p. 186.

119. *Nichi Nichi,* January 21, 1886.

120. Ibid., January 22, 1886.

121. Ibid., January 23, 1886.

122. Itō's directive is translated in *Japan Weekly Mail,* January 2, 1886, p. 11. See also Robert M. Spaulding, Jr., *Imperial Japan's Higher Civil Service Examinations* (Princeton, 1967), pp. 64–73. The examination system was not actually set up until 1887.

123. See Lebra, *Ōkuma Shigenobu,* pp. 5, 27, 34–36, 49–54.

124. The site now bears a marker as the subsequent home of the well-known painter Yokoyama Daikan, who moved there in 1906 and died in 1958. His widow still lived there in the 1970s.

125. Kawabe, *Fukuchi Ōchi,* p. 326; Tamura, *Fukuchi Ōchi,* p. 104.

126. See *Yamato Shimbun,* April 22, 1887; Nakayama, *Hennenshi,* 6: 455–456. On this occasion, Fukuchi went to a party at Itō's residence dressed as a mountain priest. See also *Kaika Shimbun,* April 19, 1884.

127. Mori Ōgai, *The Wild Geese,* trans. Kingo Ochiai and Sanford Goldstein (Rutland, Vt., 1959), p. 28.

128. *Hōchi,* February 25, 1884; Nakayama, *Hennenshi,* 5:428.

129. *Konnichi Shimbun,* May 20, 1885; Nakayama, *Hennenshi,* 6:89.

130. See Nishida, *Shimbun to zasshi,* pp. 167–168.

131. Ibid., p. 167.

132. Komiya Toyotaka, ed., *Japanese Music and Drama in the Meiji Era,* trans. E. G. Seidensticker and Donald Keene (Tokyo, 1956), p. 441.

133. See Yanagida, *Fukuchi Ōchi,* pp. 254–255, 263.

134. See Tamura, *Fukuchi Ōchi,* pp. 105–106, and Kawabe, *Fukuchi Ōchi,* pp. 311–312, among others.

135. Fukuchi, *Shimbunshi jitsureki,* p. 341.

136. Kawabe, *Fukuchi Ōchi,* p. 315.

137. *Nichi Nichi,* "Kōkoku," January 4, 1887.

138. *Nichi Nichi,* July 10, 1888; an announcement of the dismissal also ran in *Japan Weekly Mail,* July 14, 1888, p. 28. Fukuchi's informal ties to *Nichi Nichi* continued for a number of years; he wrote many novels and articles for the paper.

139. Kawabe, *Fukuchi Ōchi,* p. 278.

140. See, for example, *Nichi Nichi,* December 28, 1874.
141. Ibid., May 12, 1880.
142. Ibid., September 21, 1881.
143. Ibid., May 14, 1886.
144. Ibid., March 17, 1880.
145. Ibid., January 17, 1879.
146. Quoted in Yanagida, *Fukuchi Ōchi,* p. 242.
147. *Nichi Nichi,* January 6, 1875.
148. Robert N. Bellah, "Intellectual and Society in Japan," *Daedalus* (Spring 1972):107.
149. Nishida Taketoshi, "Ōchi no shimbun kiji ni tsuite," in Yanagida, *Fukuchi Ōchi shū,* p. 454.
150. Yanagida, *Fukuchi Ōchi,* p. 317.
151. Bellah, "Intellectual and Society," p. 108.
152. *Nichi Nichi,* August 23, 1875.
153. Ibid., March 12–16, 19, 31, April 5, 9–11, 19, 29, 30, 1879.
154. See Scalapino, *Democracy and the Party Movement,* p. 75.
155. Fukuchi, *Shimbunshi jitsureki,* p. 338.
156. *Nichi Nichi,* May 16, 1886.
157. Ibid., January 22, 1879.
158. Yanagida, *Fukuchi Ōchi,* p. 246.
159. A helpful monograph on this group is Barbara Teters, "The Conservative Opposition in Japanese Politics, 1877–1894" (Ph.D diss., University of Washington, 1953).
160. This has been discussed in such works as Fukuda Tsuneari, *Genron no jiyū to iu koto* (Tokyo, 1973); Urushiyama Shigeyoshi, *Shimbun ronchō e no hanron* (Tokyo, 1975); Kido Mataichi, ed., *Kōza Gendai jyānarizumu—shimbun* (Tokyo, 1973); and Hayashi Saburō, *Shimbun o dō yomu ka* (Tokyo, 1974). In English, see Jun'ichi Kyogoku, "The Common Sense of the Public and of the Political Establishment," *Japan Echo* 2, no. 1 (Spring 1975):13–24; Kyozo Mori, "Questionable Attitude of News Reporters," *Japan Echo* 3, no. 1 (Spring 1975):37–43.
161. Quoted from *Moshiya sōshi,* in Ozawa, "Fukuchi Ōchi no shōgai," p. 60.
162. See Irokawa, *Shimpen Meiji seishinshi,* p. 373.
163. Inukai Tsuyoshi, in *Daigaku Hyōron* (August 1917):72–73, trans. Kawabe Kisaburo, *The Press and Politics in Japan* (Chicago, 1921), p. 85.
164. Interview with Nishida, April 21, 1971.
165. Quoted by Tamura, *Fukuchi Ōchi,* p. 113.
166. Figures from Nishida, "Jūichinen—dō jūyonnen no shimbunkai," p. 400.
167. Nihon Shimbun Remmei, *Nihon shimbun hyakunenshi* (Tokyo, 1962), p. 856.
168. Quoted by Kawabe, *Fukuchi Ōchi,* p. 4.

169. Quoted by Kubota Tatsuhiko, *Nijūichi daisenkaku kisha den* (Osaka, 1930), pp. 65–66.

### Chapter Five: The After Years

1. Fukuchi Gen'ichirō, *Moshiya sōshi*, in *Fukuchi Ōchi shū*, ed. Yanagida Izumi, vol. 11 of *Meiji bungaku zenshū* (Tokyo, 1966), p. 27.
2. Basil Hall Chamberlain, *Japanese Things*, rev. reprint edition (Tokyo, 1971), p. 2.
3. Nakamura Mitsuo, *Modern Japanese Fiction, 1868–1926* (Tokyo, 1968), pp. 2–3.
4. Ibid., p. 9.
5. Kawabe Shinzō, *Fukuchi Ōchi* (Tokyo, 1942), p. 290.
6. Fukuchi Gen'ichirō, "Shomoku jisshu," *Kokumin no Tomo*, no. 48 (April 22, 1889), quoted by Yanagida Izumi, *Fukuchi Ōchi* (Tokyo, 1965), p. 326.
7. Yanagida Izumi, *Meiji shoki no bungaku shisō* (Tokyo, 1965), 1:287. Unfortunately, no one knows what he wrote.
8. See Kawabe, *Fukuchi Ōchi*, p. 29.
9. Yanagida, *Fukuchi Ōchi*, pp. 288, 292; Yanaga Chitoshi, *Japan since Perry* (New York, 1949), p. 207.
10. See, for example, *Tokyo Nichi Nichi Shimbun*, April 26, 1875 ("Nihon bungaku no fushin o tanzu"); August 29, 1875 ("Bunron"); September 10, 1875 ("Engeki jiyū ron"); July 25, 28, 1885 ("Bunsho no shinka"); and February 16, 1886 ("Bunsho kairyō no mokuteki"). All are in Yanagida, *Fukuchi Ōchi shū*, pp. 341–388.
11. See Yanagida, *Fukuchi Ōchi*, p. 290.
12. See *Chōya Shimbun*, February 24, 1889; Nakayama Yasuaki, *Shimbun shūsei Meiji hennenshi* (Tokyo, 1934–1936), 7:238.
13. Mishima Ryōzō, ed., *Kabukiza* (Tokyo, 1951), p. 3. See pp. 173–196 for a detailed list of events during Fukuchi's tenure at the Kabukiza.
14. Showa Joshi Daigaku Kindai Bungaku Kenkyūshitsu, "Fukuchi Ōchi," in *Kindai bungaku kenkyū sōsho* (Tokyo, 1958), 8:348.
15. *Minato Shimbun*, May 17, 1893; Nakayama, *Hennenshi*, 8:417.
16. Komiya Toyotaka, *Japanese Music and Drama in the Meiji Era*, trans. Edward G. Seidensticker and Donald Keene (Tokyo, 1956), p. 233.
17. See Yanagida, *Fukuchi Ōchi*, p. 227; Kawabe, *Fukuchi Ōchi*, p. 294.
18. Listed in Yanagida, *Fukuchi Ōchi*, pp. 294–299; Showa Joshi Daigaku, "Fukuchi Ōchi," pp. 342–344.
19. See, for a summary, Tamura Hisashi, *Fukuchi Ōchi*, in vol. 3 of *Sandai genronjin shū*, ed. Jiji Tsūshinsha (Tokyo, 1962), p. 104.
20. Synopsis in Faubion Bowers, *Japanese Theater* (New York, 1952), p. 166.
21. Okata Shōyū, "Fukuchi Ōchi to no kaiken," *Jimbutsu sōsho furoku*,

no. 129 (1965), quoting Mortimer Menpes, *Japan, a Record in Colour* (London, 1901), p. 13.
22. Quoted by Komiya, *Japanese Music and Drama*, pp. 33–34.
23. Ibid., pp. 234–235.
24. Yanagida Izumi, "Bungakusha toshite no Fukuchi Ōchi," in Yanagida, *Fukuchi Ōchi shū*, p. 420.
25. Yanagida, *Fukuchi Ōchi*, p. 291; see pp. 291–299 for a general evaluation of Fukuchi's drama.
26. Komiya, *Japanese Music and Drama*, p. 234.
27. Menpes, *Japan*, pp. 20–22.
28. Ibid., p. 26.
29. Komiya, *Japanese Music and Drama*, pp. 35, 236. The *kyōgen* was a short, farcical play developed centuries ago, often performed with Nō. It was usually realistic, done in colloquial language.
30. For further evaluation of Fukuchi as a dramatist, see Showa Joshi Daigaku, "Fukuchi Ōchi," pp. 348–352.
31. See Table 2, p. 180. For a complete list, see Yanagida, *Fukuchi Ōchi*, pp. 303–310; Showa Joshi Daigaku, "Fukuchi Ōchi," pp. 327–341.
32. Asahina Chisen, "Rōkisha no omoide" (1938), quoted in Kawabe, *Fukuchi Ōchi*, p. 311.
33. Fukuchi Ōchi, *Jinsei X kōsen*, in *Ōchi zenshū* (Tokyo, 1911), 2: preface.
34. Listed in Yanagida, *Fukuchi Ōchi*, pp. 305–308.
35. Ibid., pp. 308–310.
36. Ibid., pp. 302–305. Also included in Yanagida Izumi, *Meiji seiji shosetsu shū* (Tokyo, 1967), 2:465–476.
37. Yanagida Izumi, *Seiji shosetsu kenkyū* (Tokyo, 1968), 3:262.
38. Ozawa Ryōzō, "Fukuchi Ōchi no shōgai," in *Onnagata konseki dan* (Tokyo, 1941), p. 82.
39. Ibid., pp. 79–80.
40. Fukuchi, *Moshiya sōshi*, p. 3. Koji was one of Fukuchi's better-known pseudonyms.
41. Yanagida, *Fukuchi Ōchi*, p. 302.
42. See Kawabe, *Fukuchi Ōchi*, pp. 304–305.
43. Yanagida, *Seiji shosetsu kenkyū*, p. 262.
44. Showa Joshi Daigaku, "Fukuchi Ōchi," p. 358, quoting Fukuchi in *Bungei Kurabu jānāru*, no. 4 (1889). Fukuchi's general view of history is analyzed in Suzuki Shōzō, "Fukuchi Ōchi no rekishikan ni tsuite," Osaka Kyōiku Daigaku, *Rekishi Kenkyū* 7, no. 8 (1971):5–21.
45. Serialized in *Kokumin no Tomo*, nos. 114–172 (April 3, 1891, to November 13, 1892); published by Min'yūsha as a separate volume in 1892.
46. *Kokumin no Tomo*, nos. 315–364 (September 26, 1896, to December 10, 1897); published by Min'yūsha, 1898.

47. Yanagida Izumi, "Fukuchi Ōchi," in Yanagida, *Fukuchi Ōchi shū* (Tokyo, 1966), p. 415.

48. See Shibusawa Eiichi, *Tokugawa Keiki kō den*, 8 vols. (Tokyo, 1918); see also Kawabe, *Fukuchi Ōchi*, pp. 317–318.

49. See *Osaka Asahi Shimbun*, July 5, 1902; Nakayama, *Hennenshi*, 11:432. Though unfinished, the manuscript did appear posthumously in *Yamato Shimbun* under the title, "Tokugawa shi"; see note in Yanagida, "Fukuchi Ōchi," p. 415.

50. Kawabe, *Fukuchi Ōchi*, p. 317.

51. Fukuchi Gen'ichirō, *Bakufu suibō ron*, ed. Ishizuka Hiromichi (Tokyo, 1967), foreword, p. 3.

52. Ibid., preface, p. 5.

53. Ibid., main text, p. 6.

54. Ibid., pp. 256–260.

55. See Yanagida, *Fukuchi Ōchi*, p. 314.

56. Fukuchi, *Bakufu suibō ron*, preface, p. 5.

57. Chamberlain, *Japanese Things*, p. 293.

58. Tokutomi's foreword, in Fukuchi, *Bakufu suibō ron*, p. 4.

59. He translated Johann von Schiller's *Maria Stuart* from an English edition in 1888. Earlier, he had worked with Nippōsha staff members on translations of Benjamin Disraeli's *Contarini Fleming* and *Coningsby*.

60. See, for example, "Seitai to gakumon to no kankei," *Nihon Taika Zenshū* 2, no. 12 (December 10, 1890); "Bunsho no hiketsu," *Nihon Taika Zenshū* 3, no. 8 (August 10, 1891); "Mayoi no yume," *Kokumin no Tomo*, no. 178 (January 13, 1893); "Yōgaku no yunyū ni tsukite," *Taiyō* 4, no. 23 (November 20, 1898); and others.

61. For a complete list of these articles, see Showa Joshi Daigaku, "Fukuchi Ōchi," pp. 333–338.

62. *Tokyo Asahi Shimbun*, December 20, 1903; Nakayama, *Hennenshi*, 12:151.

63. Members are listed in *Hōchi*, March 5, 1904; Nakayama, *Hennenshi*, 12:202.

64. An extraordianry session was held from March 20 to March 30, 1904; the regular session lasted from November 30, 1904 to February 23, 1905.

65. *Japan Weekly Mail*, January 13, 1906, p. 28.

66. Ibid.

67. *Nichi Nichi*, January 5, 1906.

68. For a representative list of Fukuchi's editorials in this area, see James Huffman, "Fukuchi Gen'ichirō: Journalist-Intellectual in Meiji Japan" (Ph.D. diss., University of Michigan, 1972), Appendix II, pp. 453–468.

69. Ibid., pp. 469–477.

70. Tamura, *Fukuchi Ōchi*, p. 27.

71. *Nichi Nichi*, January 19, 1886.

Notes 239

72. Ibid., March 14, 1881.

73. Translation from Arthur E. Tiedemann, *Modern Japan, a Brief History* (New York, 1955), p. 110.

74. Ryusaku Tsunoda, William Theodore deBary, and Donald Keene, eds., *Sources of Japanese Tradition*, paperback (New York, 1964), 1:329–330.

75. Komiya, *Japanese Music and Drama*, p. 201.

76. Nakamura, *Modern Japanese Fiction*, p. 2.

77. Kenneth B. Pyle, *The New Generation in Meiji Japan: Problems of Cultural Identity, 1888–1895* (Stanford, 1969), p. 18.

78. Ronald P. Dore, "The Legacy of Tokugawa Education," in Marius P. Jansen, ed., *Changing Japanese Attitudes toward Modernization*, paperback (Princeton, 1969), p. 117.

79. Jansen, *Changing Japanese Attitudes*, p. 65.

80. Interview, April 21, 1971.

81. Kubota Tatsuhiko, *Nijūichi daisenkaku kisha den* (Osaka, 1930), p. 66.

82. Yanagida, *Fukuchi Ōchi*, p. 21.

83. From a Fukuchi speech commemorating the anniversary of the Iwakura mission, delivered in 1902; see *Yomiuri Shimbun*, March 22, 1902, in Nakayama, *Hennenshi*, 11:191–192.

84. Fukuchi Gen'ichirō, *Kaiō jidan*, in Yanagida, *Fukuchi Ōchi shū*, p. 313.

85. Pyle, *New Generation*, p. 76, quoting Yokoi Tokio.

86. Zushikawa, "Ōchi Koji no tsuioku," p. 21.

87. Komiya, *Japanese Music and Drama*, p. 441.

88. The classic study of the Renaissance is Jakob Burckhardt, *The Civilization of the Renaissance in Italy* (New York, 1950). See also *The Renaissance in Historical Thought* (Boston, 1948), and Denys Hay, *The Italian Renaissance in Its Historical Background* (Cambridge, 1961).

89. Fukuzawa Yukichi, *Gakumon no susume*, sec. 4, trans. D. A. Dilworth and Umeyo Hirano, *An Encouragement of Learning* (Tokyo, 1969), p. 25. For a perceptive evaluation of this and similar statements by Fukuzawa, see Earl H. Kinmonth, "Fukuzawa Reconsidered: *Gakumon no susume* and Its Audience," *Journal of Asian Studies* 37, no. 4 (August 1978):677–696.

90. Miyake Setsurei, "Ijin no ato," quoted by Yanagida, *Fukuchi Ōchi*, p. 341.

91. S. N. Eisenstadt, "Intellectuals and Tradition," *Daedalus* (Spring 1972):1.

92. Ibid., pp. 8–9. An additional role for the intellectual in a "follower society" is that of sharing "teleological insight," the capacity to "discern the future of one's own society by projecting it in accordance with conditions and trends in the 'advanced world.'" Fukuchi apparently never took up this role consciously, but his writings constantly tend in that direction. See also Ken-

neth B. Pyle, "Advantages of Followership: German Economics and Japanese Bureaucrats, 1890–1925," *Journal of Japanese Studies* 1, no. 1 (Autumn 1974):128.

93. Robert N. Bellah, "Intellectual and Society in Japan," *Daedalus* (Spring 1972):103.

94. Eisenstadt, "Intellectuals and Tradition," p. 18.

95. For an incisive account of twentieth-century "particularism," see Robert N. Bellah, "Japan's Cultural Identity: Some Reflections on the Work of Watsuji Tetsurō," *Journal of Asian Studies* 24, no. 4 (1965):573–594. His *Tokugawa Religion* also concerns itself with particularism (Glencoe, Ill., 1970).

96. Itō Hirobumi, "Some Reminiscences of the Grant of the New Constitution," in Ōkuma Shigenobu, ed., *Fifty Years of New Japan* (New York, 1909), 1:130; emphasis added by author.

# Bibliography

To adequately describe the major sources of material available on Fukuchi Gen'ichirō would demand more space than the reader would countenance. A few comments do, however, seem essential. By far the most important of his "gradualist" writings are the thousands of newspaper editorials he wrote at *Tokyo Nichi Nichi Shimbun,* all available in the collections of Meiji Shimbun Zasshi Bunko at Tokyo University. To facilitate their use, Nishida Taketoshi (former curator of the Bunko) has prepared an impressive, briefly annotated index to each of the editorials. Many of Fukuchi's more important political writings also have been included in Yanagida Izumi's *Fukuchi Ōchi shū,* while his journalistic efforts at *Kōko Shimbun* have been reprinted in their entirety in the fourth volume of Osatake Takeki's *Bakumatsu Meiji shimbun zenshū.*

Most productive of the sources on Fukuchi's career are his own memoirs, the *Kaiō jidan* and *Shimbunshi jitsureki* (both included in *Fukuchi Ōchi shū*), and the biographies by Kawabe and Yanagida as well as the provocative early chapters of Sugiura's *Shimbun koto hajime.* Also helpful, though spottily used in this study, are the manifold, thinly disguised personal references in Fukuchi's three score novels, many of which are included in his own *Ōchi shū* and *Ōchi zenshū.* Several of his historical writings (especially *Bakumatsu seijika*) also are filled with memoir-type materials.

It will be further apparent from the Notes and Bibliography that I am deeply in debt to the authors and editors of large numbers of other monographs, collected works, and essays. And I was aided—far more than my foreign-sounding Japanese deserved—by exceedingly helpful conversations with Professor Nishida at the Shimbun Zasshi Bunko and with Sugiura Tadashi, resident historian at *Mainichi Shimbun.*

Akamatsu, Paul. *Meiji 1868, Revolution and Counter-Revolution in Japan.* London: George Allen and Unwin, 1972.

Akiba Tarō. *Nihon shingeki shi* [History of new Japanese drama]. 2 vols. Tokyo: Risōsha, 1955.

Akita, George. *Foundations of Constitutional Government in Modern Japan, 1868-1900.* Cambridge, Mass.: Harvard University Press, 1967.

Alcock, Rutherford. *Capital of the Tycoon: A Narrative of a Three Years' Res-*

*idence in Japan.* 2 vols. London: Longman, Green, Longman, Roberts and Green, 1863.

Allen, G. C. *A Short Economic History of Modern Japan 1867–1937.* New York: Frederick A. Praeger, 1962.

Altman, Albert. "The Emergence of the Press in Meiji Japan." Ph.D. dissertation, Princeton University, 1965.

———. " 'Shimbunshi': The Early Meiji Adaptation of the Western-style Newspaper." *Modern Japan: Aspects of History, Literature and Society.* Edited by W. G. Beasley. Berkeley: University of California Press. 1975.

Asahina Chisen. *Asahina Chisen bunshū* [Collected works of Asahina Chisen]. Tokyo: Asahina Chisen Bunshū Kankōkai, 1927.

———. *Rōkisha no omoide* [Memories of an aged reporter]. Tokyo, 1938.

Beasley, W. G. *The Meiji Restoration.* Stanford: Stanford University Press, 1972.

———. *The Modern History of Japan.* New York: Frederick A. Praeger, 1963.

———. *Select Documents on Japanese Foreign Policy, 1853–1868.* London: Oxford University Press, 1955.

Beckmann, George M. *The Making of the Meiji Constitution.* Lawrence, Kans.: The University Press of Kansas, 1957.

Bellah, Robert N. "Intellectual and Society in Japan." *Daedalus* (Spring 1972):89–115.

———. "Japan's Cultural Identity: Some Reflections on the Work of Watsuji Tetsurō." *Journal of Asian Studies* 24, no. 4 (1965):573–594.

———. *Tokugawa Religion: The Values of Pre-industrial Japan.* Glencoe, Ill.: The Free Press, 1957.

Black, John R. *Young Japan: Yokohama and Yedo 1858–1879.* Tokyo: Oxford University Press, 1968.

Blacker, Carmen. "The First Japanese Mission to England." *History Today* (December 1957):840–847.

———. *The Japanese Enlightenment: A Study of the Writings of Fukuzawa Yukichi.* Cambridge: The University Press, 1964.

Braisted, William R., trans. *Meiroku Zasshi: Journal of Japanese Enlightenment.* Tokyo: University of Tokyo Press, 1976.

Brown, Sidney D. "Kido Takayoshi and the Meiji Restoration: A Political Biography, 1833–1877." Ph.D. dissertation, University of Wisconsin, 1952.

Bunkaidō. *Tokyo rinji fu kai bōchōroku* [Record of the extraordinary meeting of the Tokyo city assembly], no. 1 (January 1879).

Burkman, Thomas W. "The Urakami Incident and the Struggle for Religious Toleration in Early Meiji Japan." *Japanese Journal of Religious Studies* 1, nos. 2–3 (June–September 1974):143–216.

Carr, Edward H. *What Is History?* New York: Vintage Books, 1961.

Centre for East Asian Cultural Studies, ed. *The Meiji Japan through Contem-*

*porary Sources.* Vol. 1. *Basic Documents, 1854-1889.* Tokyo: Tokyo Press, 1969.

Chamberlain, Basil Hall. *Japanese Things, Being Notes on Various Subjects Connected with Japan.* Tokyo: Charles E. Tuttle, 1971.

Choi, Kee Il. "Shibusawa Eiichi and His Contemporaries." Ph.D. dissertation, Harvard University, 1958.

*Chōya Shimbun.*

Conroy, Hilary, *The Japanese Seizure of Korea: 1868-1910.* Philadelphia: University of Pennsylvania Press, 1960.

Craig, Albert M. *Chōshū in the Meiji Restoration.* Cambridge, Mass.: Harvard University Press, 1961.

Craig, Albert M. and Shively, Donald H., eds. *Personality in Japanese History.* Berkeley: University of California Press, 1970.

Davis, Sandra T. W. "Ono Azusa and the Political Change of 1884." *Monumenta Nipponica* 25, nos. 1–2 (1970):137–154.

Dore, R. P., ed. *Aspects of Social Change in Modern Japan.* Princeton: Princeton University Press, 1967.

Dower, John W., ed. *Origins of the Modern Japanese State: Selected Writings of E. H. Norman.* New York: Pantheon Books, 1975.

Earl, David. *Emperor and Nation in Japan.* Seattle, 1964.

Eisenstadt, S. N. "Intellectuals and Tradition." *Daedalus* (Spring 1972):1–9.

Emery, Edwin. *The Press and America.* Englewood Cliffs, N.J.: Prentice-Hall, 1972.

Endō Motō and Shimomura Fujio, eds. *Kokushi bunken kaisetsu* [Annotated bibliography of Japanese history]. Tokyo: Asakura Shoten, 1957.

Enomoto Haryū. *Ōchi Koji to Ichikawa Danjūrō* [Ōchi Koji and Ichikawa Danjūrō]. Tokyo: Kokkōsha, 1903.

Ernst, Earle. *The Kabuki Theatre.* New York: Oxford University Press, 1956.

Figdor, Peter. "Newspapers and Their Regulation in Early Meiji Japan, 1868–1883." *Papers on Japan.* Vol 6., pp. 1–44. Cambridge, Mass.: Harvard University East Asian Research Center, 1972.

Fraser, Andrew. "The Expulsion of Okuma from the Government in 1881." *Journal of Asian Studies* 26 (1967):213–236.

Frost, Peter. *The Bakumatsu Currency Crisis.* Cambridge, Mass.: Harvard University Press, 1970.

Fukuchi Gen'ichirō. *Bakufu suibō ron* [The decline and fall of the bakufu]. Edited by Ishizuka Hiromichi. Tokyo: Heibonsha, 1967.

————. *Bakumatsu seijika* [Political leaders of the Bakumatsu]. Vol. 8 of *Bakumatsu ishin shiryō sōsho* [Historical materials of the Bakumatsu and Restoration]. Tokyo: Jimbutsu Ōraisha, 1968.

————. "Ishin no genkun" [Elder statesmen of the Restoration]. *Taiyō* 1 (April 1895):31–37.

————. *Jinsei X kōsen* [Reflections on Life]. In *Ōchi zenshū* [Complete works of Ōchi], vol. 2. Tokyo: Hakubunkan, 1911.

————. *Kaiō jidan* [Recollections]. See Yanagida Izumi, *Fukuchi Ōchi shū:* 264-324.

————. *Kaisha ben* [Treatise on banking]. *Keizai hen* [Economics volume]. Vol. 12 of *Meiji bunka zenshū* [Collected works on Meiji culture]. Edited by Meiji Bunka Kenkyūkai, q.v. Tokyo: Nihon Hyōronsha, 1968.

————. *Moshiya sōshi* [What if . . . ]. See Yanagida Izumi, *Fukuchi Ōchi shū:* 3-91.

————. *Nagasaki sanbyakunenkan gaikō hensen jijō* [The vicissitudes of three hundred years of foreign exchange in Nagasaki]. Tokyo: Hakubunkan, 1902.

————. *Ōchi shū* [Works of Ōchi]. Tokyo: Shunyōdō, 1911.

————. *Ōchi zenshū* [Complete works of Ōchi]. 3 vols. Tokyo: Hakubunkan, 1911.

————. *Satchō ron* [On Satsuma and Chōshū]. Tokyo: Nippōsha, 1886.

————. *Shimbunshi jitsureki* [My career in the newspaper]. See Yanagida Izumi, *Fukuchi Ōchi shū:* 325-341.

————. *Takashima Shūhan* [The life of Takashima Shūhan]. See *Ōchi zenshū,* 3:847-984.

————. "Shomoku jisshu" [Ten varieties of book catalogues]. *Kokumin no Tomo* (April 22, 1889).

Fukuchi Nobuyo. *Kankon shiryō* [Data on the dead]. Privately prepared by Fukuchi family, 1918.

Fukuchi Ōchi. See Fukuchi Gen'ichirō.

Fukuda Tsuneari. *Genron no jiyū to iu koto* [Freedom of the press]. Tokyo: Shinchōsha, 1973.

Fukuzawa Yukichi. *An Encouragement of Learning.* Translated by David A. Dilworth and Umeyo Hirano. Tokyo: Sophia University Press, 1969.

————. *The Autobiography of Yukichi Fukuzawa.* Translated by Eiichi Kiyooka. New York: Columbia University Press, 1966.

Fukuzawa Yukichi. *Fukuzawa Yukichi zenshū* [Complete works of Fukuzawa Yukichi]. 21 vols. Tokyo: Keiō Gijuku Hensan, 1958-1963.

Griffis, W. Elliot. *Verbeck of Japan: A Citizen of No Country.* New York: Fleming H. Revell, 1900.

Hackett, Roger F. "Nishi Amane: A Tokugawa-Meiji Bureaucrat." *Journal of Asian Studies* 18 (February 1959):213-225.

————. "The Meiji Leaders and Modernization: The Case of Yamagata Aritomo." *Changing Attitudes toward Modernization.* Edited by Marius B. Jansen. Princeton: Princeton University Press, 1965.

————. "The Military in Japan." *Political Modernization in Japan and Turkey.* Edited by Robert E. Ward and Dankwart A. Rustow. Princeton: Princeton University Press, 1964.

————. *Yamagata Aritomo in the Rise of Modern Japan, 1838-1922.* Cambridge, Mass.: Harvard University Press, 1971.

Hall, Ivan P. *Mori Arinori.* Cambridge, Mass.: Harvard University Press, 1973.

Hall, John Whitney. *Japan: From Prehistory to Modern Times.* New York: Dell Publishing, 1970.

Hamamura Yonezo. *Kabuki.* Edited by Society of Traditional Arts. Translated by Takano Fumi. Tokyo: Kenkyūsha, 1956.

Hanazono, Kanesada. *Journalism in Japan and Its Early Pioneers.* Osaka: Osaka Shuppansha, 1926.

―――. *The Development of Japanese Journalism.* Osaka: Osaka Mainichi Shimbunsha, 1924.

Harootunian, H. D. *Toward Restoration: The Growth of Political Consciousness in Tokugawa Japan.* Berkeley: University of California Press, 1970.

Havens, Thomas Robert Hamilton. *Nishi Amane and Modern Japanese Thought.* Princeton: Princeton University Press, 1970.

Hay, Denys. *The Italian Renaissance in Its Historical Background.* Cambridge: The University Press, 1961.

Hayashida Kametarō. *Nihon seitō shi* [A history of Japanese political parties]. 2 vols. Tokyo: Dai Nihon Yūbenkai Kōdansha, 1927.

Heco, Joseph. *The Narrative of a Japanese.* Edited by James Murdoch. Yokohama, 1895.

Hirschmeier, Johannes. *The Origins of Entrepreneurship in Meiji Japan.* Cambridge, Mass.: Harvard University Press, 1964.

House, Edward H. *Japanese Episodes.* Boston: James Osgood, 1881.

―――. *The Kagoshima Affair, a Chapter of Japanese History.* 1875.

―――. *The Japanese Expedition to Formosa.* Tokyo, 1875.

Idditti Smimasa. *The Life of Marquis Ōkuma: A Maker of Japan.* Tokyo: Hokuseidō, 1940.

Ike Nobutaka. *The Beginnings of Political Democracy in Japan.* Baltimore: The Johns Hopkins University Press, 1950.

Inada Masatsugu. *Meiji kempō seiritsu shi* [History of the framing of the Meiji constitution]. 2 vols. Tokyo: Yūhikaku, 1960–1962.

Ino Tentarō. *Nihon gaikō shisō shi ronkō* [Studies in the history of Japanese diplomatic thought]. 2 vols. Tokyo: Komine Shoten, 1966–1967.

Irokawa Daikichi. *Shimpen Meiji seishin shi* [A history of the spirit of Meiji— revised edition]. Tokyo: Chūō Kōronsha, 1973.

Itagaki Taisuke, ed. *Jiyūtō shi* [History of the Liberal Party]. Revised by Tōyama Shigeki and Satō Shigerō. 3 vols. Tokyo: Iwanami Shoten, 1958.

Itō Hirobumi, *Commentaries on the Constitution of the Empire of Japan.* Translated by Itō Miyoji. 2d ed. Tokyo: Chūō Daigaku, 1906.

―――. "Some Reminiscences of the Grant of the New Constitution." *Fifty Years of New Japan.* Vol. 1. Edited by Ōkuma Shigenobu. London: Smith, Elders, 1910.

Itō Seitoku. "Sosei kara Meiji ki" [The Meiji period, from its beginnings].

*Nihon shimbun hyakunenshi* [One hundred year history of Japanese newspapers]. Edited by Nihon Shimbun Remmei. Tokyo: Nihon Shimbun Remmei, 1962.

Jansen, Marius B., ed. *Changing Japanese Attitudes toward Modernization.* Princeton: Princeton University Press, 1965.

―――. "Monarchy and modernization in Japan." *Journal of Asian Studies* 36, no. 4 (August 1977):611–622.

Jibun Taikan Kankōkai. *Ōchi bunshū* [Works of Ōchi]. Vol. 2 of *Jibun taikan* [Survey of modern writing]. Tokyo, 1910.

Jiji Tsūshinsha, eds. *Sandai genronjin shū* [The works of three generations of journalists]. 8 vols. Tokyo: Jiji Tsūshinsha, 1962–1967.

Jonas, F. M. "Foreign Influences on the Early Press of Japan." *Japan Society, London—Transactions and Proceedings.* Vol. 32 (1934–1935).

Kabukiza Shuppanbu. *Kabukiza* [The Kabukiza]. Tokyo: Kabukiza Shuppanbu, 1951.

Kada Tetsuji. *Shakai shi* [Social history]. Tokyo: Tōyō Keizai Shimpōsha, 1940.

Kamikawa Hikomatsu, ed. *Japanese-American Diplomatic Relations in the Meiji-Taisho Era.* Vol. 3 of *A History of Japanese-American Cultural Relations 1853-1926.* Translated and adapted by Kimura Michiko. Tokyo: Ōbunsha, 1958.

Kaneko Hisakazu. *Manjiro, the Man Who Discovered America.* Boston: Houghton Mifflin, 1956.

Kawabe Kisaburō. *The Press and Politics in Japan.* Chicago: University of Chicago Press, 1921.

Kawabe Shinzō. *Fukuchi Ōchi* [The life of Fukuchi Ōchi]. Tokyo: Sanseido, 1942.

Kawatake Shigetoshi. *Kabuki Japanese Drama.* Tokyo: The Foreign Affairs Association of Japan, 1958.

"Keizai chishiki no fukyū shimei" [The mission of spreading economic knowledge]. *Nihon Keizai Shimbun,* December 1, 1956, p. 12.

Kido Kōin. *Kido Kōin monjo* [The works of Kido Kōin]. Edited by Tsumaki Chūta. 8 vols. Tokyo: Kido Kō Denki Hensanjo, 1929–1931.

―――. *Kido Kōin nikki* [Diary of Kido Kōin]. 3 vols. Tokyo: Nihon Shiseki Kyōkai, 1932.

Kido Mataichi, ed. *Kōza gendai jānārizumu, II* [Lectures on modern journalism, II]. Tokyo: Jiji Tsūshinsha, 1973.

Kincaid, Zoe. *Kabuki, the Popular Stage of Japan.* London: Macmillan, 1925.

Kinmonth, Earl H. "Fukuzawa Reconsidered: *Gakumon no susume* and Its Audience." *Journal of Asian Studies* 37, no. 4 (August 1978):677–696.

Kobre, Sidney. *Development of American Journalism.* Dubuque: William C. Brown, 1969.

Koechi Haruo. "Fukuchi Ōchi kenkyū annai" [Guide to research on Fukuchi Ōchi]. *Meiji Bungaku Zenshū Geppō*, no. 17 (June 1966). Tokyo: Chikuma, 1966.

Koito Chūgo. *Nihon to kokusai komiyunikēshiyon* [Japan and international communication]. Tokyo: Jōchi Daigaku Bungakubu, 1977.

*Kōko Shimbun*. See Osatake Takeki, *Bakumatsu Meiji shimbun zenshū:* 3–82.

Komiya Toyotaka. *Japanese Music and Drama in the Meiji Era*. Translated by Donald Keene and Edward G. Seidensticker. Tokyo: Ōbunsha, 1956.

Kōsaka Masaaki. *Japanese Thought in the Meiji Era*. Translated and adapted by David Abosch. Tokyo: Pan-Pacific Press, 1958.

Kubota Tatsuhiko, ed. *Nijūichi daisenkaku kisha den* [The biographies of twenty-one pioneer reporters]. Osaka: Osaka Mainichi Shimbunsha, 1930.

Kuga Katsunan. "Kinji seiron kō" [Studies on recent politics]. In *Kuga Katsunan zenshū* [Complete works of Kuga Katsunan], vol. 1. Edited by Nishida Taketoshi and Uete Michiari. Tokyo: Misuzu Shobo, 1968.

Kusumoto Mitsuo. *Shimbun no sugao* [A frank look at newspapers]. Tokyo: Kōbundō Shuppankai, 1977.

Kyogoku Jun'ichi. "The Common Sense of the Public and of the Political Establishment." *Japan Echo* 2, no. 1 (Spring 1975):13–24.

Lanman, Charles. *Leading Men of Japan*. Boston, 1883.

––––––. *Leaders of the Meiji Restoration in America*. Tokyo: Hokuseido, 1931.

Lay, A. H. "History of the Rise of Political Parties in Japan." *Transactions of the Asiatic Society of Japan*. Vol. 30:363–462.

Lebra, Joyce. *Okuma Shigenobu, Statesman of Meiji Japan*. Canberra: Australian National University Press, 1973.

Lockwood, William W. *The Economic Development of Japan: Growth and Structural Change, 1868–1938*. Princeton: Princeton University Press, 1954.

McLaren, Walter W. "Japanese Goverment Documents." *Transactions of the Asiatic Society of Japan*. Vol. 42, pt. 1 (1914). Tokyo: Yashida Booksellers.

––––––. *A Political History of Japan during the Meiji Era, 1867–1912*. New York: Russell and Russell, 1965.

Mainichi Shimbunsha. *Mainichi Shimbun kyūjūnen* [Ninety years of *Mainichi Shimbun*]. Tokyo: Mainichi Shimbunsha, 1962.

––––––. *Mainichi Shimbun hyakunenshi* [Centennial History of *Mainichi Shimbun*]. Tokyo: Mainichi Shimbunsha, 1972.

Marlowe, John. *A History of Modern Egypt and Anglo-Egyptian Relations, 1800–1956*. Hamden, Conn.: Archon Books, 1965.

Maruyama Masao. *Studies in the Intellectual History of Tokugawa Japan.* Tokyo: University of Tokyo Press, 1974.

Matsumoto Sannosuke, ed. *Gendai Nihon shisō taikei* [Outline of modern Japanese thought]. 35 vols. Tokyo: Chikuma Shobō, 1966.

Mayo, Marlene. "The Iwakura Embassy and the Unequal Treaties, 1871–1873." Ph.D. dissertation, Columbia University, 1961.

————. "The Iwakura Mission to the United States and Europe, 1871–1873." *Researches in the Social Sciences on Japan* 2 (June 1959):28–47.

————. "The Korean Crisis of 1873 and Early Meiji Foreign Policy." *Journal of Asian Studies* 31, no. 4 (August 1972):793–820.

Meiji Bunka Kenkyūkai, series ed. *Meiji bunka zenshū* [Collected Works on Meiji Culture]. 31 volumes. Tokyo: Nihon Hyōronsha, 1968. Volumes used in this study: 1: *Kensei* [Constitutional government]; 4: *Shimbun* [Newspapers]; 9–10: *Seishi* [Constitutional government]; 12: *Keizai* [Economics]. The series was originally edited by Yoshino Sakuzō in 1928–1930, and was expanded and reissued in 1968 by Meiji Bunka Kenkyūkai.

Menpes, Mortimer. *Japan: A Record in Colour.* London: Charles Black, 1905.

Merrill, John and Heinz-Dietrich Fischer, eds. *International and Intercultural Communication.* New York: Hastings House, 1976.

Midoro Shōichi. *Meiji Taisho shi* [History of the Meiji and Taisho eras]. 6 vols. Tokyo: Asahi, 1930.

Mishima Ryōzō. *Kabukiza* [The Kabukiza]. Tokyo: Kabukiza Shuppanbu, 1951.

Miyake Setsurei. *Dōjidaishi* [An account of my times]. 6 vols. Tokyo: Iwanami Shoten, 1954.

————. "Nakae Chōmin" [Nakae Chōmin]. *Taiyō* 18, no. 9 (June 15, 1912).

Mori Kyozo. "Questionable Attitude of News Reporters." *Japan Echo* 2, no. 1 (Spring 1975):37–43.

Mori Ōgai. *The Wild Geese.* Translated by Kingo Ochiai and Sanford Goldstein. Rutland, Vt.: Charles E. Tuttle, 1959.

Mori Shina. "Meiji gannen Fukuchi Ōchi gokuchū bemmeisho" [Fukuchi Ōchi's prison defense, 1868]. *Bungaku* (November 1968):86–91.

Mossman, Samuel. *New Japan, the Land of the Rising Sun.* London: John Murray, 1873.

Mounsey, Augustus H. *The Satsuma Rebellion, an Episode of Modern Japanese History.* London: John Murray, 1879.

Murdoch, James. *A History of Japan.* 3 vols. New York: Frederick Ungar, 1964.

Najita, Tetsuo. *Japan.* Englewood Cliffs, N.J.: Prentice-Hall, 1974.

Nakagawa, T. G. "Journalism in Japan." *Forum* 29 (May 1900):370–376.

Nakamura Hajime. *A History of the Development of Japanese Thought.* Tokyo: Kokusai Bunka Shinkōkai, 1967.

Nakamura Mitsuo. *Modern Japanese Fiction, 1868–1926.* Tokyo: Kokusai Bunka Shinkōkai, 1968.

Nakayama Yasuaki, ed. *Shimbun shūsei Meiji hennenshi* [Documentary history of Meiji compiled from newspapers]. 15 vols. Tokyo: Zaisei Keizai Gakkai, 1934–1936.

Nevins, Allan. *The Gateway to History.* New York: D. C. Heath, 1938.

Nihon Dempō, ed. *Gojūnin no shimbunjin* [Fifty newspapermen]. Tokyo: Nihon Dempō Tsūshinsha, 1955.

*Nihon Keizai Shimbun,* December 1, 1956.

Nihon Shimbun Hambai Kyōkai, ed. *Shimbun hambai hyakunenshi* [One hundred year history of newspaper sales]. Tokyo: Nihon Shimbun Hambai Kyōkai, 1969.

Nihon Shimbun Kyōkai, ed. *Nihon shimbun shi chihō betsu* [Japanese newspaper history—by regions]. Tokyo: Nihon Shimbun Kyōkai, 1956.

Nihon Shimbun Remmei, ed. *Nihon shimbun hyakunenshi* [One hundred year history of Japanese newspapers]. Tokyo: Nihon Shimbun Remmei, 1962.

Nishida Taketoshi. *Meiji jidai no shimbun to zasshi* [Newspapers and magazines of the Meiji period]. Tokyo: Shibundō, 1966.

———. "Meiji jūichinen—dō jūyonnen no shimbunkai" [The newspaper world from 1877 to 1881]. *Meiji bunka no shinkenkyū* [New research on Meiji culture]. Edited by Osatake Takeki. Tokyo: Meiji Bunka Kenkyūkai, 1944.

———. "Meiji shoki shimbun ronsetsu sakuin" [Index of early Meiji newspaper editorials]. *Meiji bunka kenkyū,* nos. 5–6 (October 1934–November 1935).

———. "Ōchi no shimbun kiji ni tsuite" [Regarding Ōchi's newspaper articles]. See Yanagida Izumi, *Fukuchi Ōchi shū:* 453–456.

———. "*Tokyo Nichi Nichi Shimbun* shasetsu mokuroku" [Index of *Tokyo Nichi Nichi Shimbun* editorials]. Mimeographed. Tokyo: Kindaishi Kondankai, 1954.

———. "*Tokyo Nichi Nichi Shimbun* shasetsu sakuin" [Index of *Tokyo Nichi Nichi Shimbun* editorials]. Unpublished manuscript in Nishida's personal collection.

Noguchi Yone. "Journalism in Japan." *The Bookman* 19 (April 1904): 50–54.

Norman, E. H. *Japan's Emergence as a Modern State.* New York: Institute of Pacific Relations, 1940.

Nozaki Sukefumi. *Watakushi no mita Meiji bundan* [The Meiji literary figures I observed]. Tokyo: Shun'yōdō, 1927.

250   *Bibliography*

Oka Mitsuo. *Kindai Nihon shimbun shōshi* [A short history of recent Japanese journalism]. Kyoto: Minerubua Shobō, 1969.
Okada Akio et al., eds. *Meiji ishin* [The Meiji Restoration]. Vol. 10 of *Nihon no rekishi* [The history of Japan]. Tokyo: Yomiuri Shimbunsha, 1965.
———. *Meiji no Nihon* [The Japan of Meiji]. Vol. 11 of *Nihon no rekishi* [The history of Japan]. Tokyo: Yomiuri Shimbunsha, 1963.
Okata Shōyū. "Fukuchi Ōchi to no kaiken" [Interview with Fukuchi Ōchi], *Jimbutsu Sōsho furoku* [Supplement to *Jimbutsu Sōsho* series], no. 129 (1965).
Okazaki Yoshie, ed. *Japanese Literature in the Meiji Era*. Translated and adapted by V. H. Viglielmo. Tokyo: Pan-Pacific Press, 1958.
Ōkuma Shigenobu, ed. *Fifty Years of New Japan*. 2 vols. London: Smith, Elders, 1910.
Ono Hideo. *Kawaraban monogatari: Edo jidai masu komi no rekishi* [The *kawaraban* story: history of mass communications in the Edo period]. Tokyo: Yūzankaku, 1960.
———. " 'Moshiogusa' oyobi 'Kōko Shimbun' no kaisetsu" [An explanation of the *Kōko Shimbun* and the *Moshiogusa*]. See Osatake Takeki, ed. *Bakumatsu Meiji shimbun zenshū*: 1–3, 11–14.
———. "Shimbunjin toshite no Fukuchi Ōchi [Fukuchi Ōchi as a newspaperman]. *Meiji Bungaku Zenshū Geppō*, no. 17 (June 1966). Tokyo: Chikuma, 1966.
———. *Shimbun no rekishi* [History of the newspaper press]. Tokyo: Tokyodō Shuppan, 1961.
Osatake Takeki, ed. *Bakumatsu Meiji shimbun zenshū* [Collected newspapers of the Bakumatsu-Meiji period]. Tokyo: Taiseidō, 1934–1935.
———. *Nihon kensei shi taikō* [An outline of Japanese constitutional history]. 2 vols. Tokyo: Nihon Hyōronsha, 1939.
Ōtahara Aribumi. *Jū daisenkaku kisha den* [Ten pioneer reporters]. Tokyo: Tokyo Nichi Nichi Shimbunsha, 1926.
Ōtsu Junichirō. *Dai Nihon kensei shi* [Constitutional history of Japan]. 10 vols. Tokyo: Hakubunkan, 1945.
Ozawa Ryōzō. *Onnagata konseki dan* [Discussion of female impersonators, past and present]. Tokyo: Chikuma, 1941.
Passin, Herbert. "Writer and Journalist in the Transitional Society." *Communications and Political Development*, pp. 78–123. Edited by Lucian Pye. Princeton: Princeton University Press, 1968.
Pittau, Joseph. "Inoue Kowashi: 1843–1945, and the Formation of Modern Japan." *Monumentica Nipponica* 20 (1965):253–282.
———. *Political Thought in Early Meiji Japan, 1868–1889*. Cambridge, Mass.: Harvard University Press, 1967.
Pyle, Kenneth B. "Advantages of Followership: German Economics and Japa-

nese Bureaucrats, 1890–1925," *Journal of Japanese Studies* 1, no. 1 (August 1974):127–164.

_____. *The New Generation in Meiji Japan: Problems of Cultural Identity, 1888–1895.* Stanford: Stanford University Press, 1969.

Rosovsky, Henry. *Capital Formation in Japan.* Glencoe, Ill.: The Free Press, 1961.

Rozman, Gilbert. "Edo's Importance in the Changing Tokugawa Society." *Journal of Japanese Studies* 1, no. 1 (Autumn 1974):91–112.

Sakai Kunio. *Ijin ansatsu shi* [History of the assassination of great men]. Tokyo: Genrindō, 1937.

Sakata Yoshio. *Meiji ishin shi* [History of the Meiji Restoration]. Tokyo: Miraisha, 1960.

Sansom, G. B. *Japan: A Short Cultural History.* London: Appleton-Century-Crofts, 1962.

_____. *The Western World and Japan.* New York: Alfred A. Knopf, 1950.

Sashihara Yasuzō. *Meiji sei shi* [A political history of the Meiji period]. 3 vols. Tokyo: Fuzanbō Shoten, 1893.

Satō Shukichi, ed. *Meiyō kaifuku soshōroku* [Record of legal actions related to the restoration of honor]. Tokyo: Chissandō, 1881.

Satow, Ernest. *A Diplomat in Japan.* London: Seeley, Service and Company, 1921.

Sawada Setsuzo. "Newspapers in Japan." *Japan Society, London—Transactions and Proceedings.* Vol. 11 (1913):188–208.

Scalapino, Robert A. *Democracy and the Party Movement in Prewar Japan.* Berkeley: University of California Press, 1953.

Scott, Adolph. *Kabuki Theatre of Japan.* London: George Allen, 1955.

Shibusawa Eiichi Denki Shiryō Kankōkai, ed. *Shibusawa Eiichi denki shiryō* [Collection of materials on the life of Shibusawa Eiichi]. Tokyo: Ryūmonsha, 1955–1964.

Shibusawa Eiichi, ed. *Tokugawa Keiki kō den* [Biography of Tokugawa Keiki]. 8 vols. Tokyo: Ryūmonsha, 1918.

Shigemura Naganori. *Gendai shimbun kō* [Thoughts on modern newspapers]. Tokyo: Gakuyō Shobō, 1977.

Shimane Kiyoshi. *Tenkō: Meiji ishin to bakushin* [Conversion: bakufu retainers and the Meiji Restoration]. Tokyo: San'ichi Shobō, 1969.

Shimbun Kenkyū Dōjinkai, ed. *Shimbun handobukku* [Newspaper handbook]. Tokyo: Dabuiddosha, 1966.

Shinoda Masano. "Fukuchi Ōchi no sakugeki no ichimen" [One aspect of Fukuchi Ōchi's play writing]. *Kabuki,* no. 28 (April 1975):102–117.

Showa Joshi Daigaku Kindai Bungaku Kenkyūshitsu, ed. "Fukuchi Ōchi" [Fukuchi Ōchi]. *Kindai bungaku kenkyū sōsho* [Modern literature research series]. Vol. 8. Tokyo: Showa Joshi Daigaku, 1958.

Siemes, Johannes. *Hermann Roessler and the Making of the Meiji State.* Tokyo: Sophia University and Charles E. Tuttle, 1968.

Silberman, Bernard S. *Ministers of Modernization: Elite Mobility in the Meiji Restoration, 1868–1893.* Tucson: University of Arizona Press, 1964.

Spaulding, Robert M., Jr. "Bibliography of Western-language Dailies and Weeklies in Japan, 1861–1961." Mimeographed. University of Michigan.

Soviak, Eugene. "On the Nature of Western Progress: The Journal of the Iwakura Embassy." *Tradition and Modernization in Japanese Culture.* Edited by Donald H. Shively. Princeton: Princeton University Press, 1971.

Spencer, Herbert. "Advice to the Modernizers of Japan." *Herbert Spencer on Social Evolution: Selected Writings.* Edited by J. D. Y. Peel. Chicago: University of Chicago Press, 1972.

Steinhoff, Patricia G. "Tenkō: Ideology and Societal Integration in Prewar Japan." Ph.D. dissertation, Harvard University, 1969.

Suehiro Tetchō. "Shimbun keirekidan" [An account of my newspaper life]. *Shimbun hen.* Vol. 4 of *Meiji bunka zenshū.* Edited by Meiji Bunka Kenkyūkai, q.v. Tokyo: Nihon Hyōronsha, 1968.

Sugimura Kōtarō. *Saikin shimbunshigaku* [Studies in recent journalism]. Tokyo: Chūō Daigaku Shuppanbu, 1970.

Sugiura Tadashi. *Shimbun koto hajime* [Newspaper beginnings]. Tokyo: Mainichi Shimbunsha, 1971.

Suzuki Shōzō. "Fukuchi Ōchi no rekishikan ni tsuite" [A discussion of Fukuchi Ōchi's view of history]. *Rekishi Kenkyū* 7, no. 8 (1971):5–21. Osaka: Osaka Kyōiku Daigaku.

Tamura Hisashi. *Fukuchi Ōchi* [Fukuchi Ōchi]. Vol. 3 of *Sandai genronjin shū* [The works of three generations of journalists]. Edited by Jiji Tsūshinsha, q.v. Tokyo: Jiji Tsūshinsha, 1962.

Teters, Barbara J. "The Conservative Opposition in Japanese Politics 1877–1894." Ph.D. dissertation, University of Washington, 1955.

————. "Kuga's Commentaries on the Constitution of the Empire of Japan." *Journal of Asian Studies* 27, no. 2 (February 1969):321–338.

Tiedemann, Arthur, ed. *An Introduction to Japanese Civilization.* New York: Columbia University Press, 1974.

————. *Modern Japan, a Brief History.* New York: D. Van Nostrand, 1955.

Tōbata Seiichi, ed. *The Modernization of Japan I.* Tokyo: The Institute of Asian Economics Affairs, 1966.

Tokutomi Soho. *Kōshaku Yamagata Aritomo den* [Biography of Prince Yamagata Aritomo]. 3 vols. Tokyo: Yamagata Aritomo Kō Kinen Jigyōkai, 1933.

————. "Meiji no daikisha Fukuchi Ōchi Koji" [The great Meiji reporter, Fukuchi Ōchi Koji]. *Chūō Kōron,* April 1939.

*Tokyo Nichi Nichi Shimbun*, 1874–1888. See also occasional articles from 1889 to 1906.

Tokyo Nichi Nichi Shimbunsha, ed. *Tōnichi nanajūnen shi* [Seventy-year history of the *Tokyo Nichi Nichi Shimbun*]. Tokyo: Tokyo Nichi Nichi Shimbunsha, 1941.

Tōtenkō. *Meiji Shimbun Zasshi Bunko shozō mokuroku* [Index of materials held by the Meiji Shimbun Zasshi Bunko]. 3 vols. Tokyo: Tokyo Teikoku Daigaku, Hōgakubu, 1935.

Toyama Shigeki, ed. *Meiji no ninai te I* [Shapers of the Meiji era I]. Vol. 11 of *Jimbutsu: Nihon no rekishi* [Japanese history: its people]. Tokyo: Yomiuri Shimbunsha, 1973.

Treat, Payson. *Diplomatic Relations between the United States and Japan, 1853–1895.* 2 vols. Stanford: Stanford University Press, 1932.

Tsuchihashi, Paul Yashita. "Japanese Chronological Tables." Tokyo: Sophia University Press, 1952.

Tsuda Sōkichi. *Bungaku ni arawareta waga kokumin shisō no kenkyū* [Our thought as it appears in literature]. 4 vols. Tokyo: Rakuyōdō, 1920.

Tsukahara Jūshien. "Ōchi Koji" [Ōchi Koji]. *Taiyō* 18, no. 9 (June 1912).

Tsumaki Chūta, comp. *Kido Kōin ibun shū* [Collected writings of Kido Kōin]. Tokyo: Taizambo, 1942.

Tsunoda Ryusaku; deBary, William Theodore; and Keene, Donald, eds. *Sources of Japanese Tradition.* 2 vols. New York: Columbia University Press, 1958.

Tsurumi Shunsuke, ed. *Jiyanarizumu no shisō* [Philosophy of journalism]. Vol. 12 of *Gendai Nihon shisō takei*. Edited by Matsumoto Sannosuke, q.v. Tokyo: Chikuma Shobō, 1965.

Uchikawa Yoshimi. *Shimbunshi wa* [Historical anecdotes about the press]. Tokyo: Shakai Shisōsha, 1967.

Uchimura Kanzō. *The Complete Works of Kanzō Uchimura.* 8 vols. Tokyo: Kyobunkwan, 1973.

Umetani Noboru. *Gunjin chokuyu seiritsu shi no kenkyū* [Research on the drafting of the "Imperial precepts to soldiers and sailors"]. Osaka: Osaka Daigaku Bungakubu, 1961.

Urushiyama Shigeyoohi. *Shimbun ronchō e no hanron* [In opposition to the prevailing tone of the press]. Tokyo: Nisshin Hodō, 1975.

Ushijima Shunsaku. *Nihon genron shi* [History of the Japanese press]. Tokyo: Kawade Shobō, 1955.

Uyehara, George Etsujiro. *The Political Development of Japan, 1867–1909.* New York: E. P. Dutton, 1910.

Ward, Robert E. and Rustow, Dankwart A., eds. *Political Modernization in Japan and Turkey.* Princeton: Princeton University Press, 1964.

Watanabe Ikujirō. *Ōkuma Shigenobu: shin-Nihon no kensetsusha* [Ōkuma Shigenobu: a builder of new Japan]. Tokyo: Shorindō, 1943.

Watanabe Shujirō, ed. "Kokusai shihei shimatsu ni tsuite" [Regarding the handling of government bonds]. Compiled from *Tokyo Nichi Nichi Shimbun,* June 26–July 22, 1880.

Wataru Ichikawa. "A Confused Account of a Trip to Europe, Like a Fly on a Horse's Tail." Translated by Henry Satow. *Chinese and Japanese Repository of Facts and Events: Science, History and Art, Relating to Eastern Asia.* July–December 1865.

Whittemore, Edward P. *The Press in Japan Today: A Case Study.* Columbia: University of South Carolina Press, 1961.

Wildes, Harry Emerson. "Press Freedom in Japan." *American Journal of Sociology* 32 (January 1927): 601–614.

_____. *The Press and Social Currents in Japan.* Chicago: University of Chicago Press, 1927.

Yamada Minoru, Katō Hidetoshi, and Kuwabara Takeo. "The Intellectual Role of Journalism." *Journal of Social and Political Ideas in Japan* 2, no. 1 (April 1964):48–53.

Yamamoto Taketoshi. *Shimbun to minshū Nihongata shimbun no keisei katei* [Newspapers and the people: formative processes in Japanese newspapers]. Tokyo: Kinokuniya Shoten, 1973.

Yanaga Chitoshi. *Japan since Perry.* New York: McGraw-Hill, 1949.

Yanagida Izumi. *Fukuchi Ōchi.* Tokyo: Nihon Rekishi Gakkai, 1965.

_____. "Fukuchi Ōchi." See Yanagida, *Fukuchi Ōchi shū,* pp. 409–432.

_____. "Kuga Katsunan" [Kuga Katsunan]. In Vol. 5 of *Sandai genronjin shū.* Edited by Jiji Tsūshinsha, q.v. Tokyo: Jiji Tsūshinsha, 1962–1967.

_____. *Meiji seiji shōsetsu shū* [A collection of Meiji political novels]. Tokyo: Chikuma Shobō, 1967.

_____. *Meiji shoki no bungaku shisō* [Literary thought in early Meiji]. Tokyo: Shunjūsha, 1965.

_____. "Ōchi Koji suketsuchingu" [Sketchings of Ōchi Koji]. *Denki* 2 (February 1935):2–18.

_____. *Seiji shōsetsu kenkyū* [Research in political novels]. 3 vols. Tokyo: Shunjūsha, 1968.

_____, ed. *Fukuchi Ōchi shū* [Works of Fukuchi Ōchi]. Vol. 11 of *Meiji bungaku zenshū* [Collected works of Meiji literature]. Tokyo: Chikuma Shobō, 1966.

*Yūbin Hōchi Shimbun.*

Zumoto Motasada. "Journalism in Japan." *Japan Society, London—Transactions and Proceedings.* Vol. 6 (1902):108–122.

Zushikawa Chōko. "Ōchi Koji no tsuioku" [Recollections of Ōchi Koji]. *Denki* 2 (February 1935):19–24.

# Glossary

Abe Masahiro 阿部正弘
Aikokusha 愛国社
Aizawa Seishisai 会沢正志斎
Aizu 会津
Aku-no-ura 飽の浦
Andō Nobumasa 安藤信正
Asahina Chisen 朝比奈知泉
Asahi Shimbun 朝日新聞
Asaka Gonsai 安積艮斎

Baba Tatsui 馬場辰猪
*Bankoku Shimbun* 万国新聞
Bansho Shirabedokoro 蛮書調所
*Batabia Shimbun* バタビヤ新聞
bugyō 奉行

Chihōkan kaigi 地方官会議
chokuyu 勅諭
*Chōya Shimbun* 朝野新聞
*Chūgai Shimbun* 中外新聞

daigensha 代言者
daishimbun 大新聞
*Daitō Nippō* 大東日報
Dajōkan 太政官
*Dajōkan Nisshi* 太政官日誌
dokusai seiji 独裁政治

*Eiri Jiyū Shimbun* 絵入自由新聞
engi 衍義
Etō Shimpei 江藤新平

Fujita Mokichi 藤田茂吉
Fujita Tōko 藤田東湖
Fukuchi Gen'ichirō 福地源一郎
Fukuchi Gensuke 福地源輔
Fukuchi Kōan 福地苟庵
Fukuchi Koji 福地居士
Fukuchi Nobuyo 福地信世
Fukuchi Ōchi 福地桜痴
Fukuchi Satoko 福地さとこ
Fukuchi Yasokichi 福地八十吉
Fukuchi Yoshimasa 福地嘉昌
Fukuzawa Yukichi 福況諭吉
Furusawa Uruō 古沢滋

gaikoku bugyō 外国奉行
gesaku 戯作
*Ginkō Zasshi* 銀行雑誌
Godai Tomoatsu 五代友厚
gokenin 御家人
gosō 吾曹
Gotō Shōjirō 後藤象次郎
goyō shimbun 御用新聞

hambatsu seifu 藩閥政府
Haneda Kyōsuke 羽田恭輔
Hara Satoshi 原敬
hatamoto 旗本
Hayashi Zushonosuke 林図書助
heimin 平民
henshūjin 編集人
*Hiragana Mainichi Shimbun*
　ひらがなまいにちしんぶん

Hiraoka Kōsuke 広岡幸助
hōan jōrei 保安条例
Hotta Masayoshi 堀田正睦
*Hyōron Shimbun* 評論新聞

Ichikawa Danjūrō 市川団十郎
Ii Naosuke 井伊直弼
Inoue Kaoru 井上馨
Inukai Tsuyoshi 犬養毅
Itagaki Taisuke 板垣退助
Itō Hirobumi 伊藤博文
Itō Miyoji 伊東巳代治
Iwakura Tomomi 岩倉具視

*Jiji Shimpō* 時事新報
jiyū minken undō 自由民権運動
*Jiyū Shimbun* 自由新聞
Jiyūtō 自由党
jōi 攘夷
Jōno Dempei 条野伝平

*Kaigai Shimbun* 海外新聞
kaigisho 会議所
Kaisei Gakkō 開成学校
*Kaishin Shimbun* 改進新聞
Kaishintō 改進党
*Kampō* 官報
Kanagaki Robun 仮名垣魯文
*Kanhan Batabia Shimbun*
　官板バタビヤ新聞
*Kanhan Chūgai Shimbun* 官板中外新聞
*Kanhan Kaigai Shimbun* 官板海外新聞
Kanrin-maru 咸臨丸
Katō Hiroyuki 加藤弘之
Katsu Kaishū 勝海舟
kawaraban 瓦版
kazoku 華族
kempō 憲法
Kido Takayoshi (Kōin) 木戸孝允
kisha 記者
Kishida Ginkō 岸田吟香
kōbu-gattai 公武合体
Kōgisho 公議所

*Kokai Shimpō* 湖海新報
*Kōko Shimbun* 江湖新聞
kokugaku 国学
*Kokumin no Tomo* 国民之友
*Kokumin Shimbun* 国民新聞
kokutai 国体
kokuyaku kempō 国約憲法
Kuga Katsunan 陸羯南
kumin dōchi 君民同治
Kurimoto Jōun 栗本鋤雲
Kuroda Kiyotaka 黒田清隆
kyakuin 客員
kyūshinshugi 急進主義

Maejima Hisoka 前島密
Maruyama Sakura 丸山作楽
Matsudaira Iwami no kami
　松平石見守
Matsukata Masayoshi 松方正義
Meiji ishin 明治維新
*Meiji Nippō* 明治日報
Meirokusha 明六社
*Meiroku Zasshi* 明六雑誌
minken 民権
Mito 水戸
Mitsukuri Shūhei 箕作秋坪
Miyake Setsurei 三宅雪嶺
Mizuno Tadanori 水野忠徳
Mizuno Torajirō 水野寅二郎
mochinushi 持ち主
Mōri 毛利
Moriyama Takichirō 森山多吉郎
*Moshiogusa* もしほ草
Motoki Shōzō 本木昌造
Murayama Ryūhei 村山竜平

*Naigai Shimpō* 内外新報
Nakae Chōmin 中江兆民
Nakahama Manjirō 中浜万次郎
Namamugi jiken 生麦事件
Namura Hachiemon 名村八右衛門
Narushima Ryūhoku 成島柳北
*Nichi Nichi Shimbun* 日日新聞

Nihon 日本
Nippōsha 日報社
Nishi Amane 西周
Nishida Densuke 西田伝助
*Nisshin Shinjishi* 日新真事誌
Numa Morikazu 沿間守

ōdō 王道
Ōi Kentarō 大井憲太郎
Ōkubo Toshimichi 大久保利通
Ōkuma Shigenobu 大隈重信
Ōmeisha 嚶鳴社
Oranda fūsetsugaki 荷蘭陀風説書
Osagawa 長川
*Osaka Mainichi Shimbun* 大阪毎日新聞
*Osaka Nippō* 大阪日報
*Osaka Shimpō* 大阪新報
ōsei fukko 王政復古
Ozaki Yukio 尾崎行雄

Rai San'yō 頼山陽
rangaku 蘭学
Rikken Teiseitō 立憲帝政党
Risshisha 立志社
Rokumeikan 鹿鳴館
ronsetsu 論説

*Saifū Shimbun* 采風新聞
Saigō Takamori 西郷隆盛
Saionji Kimmochi 西園寺公望
Sakuma Shōzan 佐久間象山
Sanjō Sanetomi 三条実美
Sasaki Takayuki 佐々木高行
Seki Naohiko 関直彦
shasetsu 社説
Shibusawa Eiichi 渋沢栄一
Shimazu Nariakira 島津斉彬
shimbun jōrei 新聞条例
*Shimbunshi* 新聞紙
*Shimbun Zasshi* 新聞雑誌
Shintomiza 新富座
shōshimbun 小新聞
Soejima Taneomi 副島種臣

*Sōmō Zasshi* 草莽雑誌
sonnō-jōi 尊王攘夷
Suehiro Tetchō 末広鉄腸

Taguchi Ukichi 田口卯吉
Takashima Shūhan 高島秋帆
Takenouchi Shimotsuke no kami
　竹内下野守
tambōsha 探訪者
Tokugawa Keiki 徳川慶喜
Tokugawa Nariaki 徳川斉昭
Tokutomi Sohō 徳富蘇峰
*Tokyo Akebono Shimbun* 東京曙新聞
*Tokyo Keizai Zasshi* 東京経済雑誌
*Tokyo Nichi Nichi Shimbun*
　東京日日新聞
Tokyo Shōhō Kaigisho
　東京商法会議所
*Tokyo Shimpō* 東京新報
*Tokyo Yokohama Mainichi Shimbun*
　東京横浜毎日新聞
tōsho 投書
*Tōyō Jiyū Shimbun* 東洋自由新聞
*Tōyō Shimpō* 東洋新報
Tsubouchi Shōyō 坪内逍遙

Uemura Masahisa 植村正久
Unjōsho 運上所
Uraga 浦賀

Yamada Akiyoshi 山田顕義
Yamaga Sokō 山鹿素行
Yamagata Aritomo 山県有明
*Yamato Shimbun* 大和新聞
Yanagawa Shunsan 柳河春三
Yano Fumio 矢野文雄
*Yokohama Mainichi Shimbun*
　横浜毎日新聞
*Yomiuri Shimbun* 読売新聞
Yoshida Shōin 吉田松陰
*Yūbin Hōchi Shimbun* 郵便報知新聞

zenshinshugi 漸進主義

# Index

Index 265

Kuroda Kiyotaka, 121, 133, 135, 159
Kurokuwa (menial laborer), 21, 209n39
Kyōgen (farcical play), 181
"Kyōjaku ron" ("On strength and weakness"), 53–55, 158
Kyōkaku harusame no kasa ("Gallant in the spring rain"), 179
Kyoto, 19, 40, 46, 54, 150
Kyūshinshugi (radicalism), 82, 97–99
Kyushu Shimeikai, 150

Law of assembly (1882), 151
Li Hung-chang, 205
Li-Itō negotiations, 205
Lippincott Bookstore, 67
Literary attitudes, 177, 182, 191
London, 38, 42, 67, 70
Loyalty, 190–191, 200

Macaulay, Thomas, 186
Maejima Hisoka, 81
Maeno Ryōtaku, 11
Mainichi Shimbun, 56, 231n71
Marseilles, 36
Marubon (ancient drama texts), 74, 178, 179, 180
Maruyama Masao, 21, 99, 102
Maruyama Sakura, 148
Masuda Takashi, 128
Matsukata Masayoshi, 159
Mayo, Marlene, 69
Meiji constitution, 5, 70, 146, 153, 170. See also Constitutional movement; Zenshinshugi, constitutionalism
Meiji economic history, 126
Meiji election law, 112
Meiji emperor, 45, 103, 107, 118–119, 136, 151. See also Emperor; Zenshinshugi, imperial sovereignty
Meiji government, 46, 52, 69, 99, 159; overall policies, 6, 64; early resistance to, 46, 47, 48–49, 50–55, 57–58, 191; pragmatism, 47, 62, 63–64, 106; use and control of press, 53, 57–61, 81–82, 94–95, 96, 104–105, 114, 131, 138–139, 147, 198, 199; modernization policies, 64–68, 69–72, 73, 75–76, 106, 121, 160, 166; economic policies, 64–65, 66–68, 73, 106, 121, 123–127, 192, 194; indebtedness, 64–65, 106; foreign study, 64–68, 69–72; Korean

crisis (1873), 72–74, 82, 106; cliques, 72–73, 74, 108, 134–136, 158–162, 170, 173, 190; general press relations, 88, 93, 94; attitude toward popular assembly, 96, 101; oligarchs and oligarchy, 98, 101, 103, 108, 134, 136, 138, 158–162, 172; creation of Chihōkan Kaigi, 103–104; attitude toward constitution, 106–107, 109, 110, 113, 133, 134; autocratic tendencies, 107–108, 134–135, 160–162; attitudes toward private industry, 125; crisis of 1881, 131, 133–137; attitudes toward political parties, 145–146, 147–148, 149, 151–152; withdrawal of support from Fukuchi, 151–152, 154, 155–156; establishment of Kampō, 154
Meiji historians, 184–185, 186
Meiji intellectuals, 193, 198–199
Meiji Nippō, 148
Meiji period: general nature, 2, 3, 5, 6, 29, 140, 177, 183–184, 192, 197; feudal remnants, 177; mirrored by Fukuchi's life, 189–200; persistence of tradition, 189–192, 200; tensions created by modernization, 194–195, 200; breadth and turbulence, 195–198; role of intellectuals, 198–199; growth of particularism, 199–200
Meiji Restoration, 20, 44–47, 48, 51, 52, 61, 62, 106, 115, 126, 138, 142, 144, 155, 160, 161, 166, 185, 186, 190, 191, 196
Meiji Shimbun Zasshi Bunko, 174
Meirokusha (Meiji Six Society), 96
Meiroku Zasshi, 96, 104
Menpes, Mortimer, 181
Merchants, 10–12, 26–27, 28–29, 30, 125, 193, 195, 196
Mexican dollars, 30
Michelet, Jules, 195
Mikawa, 53
Military and politics, 140, 148, 153, 159, 160, 169, 191, 194, 195, 200
Mill, John Stuart, 42, 217n70
Minami no Seki, 117
Minamoto (Genji) family, 53
Minamoto Yoshitsune, 182
Ministry of Industry. See Kōbushō
Minting operations, 66–67
Mission to Europe (1861). See Takenouchi mission

Paris, 37, 38, 42, 71, 79
Parliament. *See* Diet
Particularism, 199–200. *See also* Nationalism
Party cabinets, 144, 145, 146, 151, 158
Pasha, Nubar, 71
Patronage politics, 189–190
Peers, 159
Perry, Matthew C., 14, 192
Philadelphia, 66, 67
Phonograph, 164, 196
Political novels. See *Seiji shosetsu*
Political parties, 144, 145–153, 158, 183. *See also* Jiyutō; Kaishintō Rikken Teiseitō
Popular assembly debate, 82, 95–102, 107, 113, 144–145, 166–168, 170, 194; timing of assembly, 96, 97, 98–99, 101, 137, 148, 166; evaluation of current government, 97, 98, 101; proposed makeup of assembly, 97, 99–102; role of *heimin* in assembly, 99–102
Popular rights, 4, 98, 99, 106, 108–109, 112, 138, 140, 143, 144, 149, 168, 170, 194. See also *Jiyū minken undō;* Popular assembly debate; *Zenshinshugi*
Popular sovereignty, 141, 145
Popular suffrage, 195, 198
Portugal, 36
Post Office (U.S.), 67
Press of Japan: historical periodization, 5; compared to Western press, 6–7, 16, 92, 93, 171, 173, 192; earliest papers, 16; antecedents, 47–48; Restoration papers, 47, 48–49, 56, 60, 214n20; governmental control, 49, 53, 57–61, 81–82, 104–105, 114, 131, 138–139, 147, 151, 154; English press in Japan, 49, 50, 104; press laws, 60, 93, 104–105, 138, 151, 216n50; early Meiji growth, 81–83, 173; ties to official world, 81, 82, 83, 91, 94, 199; struggle for independence, 82, 94, 96, 104–105, 128; popular assembly debate, 82, 95–102 (*see also* Popular assembly debate); leading public opinion, 83, 84, 85, 96, 173–174, 199; typical salaries, 84; reportorial practices, 85, 90–91, 92, 192; advertising, 85, 175; editorials, 88, 90, 120, 173–174,

192, 221n48; *daishimbun,* 89, 90, 156, 164, 175; punishments under press laws, 93, 105; politicization, 96, 120, 128, 171, 174, 192, 199; "guild" meetings, 104–105, 113–114; sovereignty debate, 111, 141–144; gaining public respectability, 114–115, 118–119, 173, 191; coverage of economics, 123–124, 125; constitutional discussions, 131 (*see also* Constitutional movement; *Zenshinshugi*); coverage of Fukuchi's legal dispute, 132–133; ties to political parties, 147; decline in early 1880s, 156, 174; increasing commercialization and independence, 163–164; *shōshimbun,* 164, 173; 1970s press, 172. *See also* names of individual papers
Press freedom. *See* Freedom of the press
Press laws, 60, 93, 104–105, 138, 151, 216n58
Private industry, 123, 125, 126, 168
"Progress and order," 2, 6, 9, 43, 56, 77, 95, 102, 108, 111, 113, 124, 148, 149, 152, 170, 175
Protectionism, 124–125. *See also* Trade
Pulitzer, Joseph, 7, 92

Radicalism. See *Kyūshinshugi*
Rai San'yō, 12
*Rakugo* (comic tales), 178
*Rangaku* (Dutch learning), 21
Red Cross, 163
Renaissance, 195, 197
Representative government, 54, 55, 82, 98, 108, 168, 170, 193, 196. *See also* Popular assembly debate
Republican Party (U.S.), 135, 160
Restoration papers, 47, 48–49, 56, 60, 214n20
Rice exchange, 124
Richardson, Charles, 39, 41, 190
Rikken Teiseitō (Constitutional Imperial Party), 145–153, 154, 158, 162, 164, 196; platform, 148–149, 168, 169–170; size, 149–150; government ties, 146, 147–148, 150, 151–152; demise, 151–152, 154, 156, 158, 159, 190, 191; evaluation, 152–153
Risshisha, 96

philosophy, 2, 97–98, 101, 102, 107, 112, 113, 138, 148–149, 166–171, 194–195; influence, 2–3; "progress and order," 2, 6, 9, 43, 56, 77, 95, 102, 108, 111, 113, 124, 148, 149, 152, 170, 175; leading gradualists, 5; early growth in Fukuchi's mind, 9–10, 43, 68, 76–77, 102; popular assemblies, 82, 95–102, 107, 110, 113, 136, 144–145, 166–168, 170, 194; dangers of rapid change, 97, 99, 101, 102, 104, 108, 126, 145, 147, 170; emphasis on order, 97, 102, 108, 109, 111, 113, 126, 143, 162, 168, 170, 171; constitutionalism, 98, 106–113, 136,

144–145, 166, 170, 194–195; imperial sovereignty, 102, 107, 109, 110–111, 112, 138, 140–145, 152, 153, 158, 169–170, 194–195; Chihōkan Kaigi, 103–104; impatience with oligarchy, 104, 107–108; pragmatism of position, 107; popular rights, 107, 108–109, 111, 112, 113, 144, 168, 170, 194–195; *kokutai,* 142–144, 149, 152, 153, 168–169, 170, 171, 194–195; role of political parties, 144–146, 147, 148–149; historical basis of position, 169. *See also same topics as independent entries*

Zojōji, 187

**⊞ Production Notes**

This book was designed by Roger Eggers and
typeset on the Unified Composing System by the
design and production staff of The University Press
of Hawaii.

The text and display typefaces are Garamond.

Offset presswork and binding were done by Halliday
Lithograph. Text paper is Glatfelter P & S Offset,
basis 55.